XENOPHON

APOLOGY

and

MEMORABILIA I

ARIS AND PHILLIPS CLASSICAL TEXTS

XENOPHON

Apology and Memorabilia
Book I

M. D. Macleod

Aris & Phillips is an imprint of Oxbow Books

First published in the United Kingdom in 2008. Reprinted in 2015 by
OXBOW BOOKS
10 Hythe Bridge Street, Oxford OX1 2EW

and in the United States by
OXBOW BOOKS
908 Darby Road, Havertown, PA 19083

Paperback Edition: ISBN 978-0-85668-712-9

A CIP record for this book is available from the British Library

For a complete list of Aris & Phillips titles, please contact:

UNITED KINGDOM	UNITED STATES OF AMERICA
Oxbow Books	Oxbow Books
Telephone (01865) 241249	Telephone (800) 791-9354
Fax (01865) 794449	Fax (610) 853-9146
Email: oxbow@oxbowbooks.com	Email: queries@casemateacademic.com
www.oxbowbooks.com	www.casemateacademic.com/oxbow

Oxbow Books is part of the Casemate Group

Printed and bound by CPI Group (UK) Ltd, Croydon, CR0 4YY

CONTENTS

Preface   vii

Introduction   1

Bibliography   2

The Works of Xenophon   5

The Life of Xenophon   7

The dating and relationships of Xenophon's Socratic Writings   13
     to each other, to works of Plato and to Polycrates

Introduction to *Apologia Socratis*   17

Apologia Socratis (Socrates' Defence)   21

Commentary on *Apologia Socratis*   40

Introduction to *Memorabilia Socratis*   58

Memorabilia Socratis (Memorabilia of Socrates) Book I   63

Commentary on *Memorabilia Socratis* Book I   126

Xenophon's Socrates   155

Supplementary Notes on the Text   162

Index   163

PREFACE

Xenophon is an author undeservedly neglected by classicists and comparatively unfamiliar to non-classicists interested in literature or philosophy. The aim of this edition is to follow the Aris and Phillips tradition and serve the needs of both classes of readers. The notes may start with some linguistic comments, when judged necessary for readers with a basic knowledge of ancient Greek, but otherwise should be of interest to all readers.

Apology and *Memorabilia* Book One make a natural pairing because all of the one and most of the first half of the other are devoted to the same subject, the rebuttal of the specific charges made against Socrates, while the rest of the *Memorabilia*, from 1.3.7 onwards, continues on an allied theme, the general vindication of Socrates. Texts that offer a 'second opinion' on Socrates are particularly attractive to students with a special interest in Greek philosophy, but I hope to focus equally much on the study of Xenophon the man, his background, predilections, motivation and literary habits.

Xenophon continually makes the point that the influence of Socrates, through his behaviour and teaching, was useful and beneficial to all, and Xenophon himself also strove to be of service to his readers, by passing on to them the benefits of his experiences and views, and has some claims to be regarded as an important educational theorist.

Like all students of Xenophon, I owe a great debt to Édouard Delebecque, to which should be added my tribute and gratitude to the joint editors of the magnificent *Budé* edition of *Memorabilia*, Book One, published in 2000, Michele Bandini for greatly improving the text and *apparatus criticus* and our knowledge of the manuscripts, and to Louis-André Dorion for his copious and valuable notes. On philosophical matters I owe most to W. K. C. Guthrie's *History of Greek Philosophy*.

Finally I must record my warm gratitude to both my editors, my friend the late Malcolm Willcock and Christopher Collard, for their careful scrutiny of my work and for many helpful and sensible suggestions for improvement, and also to Fred Williams for his valuable help with the proofs.

I dedicate this volume to Malcolm's memory and as a tribute to his services to students of the classics and users of this series.

Matthew Macleod.

INTRODUCTION

Xenophon is often underestimated, sometimes grossly, even by distinguished scholars merely interested in literary or intellectual qualities. As Delebecque well puts it, '*On le condamne parce qu'il n'est ni Platon ni Thucydide.*' Despite his shortcomings as a historian, he remains our chief source for Greek history from 410 to 362, and for classical Spartan society. And what a wealth of information about classical Greek life, thought and religion his works provide because of the wide range of his experiences and interests!

Thucydides was, of course, the better historian, but Xenophon's military record was far superior. Xenophon clearly lacked the literary charm and acute philosophical mind of Plato, but, whatever his subject, he consistently tried in his simpler way to instruct and educate, and if alive today, he would have made a far better Minister of Education than the unpractical author of *The Republic* and *The Laws* – that is if he had not already been snapped up by the Ministry of Defence to write military manuals.

Xenophon was greatly admired by the Romans, particularly Cicero, but perhaps the greatest tribute to him as author and man of action was paid four and a half centuries after his death, in the Antonine Age, by Arrian of Nicomedia. Himself the greatest literary figure of his day as historian, philosophical writer and author of military treatises, as well as a successful Roman provincial governor and soldier, he was proud to be acclaimed as a second Xenophon.

A home-spun philosopher, prone to excessive hero-worshipping, Xenophon may introduce some fictitious elements into his portraits of Agesilaus, Cyrus the Great, and even of Socrates, but Xenophon himself fully merits the epithet of ὠφέλιμος (beneficial, useful), which he accords to Socrates, *Apology*, 34, and I am sure he would be well satisfied with that.

BIBLIOGRAPHY

Adam, J. 1936. *Platonis Apologia Socratis*, 11th ed., Cambridge.

Anderson, J. K. 1974. *Xenophon*, London.

Bandini, M. see L.-A. Dorion.

Barnes, J. see C. C. W. Taylor.

Bartlett, R. C. 1996. Trans. with notes, *Xenophon, The Shorter Socratic Writings (Apology, Oeconomicus, Symposium)*, Cornell U. P.

Benson, H. H. ed. 1992. *Essays on the Philosophy of Socrates*, Oxford.

Bluck, R. S. 1961. *Plato's Meno*, Cambridge.

Bowen, A. J. 1998. *Xenophon, Symposium*, Aris and Phillips, Warminster.

Brandwood, L. 1958. *The Dating of Plato's Works by the stylistic Method; a historical and critical Survey*, London University Dissertation.

Brandwood, L. 1992. *The Chronology of Plato's Dialogues*, Cambridge.

Brickhouse, T. C. and Smith, N. D. 1989. *Socrates on Trial*, Oxford. (pp. 272–310 provide a detailed bibliography of work on Plato's *Apology*).

Brickhouse, T. C. and Smith, N. D. 1994. *Plato's Socrates*, Oxford.

Burnet, J. 1924. *Plato's Euthyphro, Apology of Socrates and Crito*, Oxford.

Calder, W. M. 1983. *The Oath by Hera in Plato*, Mélanges Édouard Delebecque, Aix en Provence, 35–42.

Cartledge, P. see R. Waterfield.

Cawkwell, G. L. 1979. Introduction and Notes to R. Warner's (1) *Xenophon, The Persian Expedition*, Penguin, 1972 and (2) *Xenophon, A History of my Times*, Penguin.

Chroust, A. H. 1955. Xenophon, Polycrates and the Indictment of Socrates, *Classica et Mediaevalia*, 16, 1–77.

Chroust, A. H. 1957. *Socrates and Myth*, South Bend, Indiana.

Cornford, P. 1932. *Before and after Socrates*, Cambridge.

Delebecque, É. 1957. *Essai sur la Vie de Xénophon*, Paris.

Delebecque, É. 1970. *Xénophon, L'Art de la Chasse*, Paris, (Budé).

Denniston, J. D. 1960. *Greek Prose Style*, Oxford.

Dillery, J. *Xenophon and the History of his Times*, Routledge, 1995.

Dorion, L.-A. 2000. Translation and detailed notes, Xenophon, *Mémorables*, *Livre 1*, Paris, (Budé), with text, apparatus criticus and copious information on mss. by M. Bandini.

Dover, K. J. 1965. The Date of Plato's Symposium, *Phronesis* (10), 2–20.

Gigon, O. 1995. *Kommentar zum ersten Buch von Xenophons Memorabilien*, Basel.

Goodwin, W. W. 1897. *Syntax of the Moods and Tenses of the Greek Verb*, London.

Graham, D. W. 1992. Socrates and Plato, *Phronesis* (37), 166–183.

Gray, V. J. 1995. Xenophon's Image of Socrates in the Memorabilia, *Prudentia* (27), 50–73.

Gray, V. J. 1998. *The Framing of Socrates, The literary interpretation of Xenophon's Memorabilia, Hermes Einzelschrift*, Stuttgart.

Guthrie, W. K. C. 1971(1). *The Sophists*, Cambridge.

Guthrie, W. K. C. 1971(2). *Socrates*, Cambridge. (Originally in Guthrie, W. K. C. 1969. *A History of Greek Philosophy, vol. iii*, Cambridge.)

Hackforth, R. M. 1933. *The Composition of Plato's Apology*, Cambridge.

Hare, R. M. see C. C. W. Taylor.

Kraut, R. 1983. *Cambridge Companion to Plato*.

Krentz, P. 1987. *Xenophon, Hellenica*, 1–2.3.10, Aris and Phillips, Warminster.

Krentz, P. 1995. *Xenophon, Hellenica*, 2.3.11–4.2.8, Aris and Phillips, Warminster.

Liddell, H. G. Scott, R. F. and Jones, H. S. 1996. *Greek Lexicon* (9th edition 1940 with New Supplement) (abbreviated to LSJ).

Marchant, E. C. 1991. *Xenophontis Opera*, vol. 2, Oxford, 13th impression.

Marchant, E. C. and Bowerstock, G. W. 1968. *Xenophon, Scripta Minora*, Loeb C. L.

Marchant, E. C. and Todd, O. J. 1968. *Xenophon, Memorabilia, Oeconomicus, Symposium, Apology*, Loeb C. L.

Morrison, D. R. 1988. *Bibliography of Editions, Translations and Commentaries on Xenophon's Socratic Writing, 1600–Present*, Pittsburgh.

Morrison, J. S. 1953. Xenophon Memorabilia 1.6: The Encounters Of Socrates and Antiphon, *Classical Review* (3), 3–6.

Morrison, J. S. 1955. Socrates and Antiphon, ibid. (5), 8–12.

Ollier, F. 1961. *Xénophon, Banquet, Apologie de Socrate*, Paris (Budé).

Parke, H. W. and Wormell, D. E. W. 1956. T*he Delphic Oracle*, Oxford.

Parke, H. W. 1967. *Greek Oracles*, London.

Phillips, A. A. and Willcock, M. M. 1999. *Xenophon and Arrian on Hunting*, Aris and Phillips, Warminster.

Pomeroy, S. B. 1994. *Xenophon, Oeconomicus*, Oxford.

Pucci, P. 2002. Introduction and commentary, *Socrates' Defence*, Amsterdam.

Reeve, C. D. 1989. *Socrates in the Apology*, Indianapolis.

Reynolds, L. D. and Wilson, N. G. 1991. *Scribes and Scholars*, 3rd ed., Oxford.

Rowe, C. J. 1988. *Plato's Symposium*, Aris and Phillips, Warminster.

Sandbach, F. H. Plato and the Socratic Work of Xenophon, *Cambridge History of Classical Literature*, vol. 1, 478–497.

Saunders, T. J. 1987. *Plato, Early Platonic Dialogues*, Penguin.

Smith, N. D. see T. C. Brickhouse.

Stokes, M. C. *Plato, Apology*, Aris and Phillips, Warminster, 1997.

Strauss, L. *Xenophon's Socrates*, Cornell, 1972.

Tatum, J. A. *Xenophon's Imperial Fiction: On the Education of Cyrus*, Princeton, 1989.

Taylor, A. E. 1963. *Plato, The Man and his Work*, London (revised reprint of 1926 edition).

Taylor, C. C. W., Hare, R. M., Barnes, J. 1990. *Greek Philosophers, Socrates, Plato, Aristotle*, Oxford.

Thesleff, H. The Interrelation and Date of the Symposia of Plato and Xenophon, *BICS* 25 (1978), 157–170.

Tredennick, H. and Tarrant, R. *Plato, The Last Days of Socrates*, Penguin, 1990.

Tredennick, H. and Waterfield, R. *Xenophon, Conversations of Socrates*, Penguin, 1990.

Tuplin, C. ed. 2004. *Xenophon and his World*, Papers from a Conference held in Liverpool in July 1999, *Historia Einzelschrift* 172, Stuttgart.

Vlastos, G. ed. 1980. *The Philosophy of Socrates, A Collection of Critical Essays*, Notre Dame U. P.

Vlastos, G. *Socrates, Ironist and Moral Philosopher*, Cambridge, 1991.

Vlastos, G. *Socratic Studies*, ed. M. Burnyeat, Cambridge, 1994.

Waterfield, R. see H. Tredennick.

Waterfield R. and Cartledge, P. *Xenophon, The Tyrant and other Treatises*, Penguin, 1997.

Waterfield, R. 2004. *Xenophon's Socratic Mission*, in Tuplin 2004, 79–113.

Willcock, M. M. see A. A. Phillips.

THE WORKS OF XENOPHON

Xenophon is one of the most important and interesting of the classical Greek authors because of the range of his experiences, and the subjects on which he writes. Quintilian is perhaps typical of later classical writers in mentioning him as a historian but thinking of him primarily as a philosopher, but he was much more than that, as will be obvious from the following list and rough categorisation of his works, of which the Latin title, the LSJ abbreviation and the English title will be given.

Socratic Writings

(1)   *Apologia Socratis* (*Ap.*) (*Socrates' Defence*): Xenophon's version of Socrates' speeches on the day of his trial and his thinking in his last days.

(2)   *Memorabilia* (*Mem.*): Xenophon's reminiscences about Socrates.

(3)   *Symposium* (*Smp.*) (*The Banquet*): Xenophon's account of the proceedings and conversation of Socrates and his friends at a banquet, showing Socrates in a less serious vein.

(4)   *Oeconomicus* (*Oec.*) (*On Estate Management*): Xenophon depicts Socrates first discussing estate management with Critobulus and then recalling an earlier conversation with Ischomachus on the subject.

History

(5)   *Historia graeca* or *Hellenica* (*HG*) (*A History of Greece*): an account of Greek history, starting where Thucydides breaks off in 411 and continuing to the Battle of Mantinea in 362. It was written in two parts, see Cawkwell 1979, with 1.–2.3.10 coming early.

Military Memoirs

(6)   *Anabasis* (*An.*) (*The March Up Country*): Xenophon's account of his adventures in 401–399.

Biography

(7)   *Agesilaus* (*Ages.*): the life of Xenophon's commanding officer, benefactor and friend, Agesilaus, the Spartan king who died in 360. Like Isocrates' *Evagoras*

which probably precedes it, it reads more like eulogy than biography in the modern sense. Xenophon stretches the truth in listing the virtues he ascribes to Agesilaus, idealising him like Socrates, Cyrus the Great and others, as an example for readers to imitate.

Political Theory

(8) *Respublica Lacedaemoniorum* (*Lac.*) (*The Spartan State*): an appreciative account of the Spartans' educational system, training them for life in general and war in particular.

(9) *Hiero* (*Hier.*): a dialogue in which Simonides of Ceos gives Hiero, the tyrant of Syracuse, advice on how to be a good ruler.

Technical Treatises

(10) *De Equitandi Ratione* (*Eq.*) (*Horsemanship*): a treatise written by an expert.

(11) *De Equitum Magistro* (*Eq. Mag.*) (*On the Duties of a Cavalry Officer*): advice by an expert.

(12) *Cynegeticus* (*Cyn.*) (*On Hunting*): on a subject dear to Xenophon, hunting with dogs.

Economics

(13) *Vectigalia* (*Vect.*) (*Ways and Means*): Xenophon's last work, offering ingenious suggestions about how Athens could improve her industrial and commercial prosperity.

Finally there is (14) *Institutio Cyri* (*Cyr.*) (*The Education of Cyrus*), a work impossible to categorise under any particular genre. Only the first book deals with the education of Cyrus and the other seven books are a blend of the fictional and the historical, describing the life, and achievements of Cyrus the Great, a figure idealised to include some features of Socrates and also of Xenophon himself. Xenophon's underlying purpose is to express his own ideas of how the perfect warrior king and ruler should be brought up, think and behave. The narrative resembles *Anabasis* for its easy flow and includes a magnificent love story. It has a good claim to be regarded as the first historical novel and as Xenophon's masterpiece.

THE LIFE OF XENOPHON

Xenophon was born early in the Peloponnesian War, perhaps about 430 B.C.,[1] and lived on till at least 355 B.C., the period when Philip of Macedon was becoming a menace to the rest of Greece. Apart from Xenophon's own works, particularly the *Anabasis* with its detailed coverage of his early military experiences from 401 to 399, our main source of information is Diogenes Laertius 2.48–59 who, writing probably very early in the third century A.D. on the lives and opinions of eminent philosophers, is valuable for his knowledge of sources now lost to us, but used these sources uncritically and was guilty of errors and inconsistencies.[2]

Xenophon's father Gryllus came from the deme of Erchia, probably near the modern Spata, not much more than ten miles from Athens, on the fringes of the Mesogeia, a rich agricultural plain enclosed by mountains. Gryllus probably farmed his own land like Ischomachus of the *Oeconomicus*; perhaps Xenophon's enthusiasm for the corn-growing potentialities of Attica, expressed late in his life in the *Vectigalia*, is based too much on memories of the locality of his early home, contrasting as it does with Thucydides' more realistic categorisation of Attica as a whole as 'thin-soiled', 1.2.5. Alternatively Anderson 10 suggests that the family may have made money out of the Laureion mines, as in *Vect.* 4 Xenophon also showed interest in their potentialities for Athens. At any rate Gryllus was comparatively well off, so that he and his son would serve Athens as knights rather than hoplites. Xenophon in Asia, 400–399 B.C., *An.* 3.3.19, had horses with him, perhaps brought from home. Much later he was to write a work on the duties of a cavalry commander, *De Equitum Magistro*, followed by a knowledgeable treatise on horsemanship, *De Equitandi Ratione*, which starts by claiming long expertise as a rider. In *Eq. Mag.* 1.11–12 Xenophon recommends that those who will have to serve later in the cavalry should be encouraged to learn to ride while still boys. Xenophon's love of horses surely started at an early age and he must have served in the cavalry towards the end of the Peloponnesian War.

Annual wartime invasions of Attica by the Spartans would have made life at Erchia difficult, if not impossible, particularly after the establishment in 413 of a permanent Spartan fort at Decelea only a few miles away, so that Xenophon presumably spent most of his early years in Athens itself. As Xenophon's *Hellenica*, though written much later, records events from 411 onwards, scholars have tried to identify particular episodes so treated by Xenophon as to suggest autopsy. Thus he may have served as a very young cavalryman with Thrasyllus in Ionia in 409, witnessed Alcibiades' return to Athens in 407, and been present at the trial of the generals after Arginusae in 406. His account in *HG* 2 of the reaction at Athens to the news of the loss of the fleet at Aegospotami in 405 also suggests his presence. It was during these last years of the war that Xenophon would have become acquainted with Socrates, if not of others connected with him, such as Alcibiades, Critias, who became one of the 'thirty tyrants', Charmides, Antisthenes, the proto-Cynic, and Aeschines, the writer of Socratic dialogues, not to mention Plato himself. The statement by Philostratus, writing in the A.D. 230s, *VS* 1.12, that Xenophon, while a prisoner in Boeotia, was let out on bail to listen to the sophist Prodicus of Ceos, is unsubstantiated elsewhere and should be treated with caution.[3]

According to an anecdote recorded by Diogenes Laertius 2.48, to start his *Life of Xenophon*, which immediately follows his *Life of Socrates*, Socrates actively conscripted Xenophon as a disciple by barring his way in an alley and asking first where every sort of food was on sale, and secondly where *kaloi kagathoi*,[4] perfect men, were produced. When this puzzled Xenophon, Socrates said 'Then follow me and learn'.

As a prosperous young man about town, Xenophon no doubt saw a great deal of Socrates, but only introduces himself as an active participant into one episode in *Mem.*, 1.3.8 ff., where he has himself reproved by Socrates for sympathising with Critobulus who had kissed a strikingly handsome young man.[5] Occasionally in *Mem.*, 1.4.2, 2.4.1, 2.5.1, 4.3.2, as in *Oec.* 1.1, and, fictitiously in *Smp.* 1.1., Xenophon claims to have heard the conversation; usually, however, he uses phrases like 'I know' or 'I remember'.

During the brief tenure of power by the 'thirty tyrants', 404–403, Xenophon seems to have served in their cavalry and presumably to have fought against the democratic forces led by Thrasybulus and by Anytus, one of Socrates' accusers, but he was able to take advantage of the general amnesty described in *HG* 2.4.43. Life in Athens under the restored democracy must have been distasteful, however, to Xenophon, a knight with oligarchical sympathies, till the welcome arrival in 401 of a letter from Proxenos, inviting him to go to Ionia and accompany Cyrus, supposedly for an expedition against the Pisidians, but in reality against Artaxerxes, Cyrus' older brother, who had recently become the Persian King on the death of their father Darius. Xenophon, in *An.* 3.1.5 ff., tells how, on Socrates' advice, he went to Delphi to consult the oracle about his proposed journey, but instead merely asked Apollo to which gods he should sacrifice to achieve the best outcome for his intended journey and a safe return home. Apollo specified the appropriate gods, but on his return to Athens Xenophon was criticised by Socrates for not asking whether he should have gone on the journey in the first place. (Socrates feared that service with Cyrus, who had helped Lysander and the Spartans towards the end of the war, would make Xenophon unpopular in Athens.) However under the circumstances Socrates told him to make the sacrifices and set out, which he did.

This Persian expedition was to be his making, affording him the chance to prove himself as a military leader and also providing him with the material for his great work, the *Anabasis*, in which he records his experiences from the spring of 401 to the spring of 399. Its title, however, is a misnomer, as the word means 'journey inland, away from the sea', and can only properly be applied to the first of the seven books, which covers the march of the 10,000 Greek mercenaries from Ionia to Cynaxa near Babylon; there, though heavily outnumbered by Artaxerxes' vast army, the Greeks won the day but lost their paymaster Cyrus who threw his life away in an unnecessary and impetuous attack on his brother, whom he wounded, before himself being killed by a member of the royal bodyguard. Book 2 describes how the 10,000 started for home under a truce but lost their five generals treacherously murdered by Tissaphernes. Thus at the beginning of Book 3 the Greeks find themselves in a desperate situation, leaderless, far from home and surrounded by enemies, but Xenophon now takes a major part in his own narrative, restoring discipline and hope to the army, giving them the sensible advice not to trust the perfidious Persians but to make for home with all speed, fighting their way when necessary. Xenophon, though previously holding no official post in the army, is now appointed one of the five new generals and, according to his own account,[6] plays a prominent part in leading them hundreds of miles northwards through Kurdestan and the snow-covered mountains of Armenia till they reach the Black Sea at Trapezus (Trebizond), and then westwards till they arrive at the Hellespont in the summer of 400. Harassed by the troops of the local satrap, Pharnabazus, and unwelcome to the Spartan admiral based at Byzantium, they entered the service of the Thracian Seuthes, spending the winter of 400 and the spring of 399 fighting his battles in Thrace. At this point Xenophon was eager to return to Athens, for, as he says, *An*. 7.7.57, he had not yet been exiled, but he was persuaded by his friends to lead the remainder of the 10,000 to Ionia to join the Spartan Thibron, to whom they were most welcome, as the Spartans were now at war with the Persian satraps.

Xenophon seems to have stayed on in the East continuously from 399, the year of Socrates' trial and death, serving with his Cyreans (the mercenaries enlisted for Cyrus) in Spartan armies, for a short time under Thibron, *cf. HG* 3.1.6, then under Dercyllidas, *cf. HG* 3.2.7, and finally with King Agesilaus, whom he idolised as a Panhellenist 'crusading' for the liberation of Asia Minor from the Persians, as is obvious from his laudatory biography, *Agesilaus*, as well as his *HG*. But Sparta had been making herself unpopular in Greece, and in 394 Agesilaus was recalled to meet the threat of an anti-Spartan alliance consisting of the Boeotian League headed by Thebes and of others including Argos, Corinth and Athens. He marched into Boeotia and won a narrow victory over the allied army of Athenians and Boeotians at Coroneia. Agesilaus' army included the Cyrean mercenaries who were under the command of Herippidas, *HG* 3.4.20 and 4.3.15. Xenophon himself was presumably involved in this battle against his fellow-countrymen, as he had accompanied Agesilaus to Boeotia, *cf. An.* 5.3.6, though only Plutarch, *Ages.* 18 expressly says so; Xenophon's reticence on the subject is understandable.

By this time Xenophon had been exiled from Athens, whether for the services to Agesilaus by Xenophon himself and his Cyreans, or perhaps even earlier for his espousal of the cause of Cyrus, who had befriended Lysander and the Spartans in the latter stages of the Peloponnesian War. Xenophon perhaps went on serving with Agesilaus till the 'King's Peace' of 386. At any rate he was rewarded by the Spartans with a home at Scillous about 2½ miles from Olympia and with the office of Spartan *proxenos*[7] at Olympia. He settled there with his wife Philasia and his twin sons Gryllus and Diodorus, and, out of part of the proceeds of the Persian expedition in fulfilment of a vow, bought a beautiful estate in a place prescribed by Delphic Apollo 'for the goddess Artemis', where he built her a temple and altar; the estate had excellent hunting for the enjoyment not only of the goddess but also of Xenophon, his two sons and his neighbours, and produced crops of which the tenth part was offered to Artemis. Nothing could have been more typical of this practical, pious man so fond of outdoor pursuits; for further details see *An.* 5.3.7 ff.

At Scillous Xenophon led the life of a gentleman farmer, no doubt in the way that Ischomachus recommends to Socrates in *Oec.* Although Agesilaus continued to lead Spartan armies till his death at an advanced age in 360,

Xenophon in his middle years had presumably retired from active soldiering, and had begun to write. Though he would have met old friends from Athens every fourth year at the Olympic Festivals, by then, as is obvious from his *HG*, he was far more interested in the fortunes of Sparta, where he was a respected figure. He sent his twin sons there to be brought up in the way that he praises in *Respublica Lacedaemoniorum*. He may even have been present for the festival of the *Gymnopaidiai* in 371, when news arrived of the disastrous defeat of the Spartans by the Thebans at Leuctra.

After their victory the Thebans became the dominant force in all mainland Greece, including even the Peloponnese, and the Elians, ever jealous of the Spartans, took advantage of the situation to evict Xenophon from Scillous. He escaped with his sons to Corinth and Diogenes Laertius 2.56 states that he settled there, implying that he remained there till his death there at an advanced age. However after Leuctra Athens' relationship with Sparta had improved because of a common hostility to Thebes, and about 367 the leading Athenian statesman Eubulus achieved the repeal of Xenophon's exile from Athens. Because in 366, *cf. HG* 7.4.6, relations between Corinth and Athens became strained, many scholars[8] believe that Xenophon now returned to Athens. To this period can be dated *Eq. Mag.*, containing advice on how to be an Athenian cavalry commander, and also the final chapter of *Eq.* These may have been for the special benefit of Xenophon's twin sons who had been sent by him to join the forces of Sparta's new ally, Athens, and were both involved in 362 in the battle of Mantinea. Diodorus survived the battle, but Gryllus died a heroic death in a cavalry engagement prior to the main battle, as described by Xenophon *HG* 7.5.15–17. Gryllus' courage was honoured at Athens by a painting by Euphranor in a colonnade near the Kerameikos which survived over 500 years to the time of Pausanias.

Xenophon's last work, *Vect.*, written not earlier than 355, offers the Athenians advice on how to improve their economy and generally supports the policy of Eubulus. This confirms the theory that Xenophon spent his last years in Athens. If Diogenes Laertius, quoting Demetrius of Magnesia, a friend of Atticus, is to be believed, Xenophon died in Corinth; if so, it may well have been on a visit. The date of his death is unknown. We need not believe the assertion of the often unreliable Pseudo-Lucianic *Longaevi* (*Octogenarians*) (written some time after A.D. 14), that he lived to be over ninety, or Diogenes Laertius' statement that he lived to a great age, as they may have been misled either by Xenophon's claim to have been present[9] at the symposium he describes or by the belief, *cf.* Strabo 9.2.7, that Xenophon had been saved by Socrates at Delium in 424;[10] the original version of the Delium episode occurs in Plato *Smp.* 221a, where Alcibiades claims to have guarded Socrates.

Notes

1. Xenophon's friend Proxenos was about 30 at his death in 400, *An.* 2.6.20, and Xenophon did not feel too young to replace him as a general, if invited, *An.* 3.1.25.
2. *E.g.* in 2.22, under *Socrates*, Diogenes Laertius says that Socrates saved Xenophon at the battle of Delium, but omits this erroneous statement in his account of Xenophon.
3. Xenophon need not have had to go to Boeotia to hear Prodikos, who often came to Athens, and it is Socrates, who had listened to Prodikos many times, whom Xenophon makes the reciter of *The Choice of Heracles*, *Mem.* 2.1.21, Prodikos' masterpiece, and one of the highlights of *Mem.* If Philostratus' statement is authentic, surety might have been provided by the family of Xenophon's friend, Proxenos, *cf. An.* 3.1.4.
4. See n. on *Mem.* 1.1.16 on *kaloskagathos*.
5. See notes on *Mem.* 1.3.8–13 questioning the historicity of several details of this passage. Xenophon, however, may well have been rebuked for having, or sympathising with, a susceptibility to handsome young men.
6. Xenophon says, *HG* 3.1.2, that the expedition of the Cyreans up to their escape to the sea had been described by Themistogenes of Syracuse. This seems to have been a pseudonym under which Xenophon published a first version of *An.* 1–4; later 'to rescue his own achievements from undeserved neglect' (Anderson 83), he may have revised 1–4, and added 5–7.
7. A *proxenos* normally represented the interests of another city in his own city.
8. Including Delebecque, author of the most detailed and scholarly biographical study of Xenophon, who believed he spent the last ten to twelve years of his life in Athens.
9. The dramatic date of Xenophon's *Smp.* is 422; *cf.* Bowen 9.
10. See note 2.

THE DATING AND RELATIONSHIPS OF XENOPHON'S SOCRATIC WRITINGS TO EACH OTHER, TO WORKS OF PLATO AND TO POLYCRATES

The successful prosecution of Socrates in 399 was followed in the late 390s by Polycrates' *Accusation of Socrates*, a sophistical exercise by an Athenian rhetorician who may have practised in Cyprus. This work, which along with Polycrates' *Defence of Busiris* is severely criticised by Isocrates in his *Busiris*, made much of the influence of Socrates on Alcibiades and Critias, which must have been one of the main contributory factors towards Socrates' condemnation, and must surely have been stressed by the three original accusers, Anytus in particular. The absence of any mention of the two politicians by Socrates in either *Apology* is surprising indeed. It must presumably be accepted as historical, and at least is consistent with other indications that even in Plato's version of his *Apology* Socrates did not try particularly hard to gain acquittal; perhaps Socrates had long disregarded both men as proper pupils. Isocrates does insist, *Busiris* 5, that Alcibiades was never taught by Socrates, though this sounds like a rival sophist speaking. M. M. Willcock suggests that the topic of Alcibiades and Critias was avoided as a weak link in the defence; the omission could thus be due to Socrates himself or to Plato reporting him. Polycrates' exercise is countered by Xenophon in *Memorabilia* 1.2.12 ff. Some scholars argue that the absence of the names of Alcibiades and Critias from both *Apologies* indicates that they preceded Polycrates. This need not be so and all that can be substantiated is that *Memorabilia* is later than Polycrates.

The precise dating of individual works of Xenophon is complicated by the fact that one does not know how, when, or where he published them, and by his habit of incorporating material from earlier works in later ones, reusing motifs, paraphrasing or repeating verbatim phrases or whole sentences, and revising or adding postscripts to works of earlier origin; see Delebecque passim.

Apology was composed long enough after the death of Socrates for other accounts of his last days to have been written, and for the (undatable) death of Anytus to have occurred. In it Xenophon was probably influenced not only by Plato's *Apology* but also by his *Meno*, as *Apology* 29–31 looks like Xenophon's reaction to Plato's surprising leniency shown in *Meno* to

Anytus, the most formidable of the three accusers. *Meno* is dated by Bluck to 386–5 and by Delebecque to shortly after the foundation of the Academy in 388.

Memorabilia similarly affords few clues for dating purposes. The influence of two early Platonic dialogues, *Lysis* and *Charmides*, may possibly be detected in 1.6.14 and 1.2.56, while that of three slightly later dialogues, *Meno*, *Protagoras* and *Euthydemus*, may be seen, of *Meno* and *Protagoras* almost certainly in 1.2.20 and of *Euthydemus* possibly in 1.2.24 ff. and more probably in 1.4.1; see notes on these passages. *Mem.* 3.5.4, with its fear of Thebes, seems to reflect the situation after the battle of Leuctra (371–362), rather than its dramatic date of 406. See pp. 58–60, *Introduction to Memorabilia*, with my summary of the contents, from which it may be concluded that the bulk of Books 1 and 2 seems to have been arranged to form a unit, with Book 3 forming a separate later unit, while Book 4 reads like a polished and mature final unit, culminating in an impressive and impassioned eulogy of Socrates. *Mem.* 4.8 uses several phrases and motifs similar to ones found in *Apology*, and it seems probable that they are echoes and that *Apology* precedes everything in *Memorabilia*, which should be regarded as a tribute to Socrates assembled in stages over the years.

The subject of *Oeconomicus*, the management of an agricultural estate, suggests that it was either written at Scillous or at least inspired by Xenophon's experiences there. Its opening reads like a continuation of *Mem.*, with Xenophon introducing a conversation of Socrates which he claims to have heard. Up to 6.12 the dialogue takes a predictable course with Socrates doing most of the talking, and Critobulus as his interlocutor, even if we are surprised to see Socrates, the haunter of the *agora*, take such an interest in agriculture and money-making despite his assertions to the contrary in Plato, *Apology* 36b. Other topics of his conversation *e.g.* the Great King, Cyrus the pretender, Lysander, horses, hunting, the beneficial effects of farming in fitting men for war, the taking of omens *etc.*, also suggest Xenophon himself rather than Socrates. The major section, however, starts at 6.12 with Socrates, unusually, made to recount at length a conversation he once had, with Socrates himself doing more of the listening than the talking. His interlocutor was the wealthy farmer, Ischomachus, who may be a real Athenian, see Pomeroy 259–264, but the significant name (= Mighty Warrior) and many of his views are strongly suggestive of Xenophon himself. The most interesting part of this section is Ischomachus' discourse on the training, treatment and duties of the good wife, but for our present purposes we should note the location of the discussion, 7.1, in the *stoa* of the temple of Zeus Eleutherios, where paintings were on display, including that of Gryllus, Xenophon's son, fighting at Mantinea, where he died a heroic death. It seems probable that the location for this conversation was chosen by the proud father and that 7.1 should be dated no earlier than 362, though this need not necessarily apply to the whole section or indeed the whole dialogue.

Xenophon mentions Plato only once, in *Mem.* 3.6.1, in which Socrates cross-questions Glaucon, son of Charmides and brother of Plato, and proves that his political ambitions are ill-founded, till he improves his knowledge and capabilities. Xenophon makes Socrates explain his decision to do this as out of goodwill towards Charmides and Plato. Plato nowhere mentions Xenophon by name, but his late work, *Laws*, seems to contain, 694c, a criticism of Xenophon's *Cyropaedia*. Their attitude to each other is discussed in Aulus Gellius, 14.3, writing in the Antonine Age, who thinks that any rivalry between them was confined to their eager admirers, whereas Pontianus, the philosopher in Athenaeus (*c.* A.D. 200), 504c, and Diogenes Laertius (perhaps of the third century A.D.), 3.34, both suggest rivalry and jealousy between them. Gellius' verdict seems the more reasonable one, as the wording of *Mem.* 3.6.1 appears respectful, rather than hostile, though the contents of Plato's *Meno* probably displeased Xenophon.

Xenophon's *Smp.* may be dated between 378 and 371 from the reference in 8.34–5 to the Theban Sacred Band (formed in 378 or soon after) and their inferiority to Spartan homosexual warriors (unlikely after the Spartan defeat at Leuctra). Orthodox scholarly opinion is that Xenophon *Smp.* is influenced by Plato *Smp.* (dated by Dover, *Phronesis*, 10, 1965, 1–20 to between 384 and 378). Bowen, however, 8–9, follows H. Thesleff, The Interrelation and Date of the Symposia of Plato and Xenophon, *BICS* 25, 1978, 157–70, believing that Xenophon's *Smp.* is the earlier work, that Plato was influenced by it, and that Xenophon, on reading Plato *Smp.*, adapted his original *Smp.* to include Socrates' discourse on *Eros* in chapter 8.

Possible connections of Xenophon's *Smp.* with *Ap.* and *Mem.* are suggested by the initial defence of his subject as *axiomnêmoneuta, cf.* title of *Mem.* and *axion...memnêsthai, Ap.* 1 (deserving to be recorded).

Probably, therefore, Xenophon's *Smp.* is later than *Ap.* and *Mem.* 1 and 2, but precedes *Mem.* 3 and 4 and *Oec.* (at least in its final form). A possible chronological framework is therefore:

(1) Plato *Ap.*
(2) Polycrates' exercise, *c.* 390.
(3) Plato *Meno, c.* 386–5?
(4) Xenophon *Ap.*, after 384?
(5) *Mem.* started.
(6) Plato *Smp.*, 384–378.
(7) Xenophon *Smp.* before 371.
(8) Continuation of *Mem.*; Books 3, 4 after 371.
(9) *Oec.*, completed after 362, but bulk of it probably written earlier.

Other Socratic writers were Aeschines of Sphettus, famed in classical times for his Socratic dialogues, Antisthenes, and Aristippus, who founded the Cyrenaic School with its emphasis on hedonism. None of these is credited with an *Apology*, though Aeschines produced an *Alcibiades*, (of which sizeable fragments remain), as did Antisthenes and also Euclides of Megara. Antisthenes, the oldest Socratic, born *c.* 455, *cf.* Bowen 12, though reputedly an offensive man who quarrelled with Plato, Guthrie, (2) 21, and portrayed as behaving rather unpleasantly at Xenophon's *Smp.*, presumably met with Xenophon's general approval for his ascetic, hardy, proto-Cynic lifestyle, *cf. Mem.* 2.5, 3.11.17, and Xenophon's writings may well have been influenced by him. Several others including Crito and Phaedo are credited by Diogenes Laertius with dialogues, presumably apologetic in purpose, though their influence on Xenophon is questionable. Diogenes Laertius, 2.40, also states that the orator Lysias wrote a defence speech for Socrates to use at his trial, but, on hearing it, Socrates rejected it as unsuitable for him. For further details of Socratic writers see C. C. W. Taylor.

INTRODUCTION TO *APOLOGIA SOCRATIS*

Xenophon's *Apologia Socratis* is of interest and importance as providing an account of Socrates on trial somewhat different from the more familiar one found in Plato. Despite their similar titles the two works differ greatly in contents and purpose.

Plato's *Apology* consists entirely of his version of what Socrates said on the day of his trial. The Greek word *apologia* means 'speech spoken in one's defence', but Plato's work in fact contains three speeches by Socrates:

(1) The *apologia* proper, the initial speech rebutting the charges (17a–35d).

(2) A second speech after Socrates has been found guilty, in which he counters Meletus' advocacy of the death penalty and makes his own proposal for his punishment. After flippantly claiming at some length that really he deserves to be maintained at Athens' expense as a public benefactor, he defers to the insistence of his friends, Plato and three others, and proposes a fine of 30 minae which his friends will guarantee (35e–38b).

(3) A final speech after he has been condemned to death (38c–42a).

Xenophon on the other hand was not at the trial and he says his account is drawn from what Socrates' friend Hermogenes had told him. Xenophon's primary purpose is to throw light on Socrates' motivation during his last days, explaining his haughty tone at his trial as based on a belief that, because of his old age, death was preferable to life. The contents of Xenophon's work are:

1–9   Introductory.
10–21   Socrates' main speech.
22–23   Xenophon's reassertion of Socrates' determination to die.
24–26   Socrates' speech after hearing the death penalty.
27–33   Socrates' cheerful behaviour while awaiting his execution and his rebuke to Anytus for failing to educate his son properly.
34   Epilogue in praise of Socrates.

Xenophon's version of Socrates' speeches is much shorter than Plato's; he says, 22, that he is only giving enough of Socrates' initial speech to prove his point about his motivation. Xenophon says that Socrates' friends also spoke in his defence, a point absent from Plato. In 23 Xenophon expressly states that Socrates refused to make any counterproposal to the death penalty advocated by Meletus and forbade his friends to do so; Plato on the other hand includes a flippant unrealistic speech by Socrates, see above, eventually suggesting a fine guaranteed by four friends.

Then there are the general differences between Xenophon's Socrates and Plato's Socrates. Plato, it is generally agreed, did eventually come to use Socrates as a mouthpiece for some of his own theories, but the Socrates of Plato's *Apology* is at least consistent with the character portrayed in *Crito* and so-called Socratic works such as *Laches* and *Charmides*, that of an unworldly intellectual and idealist. Xenophon, of course, does agree with Plato in depicting Socrates as brave, steadfast, pious and scrupulously moral, but he also credits him with other qualities that he himself admired and possessed. Xenophon's Socrates, on the evidence of *Mem.*, *Oec.* and *Smp.*, is a practical man of the world endowed with common sense and *savoir faire*. Thus in both *Mem.* and *Oec.* he shows much more interest in the problems of running a household or estate and talks a great deal more practical sense on these matters than one would expect from Plato's Socrates, who in *Ap.* 36b denies any interest in *chrêmatismos* and *oikonomia* (money-making and managing an estate). Thus Xenophon explains Socrates' behaviour at his trial as based on a commonsense reason, a desire to avoid the disadvantages of old age.

Plato and Xenophon do at least agree on many features of the actual trial, *e.g.* Socrates' refusal to court the goodwill of the jury, his general smugness (though perhaps less obvious in Plato's *Apology*, which contains more of Socrates' typical irony), the cross-examination of Meletus, and the uproar among the jurors caused at various points by Socrates' words. Then there are topics occurring in both *Apologies*, but with differences of detail, *e.g.* mentions of the *daimonion* (divine sign, see p. 42), Chaerephon at Delphi, and the oracle's response, Socrates' indulgence in prophecy in his last hours, and the prospect of meeting Palamedes. One striking omission from Xenophon's abbreviated version is the absence of any mention of Aristophanes' *Clouds* and the misconceptions it may have caused.

All the indications are that the fuller version of the eyewitness, published at Athens and probably soon after the events, and likely to be ridiculed if distorting the essential facts, and written by the one with the superior appreciation of Socrates' thought processes, is likely to contain more of the truth than the abbreviated version written after a considerable interval by an absentee claiming to reproduce what Hermogenes had told him. Xenophon's

Socrates, moreover, has several suspiciously Xenophontic features, the great stress on omens *etc.*, the mention of Lycurgus, and the elaboration of virtues dear to Xenophon's own heart praised in Xenophon's strange version of the Delphic response to Chaerephon. Probably, therefore, though it cannot be proved incontestably, differences from Plato are fictions by Xenophon, whereas common features are derived from Plato's *Apology*, whether from Xenophon having his own copy or via Hermogenes relying on a memory perhaps supplemented by having read Plato's version.

A brief note should be added here on passages in Xenophon's *Ap.* closely paralleled in *Mem.* Much of the material of *Ap.* 2–21 is also found in *Mem.* 1.2.1–20 with use not only of the same motifs but also of identical or very similar phraseology; the only difference is that in *Ap.* Socrates, as reported by Hermogenes, is the speaker, whereas in *Mem.* Xenophon himself speaks in defence of Socrates. The final chapter of *Mem.*, 4.8, with its discussion of the *daimonion*, its account of information given by Hermogenes and its eulogistic finale is particularly full of parallels with material already found in *Apology*, see pp. 156*ff.*

TEXT OF *APOLOGIA SOCRATIS*

SIGLA

B	Vaticanus graecus 1335, 12th century
B²	Corrector, 14th century
A	Vaticanus graecus 1950, 15th century
C	Mutinensis 145, 15th century
H	Britannicus Harleianus 5724, 15th century
R	Reuchlin, *editio princeps*, Genoa, A.D. 1520
Stob.	mss. of Stobaeus, a 5th century anthologist

The basis of the text printed is a reproduction of Marchant's generally reliable O.C.T., but more recently important contributions to our knowledge of the mss. and the study of the text have been made by Ollier in his excellent Budé, and by E. A. Schmoll, *GRBS* 1990, 313–321.

B has long been recognised as the most important manuscript and Schmoll argues with some justification that an editor need use only it as the basis of his/her text, and that A is ultimately derived from it via a lost manuscript, the scribe of which, B², had added corrections to A. Schmoll has also produced a theoretical stemma which may well be correct. Most of the variant readings of A, B², C, H and R do indeed look like conjectures and seem to lack authority.

B, however, though the best manuscript, is revealed as being far from perfect by the evidence of the manuscripts of Stobaeus, of the early fifth century, who in *Anthologium*, 3.7, quotes the bulk of chapters 25–28, and provides several variant readings, some worse, but a few clearly better than those of B.

What I consider improvements to Marchant are listed in *Supplementary Notes on the Text*, p. 163. Some of these have been incorporated into the text, but where this has proved too difficult, the Oxford text has been printed with marginal asterisks and translated, and the recommended change suggested and explained in the Commentary.

APOLOGIA SOCRATIS

SOCRATES' DEFENCE

ΑΠΟΛΟΓΙΑ ΣΩΚΡΑΤΟΥΣ
[ΠΡΟΣ ΤΟΥΣ ΔΙΚΑΣΤΑΣ]

Σωκράτους δὲ ἄξιόν μοι δοκεῖ εἶναι μεμνῆσθαι καὶ ὡς 1
ἐπειδὴ ἐκλήθη εἰς τὴν δίκην ἐβουλεύσατο περί τε τῆς
ἀπολογίας καὶ τῆς τελευτῆς τοῦ βίου. γεγράφασι μὲν οὖν
περὶ τούτου καὶ ἄλλοι καὶ πάντες ἔτυχον τῆς μεγαληγορίας
5 αὐτοῦ· ᾧ καὶ δῆλον ὅτι τῷ ὄντι οὕτως ἐρρήθη ὑπὸ Σωκράτους. ἀλλ᾽ ὅτι ἤδη ἑαυτῷ ἡγεῖτο αἱρετώτερον εἶναι τοῦ βίου
θάνατον, τοῦτο οὐ διεσαφήνισαν· ὥστε ἀφρονεστέρα αὐτοῦ
φαίνεται εἶναι ἡ μεγαληγορία. Ἑρμογένης μέντοι ὁ Ἱππο- 2
νίκου ἑταῖρός τε ἦν αὐτῷ καὶ ἐξήγγειλε περὶ αὐτοῦ τοιαῦτα
10 ὥστε πρέπουσαν φαίνεσθαι τὴν μεγαληγορίαν αὐτοῦ τῇ
διανοίᾳ. ἐκεῖνος γὰρ ἔφη ὁρῶν αὐτὸν περὶ πάντων μᾶλλον
διαλεγόμενον ἢ περὶ τῆς δίκης εἰπεῖν· Οὐκ ἐχρῆν μέντοι 3
σκοπεῖν, ὦ Σώκρατες, καὶ ὅ τι ἀπολογήσῃ; τὸν δὲ τὸ μὲν
πρῶτον ἀποκρίνασθαι· Οὐ γὰρ δοκῶ σοι ἀπολογεῖσθαι
15 μελετῶν διαβεβιωκέναι; ἐπεὶ δ᾽ αὐτὸν ἐρέσθαι· Πῶς; Ὅτι
οὐδὲν ἄδικον διαγεγένημαι ποιῶν· ἥνπερ νομίζω μελέτην εἶναι
καλλίστην ἀπολογίας. ἐπεὶ δὲ αὐτὸν πάλιν λέγειν· Οὐχ ὁρᾷς 4
τὰ Ἀθηναίων δικαστήρια ὡς πολλάκις μὲν οὐδὲν ἀδικοῦντας
λόγῳ παραχθέντες ἀπέκτειναν, πολλάκις δὲ ἀδικοῦντας ἢ ἐκ

Titulus πρὸς τοὺς δικαστὰς om. Stob.
15 ἔπειτα codd.: corr. Dindorf
15, 17 αὐτὸς Schenkl

SOCRATES' DEFENCE
[TO THE JURORS]

1. Socrates seems to me to be particularly memorable for the deliberate decision he took about his defence speech and about the last stages of his life after being summoned to a trial. Now others too have already written about this and they have all recaptured the proud tone of his words. From this it is obvious that the speech made by Socrates really was like that. But what they have not made clear is that he *already* considered death was preferable to life for himself, so that they make his proud tone seem rather stupid. 2. Hermogenes, however, the son of Hipponicus, was a companion of his, and his reports about Socrates were such as to make it quite obvious that his proud tone was consistent with his thinking. For Hermogenes said that, on seeing Socrates discussing anything rather than the trial, he asked 3. 'But, Socrates, shouldn't you really be considering what you'll say in your defence?' Socrates' initial reply, according to Hermogenes, was 'So you don't think I've spent all my life practising my defence?' and when he asked him 'How so?', Socrates said 'Because throughout my life I have avoided wrongdoing, and *that* I consider the best practice for a defence.' 4. Hermogenes continued that when he asked a further question 'Don't you see that the courts of the Athenian have often been misled by speeches and put innocent men to death, and often too have acquitted wrongdoers out

τοῦ λόγου οἰκτίσαντες ἢ ἐπιχαρίτως εἰπόντας ἀπέλυσαν;
Ἀλλὰ ναὶ μὰ Δία, φάναι αὐτόν, καὶ δὶς ἤδη ἐπιχειρήσαντός
μου σκοπεῖν περὶ τῆς ἀπολογίας ἐναντιοῦταί μοι τὸ δαιμόνιον.
5 ὡς δὲ αὐτὸν εἰπεῖν· Θαυμαστὰ λέγεις, τὸν δ' αὖ ἀποκρί-
νασθαι· Ἦ θαυμαστὸν νομίζεις εἰ καὶ τῷ θεῷ δοκεῖ ἐμὲ 5
βέλτιον εἶναι ἤδη τελευτᾶν; οὐκ οἶσθα ὅτι μέχρι μὲν τοῦδε
οὐδενὶ ἀνθρώπων ὑφείμην ⟨ἂν⟩ βέλτιον ἐμοῦ βεβιωκέναι;
ὅπερ γὰρ ἥδιστόν ἐστιν, ᾔδειν ὁσίως μοι καὶ δικαίως ἅπαντα
τὸν βίον βεβιωμένον· ὥστε ἰσχυρῶς ἀγάμενος ἐμαυτὸν ταὐτὰ
ηὕρισκον καὶ τοὺς ἐμοὶ συγγιγνομένους γιγνώσκοντας περὶ 10
6 ἐμοῦ. νῦν δὲ εἰ ἔτι προβήσεται ἡ ἡλικία, οἶδ' ὅτι ἀνάγκη
ἔσται τὰ τοῦ γήρως ἐπιτελεῖσθαι καὶ ὁρᾶν τε χεῖρον καὶ
ἀκούειν ἧττον καὶ δυσμαθέστερον εἶναι καὶ ὧν ἔμαθον
ἐπιλησμονέστερον. ἂν δὲ αἰσθάνωμαι χείρων γιγνόμενος
καὶ καταμέμφωμαι ἐμαυτόν, πῶς ἄν, εἰπεῖν, ἐγὼ ἔτι ἂν 15
7 ἡδέως βιοτεύοιμι; ἴσως δέ τοι, φάναι αὐτόν, καὶ ὁ θεὸς δι'
εὐμένειαν προξενεῖ μοι οὐ μόνον τὸ ἐν καιρῷ τῆς ἡλικίας
καταλῦσαι τὸν βίον, ἀλλὰ καὶ τὸ ᾗ ῥᾷστα. ἂν γὰρ νῦν
κατακριθῇ μοι, δῆλον ὅτι ἐξέσται μοι τῇ τελευτῇ χρῆσθαι
ἣ ῥᾴστη μὲν ὑπὸ τῶν τούτου ἐπιμεληθέντων κέκριται, ἀπρα- 20
γμονεστάτη δὲ τοῖς φίλοις, πλεῖστον δὲ πόθον ἐμποιοῦσα τῶν
τελευτώντων. ὅταν γὰρ ἄσχημον μὲν μηδὲν μηδὲ δυσχερὲς
ἐν ταῖς γνώμαις τῶν παρόντων καταλείπηται ⟨τις⟩, ὑγιὲς δὲ
τὸ σῶμα ἔχων καὶ τὴν ψυχὴν δυναμένην φιλοφρονεῖσθαι
ἀπομαραίνηται, πῶς οὐκ ἀνάγκη τοῦτον ποθεινὸν εἶναι; 25
8 ὀρθῶς δὲ οἱ θεοὶ τότε μὲν ἠναντιοῦντο, φάναι αὐτόν, τῇ
τοῦ λόγου ἐπισκέψει ὅτε ἐδόκει ἡμῖν ζητητέα εἶναι ἐκ παντὸς

2 αὐτός Schenkl
7 ἂν add. Stephanus, cf. Mem. 4.8.6
8 μοι C: μὲν cett.
12 ἀποτελεῖσθαι ΒΑ: corr. Marchant e Mem. 4.8.8
19 μου Reiske
22 τελευτῶν ΒΑ¹: corr. Schenkl
23 καταλίπηται codd.: corr. Stephanus, ⟨τις⟩ add. Schenkl
26 μὲν codd.: μοι Schenkl: μου Reuchlin
27 ὑμῖν Weiske

of pity engendered by their speeches or because their words have curried favour?', Socrates said 'But, by Zeus, I have twice already tried to think about my defence, but my divine sign opposes me.' 5. When Hermogenes said 'You surprise me', Socrates retorted, 'Can you really think it surprising that God too thinks it better for me to die *now*? Don't you know that to this day I would never have conceded to anyone that he had led a better life than I? For what pleases me very much is that I always knew that my whole life had been lived by me in piety and justice, so that, despite my mighty self-esteem, I found that the same opinion about me was also held by my associates. 6. But now, if my years are further prolonged, I know that it will be inevitable for me to pay the dues of old age, to have impaired vision and hearing, to be slower on the uptake and more forgetful of what I have learned. But if *I* notice myself deteriorating and find fault with myself, how' continued Socrates, 'could I continue to live a pleasant life? 7. Perhaps' he went on 'God in his kindness is looking after my interests and arranging for me to end my life not only at just the right age but also in the easiest possible way. For if I am now condemned, clearly I shall be able to avail myself of the death which has been judged by those who have attended to the matter to be easiest for the victims, but also least troublesome for their families and friends and making them feel most deeply the loss of the dying ones. For whenever anyone leaves in the minds of those present at his death no memories of anything ugly or unpleasant, but merely fades away with his body still healthy and his spirit still capable of cheerfulness, how can he fail to be sorely missed? 8. The gods were right on that occasion' continued Socrates 'to oppose my thinking about my speech, at the very time when we thought I should try to get off in any way I could. For if I had accomplished

ὅτι ἡτοιμασάμην ἂν ἀντὶ τοῦ ἤδη λῆξαι τοῦ βίου ἢ νόσοις
ἀλγυνόμενος τελευτῆσαι ἢ γήρᾳ, εἰς ὃ πάντα τὰ χαλεπὰ
συρρεῖ καὶ μάλα ἔρημα τῶν εὐφροσυνῶν. μὰ Δί', εἰπεῖν 9
5 αὐτόν, ὦ Ἑρμόγενες, ἐγὼ ταῦτα οὐδὲ προθυμήσομαι, ἀλλ'
ὅσων νομίζω τετυχηκέναι καλῶν καὶ παρὰ θεῶν καὶ παρ'
ἀνθρώπων, καὶ ἣν ἐγὼ δόξαν ἔχω περὶ ἐμαυτοῦ, ταύτην
ἀναφαίνων εἰ βαρυνῶ τοὺς δικαστάς, αἱρήσομαι τελευτᾶν
μᾶλλον ἢ ἀνελευθέρως τὸ ζῆν ἔτι προσαιτῶν κερδᾶναι τὸν
10 πολὺ χείρω βίον ἀντὶ θανάτου. οὕτως δὲ γνόντα αὐτὸν ἔφη 10
[εἰπεῖν], ἐπειδὴ κατηγόρησαν αὐτοῦ οἱ ἀντίδικοι ὡς οὓς μὲν
ἡ πόλις νομίζει θεοὺς οὐ νομίζοι, ἕτερα δὲ καινὰ δαιμόνια
εἰσφέροι καὶ τοὺς νέους διαφθείροι, παρελθόντα εἰπεῖν· Ἀλλ' 11
ἐγώ, ὦ ἄνδρες, τοῦτο μὲν πρῶτον θαυμάζω Μελήτου, ὅτῳ
15 ποτὲ γνοὺς λέγει ὡς ἐγὼ οὓς ἡ πόλις νομίζει θεοὺς οὐ
νομίζω· ἐπεὶ θύοντά γέ με ἐν ταῖς κοιναῖς ἑορταῖς καὶ ἐπὶ
* τῶν δημοσίων βωμῶν καὶ οἱ ἄλλοι οἱ παρατυγχάνοντες *
ἑώρων καὶ αὐτὸς Μέλητος, εἰ ἐβούλετο. καινά γε μὴν 12
20 δαιμόνια πῶς ἂν ἐγὼ εἰσφέροιμι λέγων ὅτι θεοῦ μοι φωνὴ
φαίνεται σημαίνουσα ὅ τι χρὴ ποιεῖν; καὶ γὰρ οἱ φθόγγοις
οἰωνῶν καὶ οἱ φήμαις ἀνθρώπων χρώμενοι φωναῖς δήπου
τεκμαίρονται. βροντὰς δὲ ἀμφιλέξει τις ἢ μὴ φωνεῖν ἢ μὴ
μέγιστον οἰωνιστήριον εἶναι; ἡ δὲ Πυθοῖ ἐν τῷ τρίποδι
ἱέρεια οὐ καὶ αὐτὴ φωνῇ τὰ παρὰ τοῦ θεοῦ διαγγέλλει; ἀλλὰ 13
25 μέντοι καὶ τὸ προειδέναι γε τὸν θεὸν τὸ μέλλον καὶ τὸ
προσημαίνειν ᾧ βούλεται, καὶ τοῦτο, ὥσπερ ἐγώ φημι, οὕτω
πάντες καὶ λέγουσι καὶ νομίζουσιν. ἀλλ' οἱ μὲν οἰωνούς τε

8　　βαρύνω codd.: corr. Hirschig
11　　εἰπεῖν del. Leonclavius
11–12　μὲν ἡ C: ἡ μὲν cett.
17　　*οἱ ἄλλοι AC: ἄλλοι B
18　　καὶ] κἂν Richards
22　　βρονταῖς codd.: corr. Gesner

that, clearly I would have secured for myself, instead of stopping living now, a painful death from illnesses or from old age, which attracts the combined flow of all troubles and everything completely joyless. 9. Good heavens no, Hermogenes,' he went on 'I won't be eager for that, but if, by making clear all the good things I think I've had from gods and men and the opinion I have of myself, I thereby annoy the jury, my choice will be to die rather than to keep on begging for life unlike a free man and so gaining instead of death a life far inferior to it.'

10. Hermogenes said that this was what Socrates had decided and so, when his opponents in the trial had accused him of not worshipping the gods worshipped by the city, but of introducing other new divinities and corrupting the young men, Socrates came forward and said, 11. 'But, gentlemen, the first thing which surprises *me* about Meletus is his source of knowledge for alleging that I don't worship the gods worshipped by the city, for I could have regularly been seen sacrificing during the public festivals and at the *communal altars by the others that happened to be there, and by Meletus * himself, had he so wished. 12. But as for new divinities, how could I be introducing them by saying that God's voice reveals itself to me signalling what I must do? For it is the same with those who use the cries of birds and the utterances of humans; *they* presumably are guided by voices. And will anyone deny that claps of thunder have a voice and are the mightiest of omens? And what about the priestess herself who sits on the tripod at Pytho? Doesn't she too use a voice to relay the messages from God? 13. But that God has foreknowledge of the future and communicates it in advance to whom he wishes, this too is what everybody says and thinks, exactly as

καὶ φήμας καὶ συμβόλους τε καὶ μάντεις ὀνομάζουσι τοὺς
προσημαίνοντας εἶναι, ἐγὼ δὲ τοῦτο δαιμόνιον καλῶ, καὶ
οἶμαι οὕτως ὀνομάζων καὶ ἀληθέστερα καὶ ὁσιώτερα λέγειν
τῶν τοῖς ὄρνισιν ἀνατιθέντων τὴν τῶν θεῶν δύναμιν. ὥς
γε μὴν οὐ ψεύδομαι κατὰ τοῦ θεοῦ καὶ τοῦτ' ἔχω τεκμήριον· 5
καὶ γὰρ τῶν φίλων πολλοῖς δὴ ἐξαγγείλας τὰ τοῦ θεοῦ
14 συμβουλεύματα οὐδεπώποτε ψευσάμενος ἐφάνην. ἐπεὶ δὲ
ταῦτα ἀκούοντες οἱ δικασταὶ ἐθορύβουν, οἱ μὲν ἀπιστοῦντες
τοῖς λεγομένοις, οἱ δὲ καὶ φθονοῦντες, εἰ καὶ παρὰ θεῶν
μειζόνων ἢ αὐτοὶ τυγχάνοι, πάλιν εἰπεῖν τὸν Σωκράτην· 10
Ἄγε δὴ ἀκούσατε καὶ ἄλλα, ἵνα ἔτι μᾶλλον οἱ βουλόμενοι
ὑμῶν ἀπιστῶσι τῷ ἐμὲ τετιμῆσθαι ὑπὸ δαιμόνων. Χαιρεφῶντος γάρ ποτε ἐπερωτῶντος ἐν Δελφοῖς περὶ ἐμοῦ πολλῶν
παρόντων ἀνεῖλεν ὁ Ἀπόλλων μηδένα εἶναι ἀνθρώπων ἐμοῦ
μήτε ἐλευθεριώτερον μήτε δικαιότερον μήτε σωφρονέστερον. 15
15 ὡς δ' αὖ ταῦτ' ἀκούσαντες οἱ δικασταὶ ἔτι μᾶλλον εἰκότως
ἐθορύβουν, αὖθις εἰπεῖν τὸν Σωκράτην· Ἀλλὰ μείζω μέν, ὦ
ἄνδρες, εἶπεν ὁ θεὸς ἐν χρησμοῖς περὶ Λυκούργου τοῦ Λακε-
δαιμονίοις νομοθετήσαντος ἢ περὶ ἐμοῦ. λέγεται γὰρ εἰς
τὸν ναὸν εἰσιόντα προσειπεῖν αὐτόν· Φροντίζω πότερα θεόν 20
σε εἴπω ἢ ἄνθρωπον. ἐμὲ δὲ θεῷ μὲν οὐκ εἴκασεν, ἀνθρώπων
δὲ πολλῷ προέκρινεν ὑπερφέρειν. ὅμως δὲ ὑμεῖς μηδὲ ταῦτ'
εἰκῇ πιστεύσητε τῷ θεῷ, ἀλλὰ καθ' ἓν ἕκαστον ἐπισκοπεῖτε
16 ὧν εἶπεν ὁ θεός. τίνα μὲν γὰρ ἐπίστασθε ἧττον ἐμοῦ
δουλεύοντα ταῖς τοῦ σώματος ἐπιθυμίαις; τίνα δὲ ἀνθρώπων 25
ἐλευθεριώτερον, ὃς παρ' οὐδενὸς οὔτε δῶρα οὔτε μισθὸν
δέχομαι; δικαιότερον δὲ τίνα ἂν εἰκότως νομίσαιτε τοῦ
πρὸς τὰ παρόντα συνηρμοσμένου, ὡς τῶν ἀλλοτρίων μηδενὸς
προσδεῖσθαι; σοφὸν δὲ πῶς οὐκ ἄν τις εἰκότως ἄνδρα φήσειεν

5   τούτου Α²C
12–15 Χαιρεφῶντος ... σωφρονέστερον citat Athenaeus
13   ἐπερωτήσαντος Athen.   περὶ] ὑπὲρ Athen.
15   μήτ' ἐλευθεριώτερον om. Athen.
17   ἀλλὰ CH: ἄλλα BA
22   πολλῶν codd.: corr. Reuchlin
27   νομίσητε vel νομίσετε codd.: corr. Schaefer

I do say, except that, whereas others name the sources of the forewarnings as birds, utterances, chance encounters and prophets, I call this source of mine 'my divine thing' and think that in using this name I am speaking with greater truth and piety than those who attribute the power of the gods to birds. Moreover I have this further proof that I am not telling lies against God; I have reported God's counsels to numerous friends, and never yet have I been proved mistaken.'

14. When, according to Hermogenes, this was heard by the jurors, and caused uproar, with some disbelieving his words, and others jealous that he was receiving greater benefits from gods than they themselves, Socrates resumed 'Come now, let me tell you something else, so that those of you so wishing may believe even less in my having been honoured by gods. For once, when Chaerephon enquired about me at Delphi before many witnesses, Apollo pronounced in reply that no man was more free-spirited or juster or more prudent than I.' 15. When, continued Hermogenes, these further statements were heard by the jurors and predictably caused still greater uproar among them, Socrates spoke again, saying 'But, gentlemen, the god had greater things to say in oracles about Lycurgus, the lawgiver to the Spartans, than he did about me. For it is said that when he was entering the temple, the god addressed him saying "I am pondering whether to call you a god or a man." But *me* he didn't liken to a god, merely judging me to be far superior to other men. However I don't want you to take the god's word about this off-hand, but to examine each of the god's pronouncements in detail. 16. For whom do you know less enslaved than me to the appetites of the body, or whom amongst men more free-spirited than I am, I who accept gifts or payment from nobody? Whom could you reasonably consider juster than the one so well adapted to his present situation as to need nothing extra from others? And how could anyone reasonably fail to call me a wise man, me who, from

εἶναι ὃς ἐξ ὅτουπερ ξυνιέναι τὰ λεγόμενα ἠρξάμην οὐπώποτε
* διέλειπον καὶ ζητῶν καὶ μανθάνων ὅ τι ἐδυνάμην ἀγαθόν; ὡς 17 *
δὲ οὐ μάτην ἐπόνουν οὐ δοκεῖ ὑμῖν καὶ τάδε τεκμήρια εἶναι,
τὸ πολλοὺς μὲν πολίτας τῶν ἀρετῆς ἐφιεμένων, πολλοὺς δὲ
5 ξένων, ἐκ πάντων προαιρεῖσθαι ἐμοὶ ξυνεῖναι; ἐκείνου δὲ τί
φήσομεν αἴτιον εἶναι, τοῦ πάντας εἰδέναι ὅτι ἐγὼ ἥκιστ'
⟨ἂν⟩ ἔχοιμι χρήματα ἀντιδιδόναι, ὅμως πολλοὺς ἐπιθυμεῖν ἐμοί
τι δωρεῖσθαι; τὸ δ' ἐμὲ μὲν μηδ' ὑφ' ἑνὸς ἀπαιτεῖσθαι
εὐεργεσίας, ἐμοὶ δὲ πολλοὺς ὁμολογεῖν χάριτας ὀφείλειν;
10 τὸ δ' ἐν τῇ πολιορκίᾳ τοὺς μὲν ἄλλους οἰκτίρειν ἑαυτούς, 18
ἐμὲ δὲ μηδὲν ἀπορώτερον διάγειν ἢ ὅτε τὰ μάλιστα ἡ πόλις
ηὐδαιμόνει; τὸ δὲ τοὺς ἄλλους μὲν τὰς εὐπαθείας ἐκ τῆς
ἀγορᾶς πολυτελεῖς πορίζεσθαι, ἐμὲ δὲ ἐκ τῆς ψυχῆς ἄνευ
δαπάνης ἡδίους ἐκείνων μηχανᾶσθαι; εἴ γε μὴν ὅσα εἴρηκα
15 περὶ ἐμαυτοῦ μηδεὶς δύναιτ' ἂν ἐξελέγξαι με ὡς ψεύδομαι,
πῶς οὐκ ἂν ἤδη δικαίως καὶ ὑπὸ θεῶν καὶ ὑπ' ἀνθρώπων
ἐπαινοίμην; ἀλλ' ὅμως σύ με φῄς, ὦ Μέλητε, τοιαῦτα 19
ἐπιτηδεύοντα τοὺς νέους διαφθείρειν; καίτοι ἐπιστάμεθα
μὲν δήπου τίνες εἰσὶ νέων διαφθοραί· σὺ δὲ εἰπὲ εἴ τινα
20 οἶσθα ὑπ' ἐμοῦ γεγενημένον ἢ ἐξ εὐσεβοῦς ἀνόσιον· ἢ ἐκ
σώφρονος ὑβριστὴν ἢ ἐξ εὐδιαίτου πολυδάπανον ἢ [ὡς] ἐκ
μετριοπότου οἰνόφλυγα ἢ ἐκ φιλοπόνου μαλακὸν ἢ ἄλλης
πονηρᾶς ἡδονῆς ἡττημένον. Ἀλλὰ ναὶ μὰ Δί', ἔφη ὁ Μέ- 20
λητος, ἐκείνους οἶδα οὓς σὺ πέπεικας σοὶ πείθεσθαι μᾶλλον
25 ἢ τοῖς γειναμένοις. Ὁμολογῶ, φάναι τὸν Σωκράτην, περί
γε παιδείας· τοῦτο γὰρ ἴσασιν ἐμοὶ μεμεληκός. περὶ δὲ
ὑγιείας τοῖς ἰατροῖς μᾶλλον οἱ ἄνθρωποι πείθονται ἢ τοῖς
γονεῦσι· καὶ ἐν ταῖς ἐκκλησίαις γε πάντες δήπου οἱ Ἀθηναῖοι
τοῖς φρονιμώτατα λέγουσι πείθονται μᾶλλον ἢ τοῖς προσ-
30 ήκουσιν. οὐ γὰρ δὴ καὶ στρατηγοὺς αἱρεῖσθε καὶ πρὸ πατέρων

---

*2   διέλειπον AB: διέλιπον C
7   ἂν add. Schneider
9   εὐεργεσίαν Stephanus
21   ὡς del. Gesner

the moment I began to understand speech, have never yet stopped seeking and learning any good thing I could? 17. And don't you find proof that my hard work was not in vain in the fact that many citizens aspiring to virtue and many non-Athenians too choose to associate with me in preference to all others? And how shall we account for the fact that all men know that I would be the least able to repay money, but yet many are eager to confer gifts on me? And what about the fact that I am never asked by anyone to repay kindnesses, whereas many acknowledge they are indebted to me for favours received? 18. And what of the fact that during the siege of Athens all others were sorry for themselves but my lifestyle was no more impoverished than when our city prospered? What of the fact that all others provide their luxuries from the market at great cost, whereas I use the resources of my own spirit to procure more delightful luxuries than theirs at no expense at all? But if no one could prove me to be lying in any of the things I've said about myself, how could I now fail to deserve to be praised both by gods and by mankind? 19. But despite that, Meletus, do you assert that by such practices I corrupt the young men? Yet I am sure we know what sorts of corruption affect young men. Tell me, Meletus, if you know of anyone who has been changed by me from piety   ety or from sensible conduct to outrageousness or from a reasonable lifestyle to extravagance or from moderation in his cups to drunkenness or from industriousness to soft living or has succumbed to any depraved pleasure.'

20. 'But, in heaven's name,' said Meletus 'I certainly know of those whom you have persuaded to obey you rather than their parents.'

'I admit it' said Socrates 'at least as regards education; for they know that's what interests me. But on matters of health people obey their doctors rather than their parents, and at meetings of the assembly all the Athenians, of course, obey those whose speeches are the most sensible rather than their relatives. For isn't it the same with your choice of generals? Don't you prefer

καὶ πρὸ ἀδελφῶν, καὶ ναὶ μὰ Δία γε ὑμεῖς πρὸ ὑμῶν αὐτῶν,
οὓς ἂν ἡγῆσθε περὶ τῶν πολεμικῶν φρονιμωτάτους εἶναι;
Οὕτω γάρ, φάναι τὸν Μέλητον, ὦ Σώκρατες, καὶ συμφέρει
21 καὶ νομίζεται. Οὐκοῦν, εἰπεῖν τὸν Σωκράτην, θαυμαστὸν καὶ
τοῦτό σοι δοκεῖ εἶναι, τὸ ἐν μὲν ταῖς ἄλλαις πράξεσι μὴ μόνον 5
ἰσομοιρίας τυγχάνειν τοὺς κρατίστους, ἀλλὰ καὶ προτετι-
μῆσθαι, ἐμὲ δέ, ⟨ὅτι⟩ περὶ τοῦ μεγίστου ἀγαθοῦ ἀνθρώποις,
περὶ παιδείας, βέλτιστος εἶναι ὑπό τινων προκρίνομαι, τούτου
ἕνεκα θανάτου ὑπὸ σοῦ διώκεσθαι;
22 Ἐρρήθη μὲν δῆλον ὅτι τούτων πλείω ὑπό τε αὐτοῦ καὶ 10
τῶν συναγορευόντων φίλων αὐτῷ. ἀλλ' ἐγὼ οὐ τὰ πάντα
εἰπεῖν τὰ ἐκ τῆς δίκης ἐσπούδασα, ἀλλ' ἤρκεσέ μοι δηλῶσαι
ὅτι Σωκράτης τὸ μὲν μήτε περὶ θεοὺς ἀσεβῆσαι μήτε περὶ
23 ἀνθρώπους ἄδικος φανῆναι περὶ παντὸς ἐποιεῖτο· τὸ δὲ
μὴ ἀποθανεῖν οὐκ ᾤετο λιπαρητέον εἶναι, ἀλλὰ καὶ καιρὸν 15
ἤδη ἐνόμιζεν ἑαυτῷ τελευτᾶν. ὅτι δὲ οὕτως ἐγίγνωσκε
καταδηλότερον ἐγένετο, ἐπειδὴ καὶ ἡ δίκη διεψηφίσθη.
πρῶτον μὲν γὰρ κελευόμενος ὑποτιμᾶσθαι οὔτε αὐτὸς ὑπετι-
μήσατο οὔτε τοὺς φίλους εἴασεν, ἀλλὰ καὶ ἔλεγεν ὅτι τὸ
ὑποτιμᾶσθαι ὁμολογοῦντος εἴη ἀδικεῖν. ἔπειτα τῶν ἑταίρων 20
ἐκκλέψαι βουλομένων αὐτὸν οὐκ ἐφείπετο, ἀλλὰ καὶ ἐπι-
σκῶψαι ἐδόκει ἐρόμενος εἴ που εἰδεῖέν τι χωρίον ἔξω τῆς
Ἀττικῆς ἔνθα οὐ προσβατὸν θανάτῳ.
24 Ὡς δὲ τέλος εἶχεν ἡ δίκη, εἰπεῖν αὐτόν· Ἀλλ', ὦ
ἄνδρες, τοὺς μὲν διδάσκοντας τοὺς μάρτυρας ὡς χρὴ 25
ἐπιορκοῦντας καταψευδομαρτυρεῖν ἐμοῦ καὶ τοὺς πειθομένους
τούτοις ἀνάγκη ἐστὶ πολλὴν ἑαυτοῖς συνειδέναι ἀσέβειαν καὶ
ἀδικίαν· ἐμοὶ δὲ τί προσήκει νῦν μεῖον φρονεῖν ἢ πρὶν κατα-
κριθῆναι, μηδὲν ἐλεγχθέντι ὡς πεποίηκά τι ὧν ἐγράψαντό

---

7   ὅτι add. Stephanus: ὃς add. Castaglio
8   εἰ post εἶναι add. C
13   τὸ Reuchlin: τότε codd.
17   κατεψηφίσθη B²

to your fathers and brothers, and indeed to yourselves as well, those whom you think wisest in military matters?'

'Yes, Socrates' said Meletus 'for that is both expedient and customary.' 21. 'Then' said Socrates 'don't you also find it surprising that in all other activities the ablest men don't just enjoy an equal footing with others but have even been honoured above them, whereas, because in matters concerning the greatest boon to mankind, namely education, I am judged by some to excel all others, for that I am prosecuted by you on a capital charge?'

22. Obviously more than this was said by Socrates and by the friends who spoke on his behalf. I, however, have not been at pains to report everything from the trial, but am satisfied with making it clear that Socrates thought it all-important to avoid appearing to have been impious to the gods and unjust to men, but did not think he should plead to be spared from death, already in fact considering it was the right time for him to die. 23. That these were his views became more obvious after the verdict had been given; for in the first place, when instructed to suggest an alternative penalty, he refused to do so himself or let his friends do so, but kept on saying that suggesting a penalty was tantamount to admitting guilt; and secondly when his friends wished to sneak him out of prison, he would not follow them but appeared to make a joke of the matter, by asking if they knew anywhere outside Attica inaccessible to death.

24. We are told by Hermogenes that, when the case was coming to an end, Socrates said 'But, gentlemen, those who instructed the witnesses that they must forswear themselves and bear false witness against me and those who believed them can't help feeling in their hearts guilty of great impiety and injustice. But, as for me, why should my self-esteem be any less now than before the verdict went against me, as I have not been proved to have done

με; οὐδὲ γὰρ ἔγωγε ἀντὶ Διὸς καὶ Ἥρας καὶ τῶν σὺν τούτοις
* θεῶν οὔτε θύων τισὶ καινοῖς δαίμοσιν οὔτε ὀμνὺς οὔτε νομίζων *
ἄλλους θεοὺς ἀναπέφηνα. τούς γε μὴν νέους πῶς ἂν δια- 25
φθείροιμι καρτερίαν καὶ εὐτέλειαν προσεθίζων; ἐφ' οἷς γε
5 μὴν ἔργοις κεῖται θάνατος ἢ ζημία, ἱεροσυλία, τοιχωρυχία,
ἀνδραποδίσει, πόλεως προδοσία, οὐδ' αὐτοὶ οἱ ἀντίδικοι
τούτων πρᾶξαί τι κατ' ἐμοῦ φασιν. ὥστε θαυμαστὸν ἔμοιγε
δοκεῖ εἶναι ὅπως ποτὲ ἐφάνη ὑμῖν τοῦ θανάτου ἔργον ἄξιον
ἐμοὶ εἰργασμένον. ἀλλ' οὐδὲ μέντοι ὅτι ἀδίκως ἀποθνήσκω, 26
10 διὰ τοῦτο μεῖον φρονητέον· οὐ γὰρ ἐμοὶ ἀλλὰ τοῖς κατα-
γνοῦσι τοῦτο αἰσχρόν [γάρ] ἐστι. παραμυθεῖται δ' ἔτι με
καὶ Παλαμήδης ὁ παραπλησίως ἐμοὶ τελευτήσας· ἔτι γὰρ καὶ
νῦν πολὺ καλλίους ὕμνους παρέχεται Ὀδυσσέως τοῦ ἀδίκως
ἀποκτείναντος αὐτόν· οἶδ' ὅτι καὶ ἐμοὶ μαρτυρήσεται ὑπό τε
15 τοῦ ἐπιόντος καὶ ὑπὸ τοῦ παρεληλυθότος χρόνου ὅτι ἠδίκησα
μὲν οὐδένα πώποτε οὐδὲ πονηρότερον ἐποίησα, εὐηργέτουν
δὲ τοὺς ἐμοὶ διαλεγομένους προῖκα διδάσκων ὅ τι ἐδυνάμην
ἀγαθόν. εἰπὼν δὲ ταῦτα μάλα ὁμολογουμένως δὴ τοῖς 27
εἰρημένοις ἀπήει καὶ ὄμμασι καὶ σχήματι καὶ βαδίσματι
20 φαιδρός. ὡς δὲ ᾔσθετο ἄρα τοὺς παρεπομένους δακρύοντας,
Τί τοῦτο; εἰπεῖν αὐτόν, ἢ ἄρτι δακρύετε; οὐ γὰρ πάλαι ἴστε
ὅτι ἐξ ὅτουπερ ἐγενόμην κατεψηφισμένος ἦν μου ὑπὸ τῆς
φύσεως ὁ θάνατος; ἀλλὰ μέντοι εἰ μὲν ἀγαθῶν ἐπιρρεόντων
προαπόλλυμαι, δῆλον ὅτι ἐμοὶ καὶ τοῖς ἐμοῖς εὔνοις λυπη-
25 τέον· εἰ δὲ χαλεπῶν προσδοκωμένων καταλύω τὸν βίον, ἐγὼ
μὲν οἶμαι ὡς εὐπραγοῦντος ἐμοῦ πᾶσιν ὑμῖν εὐθυμητέον εἶναι.
παρὼν δέ τις Ἀπολλόδωρος, ἐπιθυμητὴς μὲν ὢν ἰσχυρῶς 28

---

1   οὔτε codd.: corr. Hartung
*2   νομίζων Schaefer: ὀνομάζων codd.
5-6 ἱεροσυλίαι τοιχωρυχίαι ἀνδραποδίσις...προδοσίαι codd.: corr. Zeune
7-23 θαυμαστὸν...θάνατος citat Stobaeus
8   ὅπως Stob.: ὅπου nostri
11   γὰρ om. Stob.
14   μαρτυρήσετε Stob., nostri: corr. Stephanus
27   παρὼν...διαπέπρακται, chs. 28, 29 citat Stob.

any of the things of which they accused me? For I haven't been revealed as sacrificing to any new deities in place of Zeus and Hera and the gods who bear them company, or as swearing by or worshipping* other gods. 25. Moreover how could I corrupt the young by accustoming them to endurance and frugality? But as for the activities for which the penalty is death, I mean robbing temples, housebreaking, kidnapping, and betraying one's city, not even my opponents themselves accuse me of having done any of these things. So I can only wonder how you ever were convinced that I had done anything deserving death. 26. Nor yet should I think any less of myself because of the injustice of my death; for this brings disgrace not on me but on those who condemned me, and I get some further comfort from thinking of Palamedes who died a similar death to mine; for he still to this day provides material for finer hymns of praise than Odysseus who unjustly brought about his death. I know that I shall be supported by the testimony of both the future and of the past to prove that never to this day have I done wrong to anyone or made anyone more depraved, but have ever striven to benefit those who conversed with me by teaching them free of charge every good thing I could.'

27. That was what he said and his behaviour fully matched his words, for, as he left, the look in his eyes, his bearing and his gait were all equally cheerful. But when he noticed those accompanying him to be weeping, we are told, he said, 'What's this? Is it *now* that you weep? Haven't you long known that, from the moment I was born, I had been condemned by Nature to die? If indeed my death is premature with blessings still pouring in upon me, clearly I and my well-wishers have cause for grief, but, if I end my life at a time when only hardships can be expected, *my* opinion is that you all should think me fortunate and so feel cheerful.' 28. There was present one

αὐτοῦ, ἄλλως δ' εὐήθης, εἶπεν ἄρα· Ἀλλὰ τοῦτο ἔγωγε, ὦ
Σώκρατες, χαλεπώτατα φέρω ὅτι ὁρῶ σε ἀδίκως ἀποθνήσκοντα. τὸν δὲ λέγεται καταψήσαντα αὐτοῦ τὴν κεφαλὴν
* εἰπεῖν· Σὺ δέ, ὦ φίλτατε Ἀπολλόδωρε, μᾶλλον ἐβούλου *
με ὁρᾶν δικαίως ἢ ἀδίκως ἀποθνήσκοντα; καὶ ἅμα ἐπιγε- 5
29 λάσαι. λέγεται δὲ καὶ Ἄνυτον παριόντα ἰδὼν εἰπεῖν· Ἀλλ'
ὁ μὲν ἀνὴρ ὅδε κυδρός, ὡς μέγα τι καὶ καλὸν διαπεπραγμένος,
εἰ ἀπέκτονέ με, ὅτι αὐτὸν τῶν μεγίστων ὑπὸ τῆς πόλεως
ὁρῶν ἀξιούμενον οὐκ ἔφην χρῆναι τὸν υἱὸν περὶ βύρσας
παιδεύειν. ὡς μοχθηρὸς οὗτος, ἔφη, ὃς οὐκ ἔοικεν εἰδέναι 10
ὅτι ὁπότερος ἡμῶν καὶ συμφορώτερα καὶ καλλίω εἰς τὸν ἀεὶ
30 χρόνον διαπέπρακται, οὗτός ἐστι καὶ ὁ νικῶν. ἀλλὰ μέντοι,
φάναι αὐτόν, ἀνέθηκε μὲν καὶ Ὅμηρος ἔστιν οἷς τῶν ἐν
καταλύσει τοῦ βίου προγιγνώσκειν τὰ μέλλοντα, βούλομαι
δὲ καὶ ἐγὼ χρησμῳδῆσαί τι. συνεγερόμην γάρ ποτε βραχέα 15
τῷ Ἀνύτου υἱῷ, καὶ ἔδοξέ μοι οὐκ ἄρρωστος τὴν ψυχὴν εἶναι·
ὥστε φημὶ αὐτὸν ἐπὶ τῇ δουλοπρεπεῖ διατριβῇ ἣν ὁ πατὴρ
αὐτῷ παρεσκεύακεν οὐ διαμενεῖν· διὰ δὲ τὸ μηδένα ἔχειν
σπουδαῖον ἐπιμελητὴν προσπεσεῖσθαί τινι αἰσχρᾷ ἐπιθυμίᾳ,
31 καὶ προβήσεσθαι μέντοι πόρρω μοχθηρίας. ταῦτα δ' εἰπὼν 20
οὐκ ἐψεύσατο, ἀλλ' ὁ νεανίσκος ἡσθεὶς οἴνῳ οὔτε νυκτὸς
οὔτε ἡμέρας ἐπαύετο πίνων, καὶ τέλος οὔτε τῇ ἑαυτοῦ
πόλει οὔτε τοῖς φίλοις οὔτε αὑτῷ ἄξιος οὐδενὸς ἐγένετο.
Ἄνυτος μὲν δὴ διὰ τὴν τοῦ υἱοῦ πονηρὰν παιδείαν καὶ διὰ
τὴν αὑτοῦ ἀγνωμοσύνην ἔτι καὶ τετελευτηκὼς τυγχάνει 25
32 κακοδοξίας. Σωκράτης δὲ διὰ τὸ μεγαλύνειν ἑαυτὸν ἐν τῷ
δικαστηρίῳ φθόνον ἐπαγόμενος μᾶλλον καταψηφίσασθαι
ἑαυτοῦ ἐποίησε τοὺς δικαστάς. ἐμοὶ μὲν οὖν δοκεῖ θεοφιλοῦς

*4   μᾶλλον H, Marchant: μᾶλλον ἂν A, Stob.: μάλ' ἂν B
10   ὃς Stob.: ὡς nostri
24   Ἄνυτος C: αὐτὸς cett.
27   ἐπαγαγόμενος Cobet

Apollodorus, a man intensely devoted to Socrates, but otherwise naïve, and he said 'But what I find hardest to bear, Socrates, is that I see you being put to death unjustly.' But Socrates is said to have stroked Apollodorus' head, saying 'But, my dearest Apollodorus, did you prefer to see me executed * justly rather than unjustly?', and he is said to have smiled as he spoke.

29. It is also said that Socrates, on seeing Anytus passing, remarked 'But here is a man basking in glory, as though he has accomplished something mighty and noble by killing me, because, when I saw him honoured by the state with its highest offices, I said he ought not to be educating his son in tannery. What a poor specimen we have here, for he doesn't seem to know that of the two of us the one, whose achievements prove the more beneficial and nobler for all time, is really the victor! 30. However,' he is said to have continued, 'just as Homer attributed to some men at the end of their lives foreknowledge of the future, so I too wish to make a prophecy. I did once have a brief association with Anytus' son and he seemed to me to have some strength of spirit. So I say that he won't remain long in the servile occupation his father has arranged for him, but that because he has no one of good character to keep an eye on him, he will fall victim to some base craving and travel far in the paths of vice.'

31. These words of his turned out to be true; the young man succumbed to the delights of wine and wouldn't stop drinking night or day and finally became quite worthless to his own city, his friends and himself. So Anytus, thanks to the vile way he brought up his son and his own want of understanding, though now dead, still to this day enjoys a bad reputation.

32. Socrates, by glorifying himself at his trial, to bring the ill-will of the

μοίρας τετυχηκέναι· τοῦ μὲν γὰρ βίου τὸ χαλεπώτατον
ἀπέλιπε, τῶν δὲ θανάτων τοῦ ῥᾴστου ἔτυχεν.   ἐπεδείξατο 33
δὲ τῆς ψυχῆς τὴν ῥώμην· ἐπεὶ γὰρ ἔγνω τοῦ ἔτι ζῆν τὸ
τεθνάναι αὐτῷ κρεῖττον εἶναι, ὥσπερ οὐδὲ πρὸς τἀλλ' ἀγαθὰ
5 προσάντης ἦν, οὐδὲ πρὸς τὸν θάνατον ἐμαλακίσατο, ἀλλ'
ἱλαρῶς καὶ προσεδέχετο αὐτὸν καὶ ἐπετελέσατο.   ἐγὼ μὲν 34
δὴ κατανοῶν τοῦ ἀνδρὸς τήν τε σοφίαν καὶ τὴν γενναιότητα
οὔτε μὴ μεμνῆσθαι δύναμαι αὐτοῦ οὔτε μεμνημένος μὴ οὐκ
ἐπαινεῖν.   εἰ δέ τις τῶν ἀρετῆς ἐφιεμένων ὠφελιμωτέρῳ
10 τινὶ Σωκράτους συνεγένετο, ἐκεῖνον ἐγὼ τὸν ἄνδρα ἀξιο-
μακαριστότατον νομίζω.

4   ἀγαθὰ Richards: τἀγαθὰ codd.

jurors upon himself, made them readier to condemn him; but to *me* he seems to have met with a fate favoured by the gods; for he left the most difficult part of his life, but gained the easiest of deaths.

33. He put the strength of his spirit on display for all to see, for, once he realised that for him death was preferable to going on living, just as he didn't stand out against all other good things, so too he didn't weaken in the face of death either, but awaited it cheerfully and duly saw it through. 34. For my part when I reflect upon Socrates' wisdom and nobility, I can't help remembering him, and, when remembering him, praising him; but, if anyone more beneficial to his companions than Socrates has ever been found by any eager aspirant after virtue, he's the man in my opinion who best deserves to be acclaimed as supremely fortunate.

COMMENTARY ON
APOLOGIA SOCRATES

TITLE **DEFENCE:** *apologia* is a speech made in one's defence and *apologeisthai* means to make such a defence. The normal meaning of 'apologise' in English is completely different; Socrates is far from saying he is sorry or expressing regrets about his behaviour.

Chapter 1 Socrates: note Xenophon's effective use of word order to give his hero pride of place as first word in his text; see Denniston 44–45.

Socrates...took: a literal translation would be 'it seems proper' (whether 'merited by Socrates' or 'worthwhile') 'to remember' (or 'talk about'; *cf.* Latin *memorare*) 'Socrates and how he decided' (probably not 'the manner of his decision' but its nature, 'what he decided to do'; the instantaneous aorist ἐβουλεύσατο denotes the decision was clear-cut).

axion...memnêsthai: *cf.* Xenophon's initial justification of the contents of his *Symposium*, as *axiomnêmoneuta* (things worth recording).

the last stages of his life: Plato's *Euthyphro* depicts Socrates, when awaiting trial, as not thinking about his defence, but persisting in his normal habit of pursuing a definition, in this case of piety, from Euthyphro. After his conviction execution was delayed (for 30 days, according to *Mem.* 4.8.2), as nobody could be executed during the Delia, the interval between the departure of a state ship on a sacred mission to Delos and its return, and the ship had left on the day before the trial, see Plato, *Phaedo* 57b. Plato's *Crito* is set on the day the ship is due to return and records Socrates' rejection of Crito's offer to engineer his escape, while *Phaedo* records his courage, conversation and death; see also ch. 23 and note.

others too: notably Plato, whose *Apology* almost certainly preceded that of Xenophon, as probably did his *Euthyphro* and *Crito*; *Phaedo*, however, is usually dated rather later, and whether it preceded Xenophon's *Apology* is uncertain.

Note how Xenophon avoids mentioning Plato's name here. It may be because of temporary pique, occasioned by Plato's *Meno*, see p. 15, or he may be reluctant to acknowledge the achievements of a rival writer about Socrates. The fact remains, however, that only once does he mention Plato, in *Mem.* 3.6, where the ill-founded political ambitions of Plato's brother Glaucon are exposed by Socrates; there at least Xenophon does acknowledge Socrates' good will towards Plato. See also p. 16 for details of Socratic writings by other disciples, of whom Aeschines is the most important, with several fragments of his work surviving. He may have written a work covering the same subject as Plato's *Crito*, or, according to Diogenes Laertius 2.60, may have played the role given to Crito in the dialogue bearing his name, on which see note on *Mem.* 1.3.8. Crito himself is also credited with an *Apologia for Socrates*, though presumably retrospectively. Diogenes Laertius 2.40 also says that the orator Lysias wrote a speech for Socrates' defence, but Socrates rejected it as unsuitable for him.

recaptured: *tynchanô* with the genitive is used to mean hit one's mark with an arrow, spear *etc.*, implying successful aim, as in *Anabasis* 3.2.19.

proud tone: *megalêgoria*, 'talking big', usually has an uncomplimentary implication, suggesting *hybris* which may incur divine retribution, *cf. Od.* 22.288, Plato *Phaedo* 95b, Xenophon *An.* 6.3.18. Xenophon's word here, however, is ambivalent; *cf. megalêgorô* in *Cyr.* 4.4.2 and 7.1.17, of the justifiable pride of good soldiers and of Cyrus himself. Socrates' proud tone does fulfil his purpose in annoying the jurors, but the pride is justified. Aristotle *EN* 4.7.2, discussing truthfulness, condemns *alazoneia*, unjustified boasting, but approves of the man who gives a true assessment of himself without either exaggeration or *eirôneia*, self-depreciation, false modesty (with intent to deceive). *Eirôneia* was a notorious attribute of Socrates, but even in the Platonic *Apology* there are only occasional touches of Socratic irony and he sounds consistently smug in all three speeches of that work, though most obviously in the second speech assessing his punishment. In Plato *Ap.* 20e, Socrates, when about to introduce the topic of Chaerephon's visit to Delphi, is afraid of causing uproar among the jury, by seeming to them to be boastful, *mega legein*. See Guthrie (2) 126–129 for a kindly interpretation of Socratic irony, stressing the 'intellectual humility' of the 'true Socratic'.

A less likely translation is 'nobility of speech', 'expression of noble sentiments', *cf. megalêgoros*, Longinus 8.4; thus in chs. 1–2 Todd in his Loeb offers 'the loftiness of his words', 'his lofty utterance', 'the sublimity of his speech.'

death was preferable to life: Plato gives a different picture of Socrates' attitude. He would have preferred to go on living at Athens and serving God, *Ap.* 23c, 30a, though saying that death might be a blessing, ibid. 29b, 40c ff., and not to be feared.

rather stupid: because, unlike Xenophon, they had failed to realise he was *deliberately* antagonising the jury.

CHAPTERS 2–29 Xenophon's account of what Hermogenes had told him. *Mem.* 4.8.4-10 contains Xenophon's brief recapitulation of this passage, repeatedly using similar or identical phrases or motifs, introduced to lead up to Xenophon's final eulogy of Socrates as the culmination of the *Memorabilia*.

Chapter 2 Hermogenes: one of Socrates' most devoted companions; he was a son of Hipponicus, and probably illegitimate, and as poor as his brother Callias, the extravagant host of Xenophon's *Smp.*, was rich. Xenophon names him in *Mem.* 1.2.48 with Crito and five others as true disciples of Socrates, associating with him to improve their characters rather than to further their political ambitions. Xenophon in *Mem.* 2.10.3 and *Smp.* 8.3 makes Socrates praise him for his piety and other sterling qualities. Plato, *Phaedo* 52b names him among those present at Socrates' death and makes him an interlocutor in *Cratylus*. According to Diogenes Laertius 3.6, after Socrates' death, Plato attached himself to Cratylus and to Hermogenes 'whose philosophy was that of Parmenides'.

discussing anything rather than the trial: the first of many phrases to be reused in
Mem. 4.8.4 ff.

τὸν δὲ ἀποκρίνεσθαι: the accusative and infinitive construction is used, because
from now on we have *oratio obliqua*, indirect discourse reporting what Hermogenes
said, as *e.g.* with φάναι αὐτόν, chs. 5, 8.

Chapter 3 ***and when:*** translating Dindorf's *epei* for *epeita* of the manuscripts,
as the same construction, the assimilation in *oratio obliqua* of the main verb in a
subordinate clause into the infinitive occurs in chapters 4 and 5; for parallels see
Goodwin, § 755; *auton* here refers to Hermogenes, the narrator and questioner,
hence Schenkl's suggestion of the more grammatically correct *autos*.

Chapter 4 ***often been misled:*** factors conducive to the miscarriage of justice
included the size of citizen juries (500 or 501 in this case, see Brickhouse and Smith
26–7) and their composition, as they were drawn by lot from volunteers, mainly old
men; nor did they have a judge to guide them.

often...often too: the parallel passage in *Mem.* 4.8.5 ... ; *cf. Ap.* 17. Denniston,
1960, 84 says anaphora is not a stylistic feature of the rhetorician Gorgias, but
used mainly by writers 'who aim at vividness, force and pathos', including
Lysias, Demosthenes, Plato and Xenophon; *cf.* Xenophon *An.* 3.4.45. So perhaps
Hermogenes is portrayed by Xenophon as waxing emotional at the thought of his
beloved Socrates suffering injustice, but the anaphora may equally well originate
with Xenophon, not Hermogenes.

pity engendered by their speeches: defendants often made tearful appeals to the
pity of the jurors, producing weeping relatives in court, a procedure rejected by
Socrates in Plato *Ap.* 34d, though at least he does go on to mention his three sons.

curried favour: in neither *Apology* does Socrates make the slightest attempt to
humour the jurors.

twice: 'twice' is absent from *Mem.* 4.8.5.

my divine sign: I translate δαιμόνιον *faute de mieux* as 'divine sign', though I was
also tempted by Vlastos' 'divine mentor'. *daimonion* could be a neuter adjective
meaning 'divine thing' and that is probably how Socrates understood it, *cf.* Plato *Ap.*
31d, *theion ti kai daimonion*; alternatively it could be a noun meaning 'divinity' and
that was how his accusers intended it to be taken, *cf. Mem.* 1.1.2, and the basis of
the charge that Socrates didn't believe in the gods of the state, but introduced other
strange new *daimonia*, *cf.* chs. 10–12, Plato *Ap.* 26b, *Euthphr.* 3b. Both Xenophon
and Plato refer to it as a voice, and Plato *Ap.* 40b also calls it *to tou theou sêmeion*,
the sign sent by the god. Xenophon *Ap.* 13 and Plato *Ap.* 40a credit it with prophetic
powers. Plato, *Ap.* 31d, 40a,b makes Socrates say that it started coming to him
in his boyhood, came very frequently, and opposed him even on minor matters,
if he was going to act wrongly. Plato consistently portrays it as a negative force,
always opposing, never advocating particular lines of action; Xenophon implies in
five passages, *Ap.* 12, *Mem.* 1.1.4, 1.4.15, 4.3.12 and 4.8.1 that its advice could be
positive as well as negative, but gives no instances of such positive advice.

σημεῖον: as *sêmeion* is often used of a military signal relaying an order, and from

Homer onwards the cognate verb σημαίνω can have the meaning of 'order by a signal' or even simply 'order' it follows that the message sent must be obeyed; *cf. Mem.* 1.1.2.

Chapter 5 surprising that: the adjective *thaumastos* and the verb *thaumazô*, 'surprising', 'I am surprised' respectively, are commonly followed by *ei* ('if'), where English would expect 'that'.

God: translating τῷ θεῷ, literally 'to the god'. The ancient Greeks, though polytheistic, often seem to lapse into monotheism by referring to ὁ θεός, or sometimes, particularly in verse to θεός (= 'the god'), presumably the supreme god and so equivalent to Zeus. Plato too is not immune from this inconsistency, so that Cornford, *The Republic of Plato*, 67, can complain with some justification 'He uses the singular 'god' and the plural 'the gods' with an indifference startling to the modern monotheist.' See also Guthrie (2) 156. In both *Apologies* references to ὁ θεός in the singular predominate, but particularly in the Platonic version, where Socrates repeatedly stresses his service to 'the god'; indeed the last words of Plato's *Apology* are τῷ θεῷ. So too Xenophon in his *Ap.* uses ὁ θεός in the singular more often than not (chs. 5, 7, 12, 13 twice, 15), though there are mentions of *theoi* in chs. 9, 14, 18, and he speaks of οἱ θεοί in ch. 8 and in ch. 24, in his final speech to the jury, where 'Zeus and Hera and the other gods with them' suggests that *hoi theoi* = 'the Olympian gods.'

The one god of Xenophon's Socrates knows the future and reveals it to anyone he wishes, by omens and oracles and, in Socrates' case, by the *daimonion*. He seems to have some control over human events, and to exercise providence, at least to favoured individuals such as Socrates, so that he has something in common with the later Stoic concept of one god. Apollo is mentioned in ch. 14, and some of the references, *e.g.* in chs. 12, 15, to 'the god' after mention of Delphi or the Pythia could be Apollo in the limited sense of 'the god in question'. Socrates' one god could conceivably be Apollo, but more probably he is the supreme god who gives Apollo his orders and uses him as his mouthpiece, *cf.* Aeschylus, *Eumenides* 616–8. Aeschylus' supreme god is of course Zeus, but, neither here nor in *Mem.* 1.4.2–18, where Xenophon makes Socrates give a fuller account of his providential deity to Aristodemos, is the name Zeus used. Guthrie, (2) 156, accepts these views attributed to Socrates by Xenophon as genuinely Socratic and concludes 'Socrates believed in a god who was the supreme Mind, responsible for the ordering of the universe and at the same time the creator of men.' (*Cf.*, however, *Mem.* 4.3, which looks like a reworking of *Mem.* 1.4, with Socrates conversing, not with Aristodemos but with Euthydemus, again on divine providence, but this time exercised throughout by *hoi theoi* in the plural, so that Xenophon is at least open to the charges of vagueness or inconsistency.)

God too: kai, 'too', 'also', is missing from the parallel version in *Mem.* 4.8.6. If retained, it suggests that Socrates had already decided on the matter before the voice came.

better for me to die now: cf. the similar phraseology in *Ap.* 41d where Plato's

Socrates argues that divine providence, aided by the failure of his *daimonion* to intervene during his defence, had ensured his death as the best thing for him.

I would: the particle ἄν, absent from the mss., but necessary in the apodosis of a past unfulfilled condition, is restored from *Mem.* 4.8.6.

by me: following C in reading μοι, dative of the agent with a perfect participle passive, for μὲν of the other mss. printed by Marchant.

in piety: the confident pride in his piety expressed by Xenophon's Socrates in both *Apology* and *Mem.* contrasts with his attitude in Plato's *Euthyphro* where he is represented, while awaiting trial, as questioning Euthyphro about piety in an attempt to define it, and as posing with his notorious brand of irony as a pupil wanting to learn about piety from Euthyphro.

and justice: for Socrates discussing justice cf. Plato *Republic* Book One, and Xenophon *Mem.* 4.2.12–20, 4.4, 4.6. In *Republic* Books 2–10 Plato uses Socrates as his mouthpiece on the subject of justice on a large scale, viz. in a state, but Book 1 has a better claim to be regarded as depicting the real Socrates, as he picks holes in others' attempts to define justice, and offers a few positive suggestions of his own, e.g. that justice is a virtue of the soul. Unlike Plato's Socrates, Xenophon's Socrates believes it is just to harm enemies, though in *Cyr.* 3.1.38, the fictitious sophist, presumably modelled on Socrates, forgives the ignorant enemy who executes him. See Vlastos, 1991, 299–300.

the same: ταὐτὰ, crasis for τὰ αὐτὰ, is the object of γιγνώσκοντας; note Xenophon's skilful use of hyperbaton (unnatural word order) by introducing ταὐτὰ before its natural place to emphasise it. See Denniston.

Chapter 6 *to pay the dues of old age:* I follow LSJ in taking *epiteleisthai* as middle with τὰ as its object; cf. chapter 33 *thanaton epetelesato* and *Mem.* 4.8.8. Alternatively the verb could be passive and the meaning be 'that the dues of old age be fully paid' or 'that the things' (sc. concomitant evils) 'of old age come in full measure' (literally, 'be completed').

continue to live: note the mixed conditional sentence. After the open future protasis (ἄν with the subjunctive), the future indicative without ἄν would be expected, but instead we find a remote (unlikely) future (ἄν without the optative) apodosis.

Chapter 7 *looking after my interests and arranging:* *proxenô* means to act as a *proxenos*, a patron or protector, originally used of a citizen who looked after the interests of another state and its nationals in his own city, as Cimon had done, as the Spartans' *proxenos* at Athens. Here *proxenei* is transitive with *to...katalusai* the neuter article and infinitive used substantively as its object.

in the easiest possible way: Xenophon uses ᾗ with the superlative several times instead of the more common ὡς, ὅτι or ὅπως to mean 'as... as possible'.

I am now condemned: following the manuscripts and LSJ in reading *moi*. Reiske's emendation to the genitive *mou*, because of the force of *kata* (= 'against') in the verb is unnecessary. Cf. Herodotus 7.1.46 τοῖσι κατεκέκριτο θάνατος, and 2.133. LSJ explains the verb as impersonal, but the subject understood could be the preceding τὸ... καταλῦσαι or the following τῇ τελευτῇ, i.e. death.

the dying ones: Schenkl's emendation of τελευτῶν to τελευτωντῶν seems certain; των has been transmitted once instead of twice by haplography, an error common in manuscripts.

anyone leaves: editors follow Stephanus in writing the present middle instead of the aorist middle καταλίπηται of the manuscripts. ει and η are often confused by scribes who pronounced them in the same way. See Reynolds and Wilson, 225, and active and middle imperfects and aorists of λείπω are often confused in this way. τις is absent from the manuscripts, but conjectured by Schenkl as the subject of the verb; a scribe may well have omitted τις, thinking the verb passive with μηδὲν as its subject. τις certainly simplifies the sense, but it may not be absolutely necessary, as a subject for the verb may be supplied from the τοῦτον which follows.

spirit: translating ψυχήν. The *psychê* is the non-physical side of a human being, as opposed to his body, giving him life by its presence. It is often contrasted with the body or mentioned along with it, so that the translation 'soul' or 'spirit' is often appropriate. For Socrates and Plato *psychê* also included a man's intellectual and rational side, see n. on *Mem.* 1.4.13, and so as a whole it may be taken to suggest his true self, his personality and character, see Guthrie 1971(2), 147–150. Socrates continually stressed the need to look after one's *psychê*, from which the obvious conclusion is, though some scholars would disagree, that he, like Plato, believed that the *psychê* was immortal, as indeed Socrates is represented as suggesting as a strong probability in Plato, *Apology* 40 ff. and believing in Plato, *Phaedo.*

Chapter 8 *The gods were right:* as their opposition is presumably via the *daimonion*, normally described by Socrates as controlled by *ho theos*, Socrates as portrayed by Xenophon could be regarded as inconsistent, but see note on *c.* 5.

on that occasion: *Text. Retain μὲν of the manuscripts (after τότε), as implying a contrast (= 'on that occasion at least'), which remains undeveloped by an antithetical clause introduced by δὲ; *cf.* Xenophon's πρῶτον μὲν on its own in *An.* 1.9.14; τότε, however, has also to serve us as the correlative with the ὅτε clause which follows; neither Schenkl's μοι (involving an extra dative) nor Reuchl's μου (a difficult possessive, whether with *hoi theoi* or with *episkepsei*) seems necessary, though printed in the Oxford text, or any improvement.

which attracts…joyless: literally 'into which flow together all things that are difficult (troublesome, grievous) and very much bereft of things of joy.'

Chapter 9 *the opinion I have of myself:* the pride displayed in both *Apologies*, and that of Xenophon in particular, is far removed from the irony normally associated with Socrates. See n. on 'proud tone' in ch. 1.

annoy the jury: see n. in ch. 14 on 'caused uproar'.

unlike a free man: throughout *Mem.* Xenophon stresses Socrates' abhorrence of servile attitudes and actions, and emphasises the freedom of his spirit and behaviour guaranteed by his high standards, self-control, simple lifestyle and self-sufficiency, and even incorporates a compliment to Socrates' freedom of spirit into his version of the Delphic response to Chaerephon in ch. 14 and Xenophon's support of the Delphic verdict in ch. 16.

Chapter 10 Editors delete *eipein* after *ephê*, as it occurs more appropriately at the end of the chapter.

his opponents in the trial: Meletus, Anytus and Lycon, exasperated with him according to Plato *Ap.* 23e, Meletus on behalf of the poets, Anytus for the craftsmen and politicians, and Lycon for the orators. Meletus who led the three at the trial, is described by Plato's Socrates in *Euthyphro* 1 as an unknown young man, and Lycon seems to have been equally obscure.

The real power behind the accusation was Anytus, the tanner, who had played a prominent part four years previously in the overthrow of the 'thirty tyrants', some of whom had been associated with Socrates, and in the restoration of the democracy. At the trial, according to Plato, *Ap.* 29c, Anytus had advocated the death penalty, to put an end to further corrupting of the young men by Socrates, and that accounts for the tirade made by Xenophon's Socrates in chs. 29–31 on Anytus' failure to educate *his* son properly. Plato in his *Meno*, written *c.* 386–5?, but recording a discussion on whether *aretê*, goodness, could be taught, to be dated to soon after the restoration of the democracy in 403, gives Anytus a none too unfavourable part in the dialogue, though his aversion to intellectuals and sophists is stressed. Perhaps, therefore, Anytus' accusation of Socrates was inspired by hatred of sophists, as, rightly or wrongly, he regarded him as a sophist, but more probably he was mainly politically motivated.

worship the gods: see Burnet's excellent note on Plato *Ap.* 24c, explaining θεοὺς νομίζειν as acknowledging the gods 'by giving them the worship prescribed by νόμος, use and wont'. Xenophon here makes Socrates reject the charge by stressing that he could be seen sacrificing in public and at state festivals; *cf. Mem.* 4.3.16 where Xenophon's Socrates defines the νόμος of a city as 'conciliating the gods by sacrifice to the best of one's ability.'

Herodotus regularly uses νομίζω to mean 'practise, observe as a custom', *cf.* Xenophon's use of the verb with *mantikên* (divination) in *Mem.* 1.1.3.

new: translating καινά, which, though basically meaning 'new', often has the implication of 'new-fangled', 'strange' used pejoratively; *cf.* the similar use of νέος, particularly in tragedy.

divinities: one of the strange new divinities would certainly be Socrates' own *daimonion*, see note on ch. 4. Then there were the gods, which Socrates was misrepresented as believing in and swearing by in the *Clouds* of Aristophanes, in lines 264–5, 570, *etc.*: note how Socrates in Plato's *Ap.* was at pains to reject Aristophanes' picture of him, and specifically disassociated himself, if not from Diogenes of Apollonia, at least from Anaxagoras in his *elenchos*, refutation, of Meletus in 26d, though Plato *Phaedo* 97c, suggests he had once shown some interest in Anaxagoras. Socrates' strange oaths also became proverbial, see *M.* 1.5.5 n., but in Xenophon he uses none at all, in Plato only one 'by the dog', once calling it *Grg.* 482b, 'the god of Egyptians'.

Diogenes Laertius, quoting Favorinus (fl. *c.* A.D. 125) gives the official version of the charge, and it is identical with that in Xenophon, *Mem.* 1.1, except that

Xenophon has *eispherôn* for *eishêgoumenos*. Plato's version in *Ap*. 24b, though on the same lines is less accurate, (understandably, as it is introduced by a phrase suggesting more approximation) and in particular makes the corruption of the youth the first item.

CHAPTERS 11–13 Xenophon makes Socrates tackle Meletus' charge of impiety at once without any preliminaries, but *cf. c.* 22 where Xenophon disavows complete coverage of Socrates' speech in his defence. Plato, on the other hand, makes Socrates start with an ironical claim to be completely ignorant of forensic and rhetorical practices, and then parody them; he continues with a rejection of his 'old accusers', the comic poets and those who took their portrait of himself at face value, and with an account of Chaerephon's visit to Delphi, and the unpopularity he engendered by his attempts to disprove the oracle's verdict on his wisdom; only after all that does Plato's Socrates tackle Meletus' charge. Moreover Plato's method of rejecting the charge of impiety is completely different, consisting of a cross-examination of Meletus to make him contradict himself.

The gist of chapters 11–13 recurs in *Mem*. 1.1.2–5 with Xenophon, as is his habit, using similar or even identical phraseology, with the difference that, whereas here Socrates is speaking, there Xenophon himself is writing in defence of Socrates.

Chapter 11 *gentlemen:* Plato differs in making Socrates usually address the jurors as 'men of Athens.'

the others: οἱ ἄλλοι should mean 'all others'. Read ἄλλοι, 'others', with B.

Chapter 12 *God's voice:* the *daimonion* or σημεῖον.

signalling: σημαίνω, a verb cognate with σημεῖον is also a military term, often approximating to ordering; see notes on ch. 4.

what I must do: this vague phrase implies positive instructions, but see note on *c*. 4.

those who use the cries of birds: not only the movements and behaviour of birds but also their cries could portend good or evil; *cf*. Tiresias' speech in Sophocles *Ant*. 998 ff., and particularly 1001–2, 1021.

the utterances of humans: any chance utterance could contain an omen, *cf. PV* 486–7. Words which could be interpreted as of evil omen were particularly dangerous at sacrifices and other religious occasions; hence the exhortation *euphêmeite* (Latin *favete linguis*), though literally meaning 'speak words of good omen', in practice enjoined silence, much the safest policy.

claps of thunder have a voice: to the Greeks Zeus was the god of thunder and could use it to send omens; thus Zeus accords Cyrus thunder and lightning on the right as a favourable omen before his decisive battle with Croesus, *Cyr*. 7.1.3, *cf*. ibid. 1.6.1.

the priestess...tripod...Pytho: Pytho was another name for Delphi, the place where Apollo was reputed to have killed Pytho, a monstrous serpent. Hence the Delphic priestess who gave oracles on behalf of Apollo was called the Pythia. She prophesied sitting in the centre of a tripod. The Delphic tripod was particularly dear to Apollo and particularly celebrated. In Socrates' time the Pythia was a respectable peasant woman of at least 50. She seems to have uttered her prophecies in a trance which may have come from chewing leaves of the laurel, Apollo's sacred tree, or from drinking local spring water or possibly from inhaling vapours. See Parke, 72–88.

Chapter 13 *God has foreknowledge of the future:* the general idea that God knows the future and gives premonitions of it by various omens *etc.*, though here ascribed to Socrates, is given by Xenophon as his own, in a parallel passage in *Mem.* 1.1.3–4, and ascribed by him to Cyrus in *Cyr.* 8.7.2 ff.; Socrates of course is special in having an extra source of communications from God in his *daimonion*.

chance encounters: for *sumbolous* as a noun with this meaning *cf.* parallel passage in *Mem.* 1.1.3–4, where *tous ornithas* and *tous apantôntas* are differentiated; LSJ seems wrong to take it here as an adjective understanding *oiônous* and meaning 'omens', as it should differ from, not be repetitive of, the preceding *oiônois*.

a divine thing: translating *daimonion*, see note on chapter 4.

Chapter 14 *caused uproar:* that Socrates' words generated noisy, unfavourable reactions can hardly be doubted in view of the composition and large number of the jury, see note on *often been misled*, ch. 4, and Socrates' uncompromising approach as recorded by both Plato and Xenophon. Whereas Xenophon here ascribes their protests to Socrates' claims of divine favour via the *daimonion*, Plato, *Ap.* 20e and 21a, notes them as occasioned by Socrates' allusions to Chaerephon's visit to Delphi and the complimentary response from the oracle; later, *Ap.* 30b, Plato records a similar reaction when Socrates avows that, whether acquitted or not, he won't change his ways.

may believe even less: the irony here is sarcastic, rather than of the self-deprecatory type, usually associated with Socrates: see note on 'proud tone' in ch. 1.

once: the date is uncertain; this is unfortunate as it marks the start of Socrates' 'service to God'. Guthrie, (2) 85–6, suggests 'some time in his thirties', *i.e.* between 439 and 429.

Chaerephon: a long-standing and devoted friend and companion of Socrates *cf.* Plato, *Charmides* 15b, *Apology* 21a. According to Xenophon, *Mem.* 1.2.48, like Hermogenes, he associated with Socrates to improve his character rather than his political capabilities. Aristophanes makes him an associate of Socrates in the *Clouds* and mocks him several times for his emaciated appearance. A man of democratic sympathies, according to Plato *Ap.* 21a, he was exiled by the 'thirty tyrants' but returned in 403 with the restoration of the democracy; he had however died by the time of Socrates' trial. His notorious impetuosity may have been the explanation of his consultation of the oracle.

in the presence of many witnesses: this detail, whether true or not, is absent from Plato *Ap.* 21a. Parke, 87, accepting Xenophon's veracity without question, argues that this refers to a more commonly used and less prestigious form of consultation, whereby the Pythia merely drew lots to decide between two alternative answers.

Apollo answered: according to Plato Chaerephon asked whether anyone was wiser than Socrates , and got the answer that nobody was. This longer response looks like Xenophon's own embroiderment, as he incorporates three virtues that figure repeatedly in his moralising writings. Later Cicero's tutor, Apollonius Molo, and Diogenes Laertius 2.37, had versified forms of the response to the effect that Socrates was the wisest of all men, not, however, in the oracle's normal Homeric hexameters, but in an iambic trimeter.

Most scholars reasonably prefer Plato's version of the response, including Vlastos, 1991, 288–9, who agrees with Parke that kleromancy (divination by drawing lots between two beans) was used, but Stokes, 115–6 argues that the whole story of the visit to Delphi was a Platonic fiction.

free-spirited: eleutherios implies 'having the virtues and instincts of a free man, as opposed to those of a slave', see notes on ch. 9 and *Mem.* 1.3.7. It often suggests generosity, both of spirit and with gifts, money *etc.* Thus the adjective combines the notions of independence, generosity and liberality.

more prudent: sôphrôn, literally 'sound of mind' means 'possessed of *sôphrosynê*', a virtue involving not only prudence, but also sensible moderation, temperance and self-discipline, particularly with regard to the pleasures of the flesh, so that it includes *enkrateia* (self-control), see note on *Mem.* 1.3.7. For a discussion of *sôphrosynê* see Plato *Chrm.* A slight difficulty arises in ch. 16, where Xenophon's Socrates introduces an examination of each detail of the oracular response and, with a pride very different from the mock humility of Plato *Ap.* 23b ff., praises himself for the three specified virtues but in a different order, first as *sôphrôn*, secondly as free, and thirdly as just, but then seems to add a fourth virtue, praising himself as *sophos* (wise). The simplest explanation is that for Xenophon's Socrates there is little distinction between *sôphrosynê* and *sophia* (wisdom), *cf. Mem.* 3.9.4, and that *sophia*, 3.9.5, also embraces justice and all other aspects of virtue. What Xenophon seems to have done is to take the Platonic version of the Delphic response and to enlarge on its tribute to Socrates as *sophos*; see also note on **cleverness**, *Mem.* 1.4.2.

An alternative explanation might be to speculate that by an error common to scribes μήτε σοφώτερον has fallen out after, or less probably, before μήτε σωφρονέστερον; both phrases are of similar appearance, and the comparative adjectives have similar beginnings and identical endings, see Reynolds and Wilson, 1991, 226, on haplography, homoearcton, and homoeoteleuton (writing something similar once instead of twice, omission of one of two phrases with similar beginnings or endings). If this omission occurred, it was before the time of Athenaeus, fl. c. A.D. 200, who 5.218e ff. quotes Xenophon's version of the Delphic response without μήτε σοφώτερον, but our trust in him isn't improved by his omission of μήτε ἐλευθεριώτερον.

Chapter 15 The topic of Lycurgus is absent from Plato's *Apology*; presumably it didn't come from Hermogenes but from Xenophon himself with his great interest in things Spartan.

Lycurgus: famed amongst the Greeks and particularly praised by Xenophon, *Lac. passim*, as the deviser of Sparta's distinctive institutions and way of life. Plutarch accorded him a biography, but he is a shadowy figure, about whom little is known for certain. If a historical figure, he is perhaps to be dated to the early seventh century B.C.

the lawgiver: a *nomothetês* normally framed written laws, as did Dracon and Solon at Athens, but Lycurgus' *nomoi* were unwritten.

it is said: Herodotus 1.65 records Lycurgus visiting Delphi and being greeted by the Pythia with four hexameter lines.

I am pondering...man: Xenophon's prose version of the third line of the Delphic hexameters.

CHAPTERS 16–21 show Socrates boasting about himself with the 'proud tone', *cf.* chs. 1–2, ascribed to him by Xenophon on the testimony of Hermogenes. Socrates' praises in chapter 16 of his own self-control, freedom of spirit, justice and wisdom are in vindication of the compliments paid to him by Delphi in Xenophon's version of the oracular response. Chapters 17–21 have Socrates proudly portraying himself as possessing the same virtuous qualities which are described more fully by Xenophon himself in justification of Socrates *passim* in *Mem.* Throughout this section one has the distinct impression that these are not the actual words of Socrates at his trial, nor yet the words ascribed to him by Hermogenes in his report, but words put into Socrates' mouth, briefly praising himself along the same lines as Xenophon will do more elaborately in *Memorabilia*.

Chapter 16 *less enslaved...to the appetites of the body:* *cf.* the similar phrases in *Mem.* 1.5.5 and 4.5.3 in sections discussing *enkrateia*, usually translated as 'self-control' *cf. Mem.* 2.1.1, and so equivalent to one aspect of *sôphrosynê*, see note on chapter 14. Here Socrates' boast of being free from slavery to appetites leads naturally to the next topic, his *eleutheriôtês*, freedom of spirit.

free-spirited: see note on ch. 5. Socrates could equally well have here claimed self-sufficiency, αὐτάρκεια, *cf. Mem.* 2.14 *etc.*, a Socratic quality particularly valued by his disciple, Antisthenes, *cf. Mem.* 2.5, 3.11.17 and *Smp.* 4.34 ff. and by the Cynics.

gifts or payment: *cf. Mem.* 1.2.60–61 *etc.*, Plato *Ap.* 19a, 31c.

a wise man: here Xenophon may be reverting to the Platonic version of the Delphic response, but see note on **more prudent** in ch. 14 and on wisdom embracing the three virtues just enumerated.

*I have never yet stopped: read the aorist with perfect meaing; ει and ε are often confused by scribes, particularly with the verb λείπω, see note on **anyone leaves**, ch. 7.

Chapter 17 *many...many:* a favourite anaphora of Xenophon's; see n. on ch. 4.

non-Athenians: including the Thebans Simmias and Cebes who figure in *Phaedo*.

least able to repay money: for Socrates' poverty see *Mem.* 1.2.14, Plato *Ap.* 23b.

τοῦ πάντας εἰδέναι: the article with the accusative and infinitive used substantivally and in apposition with the neuter genitive ἐκείνου.

but yet: translating ὅμως, though one would expect ἀλλ' ὅμως, as ὅμως is an adverb meaning 'however' not a conjunction meaning 'but'; πολλοὺς ἐπιθυμεῖν is parallel with πάντας εἰδέναι.

Chapter 18 *during the siege:* when Athens was being blockaded by land and sea by the Spartans after she had lost her fleet at Aegospotamoi in 405, until the end of the war.

luxuries from the market...my own spirit: in *Smp.* 4.41 Xenophon attributes very similar words and sentiments to Antisthenes; see p. 16 and note on ch. 16.

CHAPTERS 19–21 switch to the 'bare bones' of a cross-examination of Meletus. Xenophon's Socrates continues to do most of the talking with Meletus only vouchsafed two short answers to questions from Socrates. Xenophon's Socrates briefly dismisses the charge of corrupting the young and stresses his own merits as a purveyor of the most important asset of all, education, and completely avoids the theological charge, except for denying making any young man impious. Plato, *Ap.* 24c–28a contains a much fuller elenchus of Meletus, with Socrates first tackling the charge of corrupting the young, on which he makes Meletus contradict himself, before discussing the religious charge, on which he traps Meletus into the inconsistency of accusing him of complete atheism. (On the vexed question whether the details of Plato's elenchus are historically accurate and really Socratic rather than a Platonic fiction see Stokes 127 ff.).

Chapter 19 *corrupt the young men: cf. Mem.* 1.2.1–8 *etc.*

Chapter 20 *to obey you rather than their parents:* the influence of the 'new education', the generation gap and disrespect of the young for their parents are favourite themes of Aristophanes, especially in *Clouds* and *Wasps*; see in particular Pheidippides' attitude and behaviour to his father in *Clouds* 1399 ff., after having attended Socrates' Thinkery. Though other comic poets also exploited Socrates for their humorous purposes, it is the misrepresentation of himself in Aristophanes' *Clouds* that Socrates is at pains to contradict right at the beginning of Plato's *Apology*, before dealing with Meletus' charges.

on matters of health...doctors: Socrates regularly stressed the importance of experts with specialised knowledge and skills. Thus here he approves of using doctors for health problems; *cf. Mem.* 3.3.9–11, where the appropriate use not only of doctors, but also of pilots and farmers is recommended. Socrates frequently introduced into the discussion mentions of experts in humbler occupations such as cobblers, carpenters and metal-workers, *cf. Mem.* 1.2.37. Xenophon's Socrates in *Mem.* 3.1, 2, 4–6 stresses the need for expert knowledge in generals and statesmen, implying its frequent absence. *Cf.* also *Protagoras* 319d, where Plato's Socrates complains of the way that the Athenians at the *ecclêsia* (assembly) allow any carpenter, metal-worker, cobbler *etc.* to speak and advise them on matters of state.

meetings of the assembly: the *ecclêsia*, the chief organ of Athenian direct democracy, which met at least forty times per annum and was open to all male Athenian citizens to attend, to address, if they wished, and to vote *inter alia* on policy decisions and legislation. Here at least Socrates gives it credit for taking the advice of the most sensible speakers; but *cf. Mem.* 3.7.5–7, where he says it comprised the most senseless of men, who never give a thought to public affairs.

your choice of generals: stratêgoi (etymologically = army-leaders) had a dual role in classical Athens, being not only military (and naval) commanders but also political leaders. There were ten of them, normally one from each of the ten tribes, holding office for one year, though they could be re-elected as Pericles regularly was. Unlike most Athenian magistrates, they were not selected by lot, but chosen by vote, hence Socrates' approval here.

Chapter 21 Socrates complains that, though in all other activities the ablest men are honoured above others, this is not so in the area most beneficial to men, namely education. Although he is judged by some to excel as an educator, his reward is to be prosecuted on a capital charge. The whole line of argument of chs. 20–21 is absent from Plato's *Apology*, though Plato's Socrates is at least equally proud in claiming that really he deserves maintenance at the public expense.

Chapter 22 *the friends who spoke on his behalf:* no such speeches are mentioned in Plato *Ap.*, though, in 33e, 34a, Socrates claims to have many supporters present in court, naming eleven of them, including Crito, Critobulus, Aeschines, Adeimantus, Plato and Apollodorus, who could testify he had not corrupted them or their relatives, and were all ready to help him.

appearing to have been impious to the gods and unjust to men: i.e. appearing guilty on both of the charges. It seems better to take ἀσεβῆσαι and ἄδικος as both dependent on φανῆναι; most translators, however, take ἀσεβῆσαι and φανῆναι as parallel.

Chapter 23 Xenophon again differs from Plato in stating categorically that Socrates suggested no alternative penalty, whereas Plato's Socrates first claims at some length that he really deserves maintenance at the Athenians' expense as a state benefactor, and stating that all he could afford to pay was one mina, but continuing that on the advice of Plato, Crito and Critobulus, he proposes a fine of 30 minas, for which these three would be trustworthy guarantors. This was a considerable sum, as two generations later Aristotle *NE* 1134b21 gives one mina as the customary ransom for a prisoner of war.

in the first place...and secondly: πρῶτον μὲν...ἔπειτα δὲ do double duty not only as giving two proofs of Xenophon's assertion of Socrates' desire for death, but also as contrasting the times involved.

the verdict has been given: or more literally 'the case had been decided by vote', translating ἡ δίκη διεψηφίσθη. This verb has better ms. authority than κατεψηφίσθη, a correction added by the scribe of B, for which *cf.* ch. 27 and Thuc. 2.53.

but kept on saying: even by Xenophon's account Socrates had something to say on this occasion; this could be Xenophon's abbreviation of Plato *Ap.* 36b–38a. Xenophon probably omits the proposal of a fine, as contrary to his thesis that Socrates wanted death.

That Socrates did make a smug counter-proposal speech, as Plato in his *Apology* maintains, and did thereby antagonise the jury seems very probable. On the evidence of *Ap.* 36e, the original verdict had been a close-run thing and, if 30 jurors had voted differently, Socrates would have been acquitted. Thus 280 out of 500 (or 281 out of

501) might have found him guilty and 220 (or 221) found him innocent. If Diogenes Laertius, 2.42, can be trusted, 80 who had originally acquitted him voted for his death; this would mean 360 (or 361) votes for the death penalty. (Diogenes Laertius' unreliability, however, is clear from his statement that Socrates was found guilty by a majority of 281 votes; probably he misinterpreted the point of the figure 281. For further discussion see Stokes 168–171.)

when his friends wished to sneak him out of prison: Plato in his *Crito* describes the situation and Crito's attempt to persuade Socrates to escape. It is just before dawn on the day when the sacred ship will return from Delos, necessitating Socrates' death on the following day. Crito has already provided Socrates with money to bribe his gaolers. Other friends present include two young men with prominent roles in Plato's *Phaedo*, Simmias, who has brought money with him and Cebes, who like many others is willing to help. Plato bases Socrates' refusal to escape mainly on Socrates' imaginary conversation with the Laws of Athens who tell him it would be unjust to oppose them by escaping and, if he does so, wherever he goes, he won't escape the wrath of the Laws of Hades. The only close connection here with *Crito* is Xenophon's use of the word *ekkleptô* (sneak out), also found in Plato, *Cri.* 45a.

CHAPTERS 24–26 Xenophon's version of Hermogenes' account continues with Socrates' address to the jury after the death verdict. In this brief speech he merely repeats his claim to be innocent of the two charges, complains that legally the death penalty should be reserved for proper villains, rebukes those who voted against him, because the injustice of his death resembles that of Palamedes, wrongly brought to death by Odysseus, and ends by saying that posterity will show that he never harmed anyone, but instead benefited men by his conversing with them and teaching them unpaid every good thing he could.

This short speech lacks the literary artistry of the much longer speech in Plato, *Apology* 38c–42 in which Socrates repeats many of the main motifs of the two earlier Platonic speeches, prophesies that those who condemned him to death will be punished with immediate ignominy, argues that death may well be a good thing, since his *daimonion*, 40a–c, did not oppose him in any way during his defence; indeed death may be a dreamless sleep, or, if it involves moving elsewhere, he may meet the proper judges of Hades, great poets, or men like Palamedes or Ajax unjustly brought to death by men like Odysseus. Indeed God does not neglect good men and he can now see clearly that his death has been brought about by divine providence and that it is better for him (41d, *cf.* note on ch. 5) to die now and be freed from troubles. He appeals to the Athenians to keep an eye on his sons and rebuke them *if they neglect virtue*, saying 'I go to death but you live on, but which is the better is known only to God.'

For an excellent appreciation of this third Platonic speech see Stokes 179 who notes that apart from the Platonic and Xenophontean *Apologies* there are no extant parallels for speeches addressed to dikasts after decision of the penalty, and has reason to be sceptical about the possibility of such speeches being made.

Xenophon's version of this speech only resembles the Platonic one in the rebuke of the jurors who voted for his death, the complaint about injustice and the mentions of Palamedes and Odysseus. These details are probably derived from the Platonic version, but the influence of Plato *Ap.* 38c–42a may perhaps also be detected in earlier parts of Xenophon's *Apology*, notably in the motif that death now frees Socrates from troubles. Xenophon's adaptation, if that is what it is, is to make the *pragmatôn* (difficulties) of Plato *Ap.* 41d those of old age, *cf.* also Plato *Cri.* 43c, and to make the providential behaviour of the *daimonion*, *Ap.* 4, precede the trial, and to credit Socrates with some of his, Xenophon's, own practical common sense, in deciding to avoid the troubles of old age by ensuring his own conviction.

Chapter 24 *great impiety:* note Xenophon's use of hyperbaton to increase the force of the adjective; see notes on chs. 1, 5, and Denniston 50–51, 58–59.

worshipping: but ὀνομάζων, naming, should be retained with the codices.

Chapter 25 *robbing temples…: cf. Mem.* 1.2.62.

   The end of ch. 25 and most of chs. 26–8 are available in an alternative text with several significant variations provided by Stobaeus in his *Anthologium*. Stobaeus, probably writing in the early fifth century, provided four books of chosen extracts from classical authors, mainly on moral themes for the edification of his son. His citations of chs. 25–27 and chs. 28–9 come from sections of *Anthologium* Book 3 entitled respectively Περὶ Ἀνδρείας (*On Courage*) and Περὶ Ἀρετῆς (*On Virtue*).

Chapter 26 *Palamedes:* famed as one of the cleverest of the Greeks of the heroic age and the inventor, amongst other things, of the letters of the alphabet. According to most versions of the myths about him he forced a reluctant Odysseus into joining the Trojan War and Odysseus in revenge engineered his death by planting false evidence against him and having him convicted of treachery for conspiring with Priam.

material for finer hymns of praise: Palamedes wasn't mentioned in the *Iliad* or *Odyssey* but figured in the lost epic, the *Cypria*. All three main tragic poets wrote plays entitled *Palamedes*, and Sophocles wrote at least two more plays on the myth, so that the unjustness of his death would be familiar to the Athenians. The sophist Gorgias also composed a *Defence of Palamedes*, probably before 411.

than Odysseus: the image of Homer's hero seems to have suffered in the late fifth century, at least on the evidence of tragedy. In *Rhesus* (not necessarily early or by Euripides), he resembles Odysseus of the *Iliad*. In Sophocles' earliest extant play, *Ajax*, he is decent and honourable, but he is cruel and heartless in *Hecuba*, and the most hateful of the Greeks in *Troades* of 415, while he plumbs the depths of unscrupulous villainy in Sophocles' *Philoctetes* of 409; *cf.* also ll. 524–30 of Euripides' last play *Iphigenia in Aulis*. He would also be less popular with Athenians as the victor over the local hero Ajax of Salamis in the contest for the Arms of Achilles, dramatised by Aeschylus in the first play of a lost trilogy. In Plato's *Apology* Socrates couples Ajax with Palamedes as a victim of an unjust verdict.

shall be supported by the testimony: Stephanus' correction of the future active to the future middle is confirmed by (1) the frequency of confusion of *ai* and *e* by scribes because of their similar pronunciations (2) the future middle infinitive form in the parallel passage in *Mem.* 4.8.10. The use of the impersonal passive construction with *marturô* is found in Plato and the orators and the use of the future middle with passive meaning is paralleled in Demosthenes 57.37.

every good thing: Socrates' final speech at his trial is made by Xenophon to end with *agathon* (good), a theme pervading *Mem.*, whereas Plato makes Socrates end the corresponding speech with an equally important word, ϑεός, God.

CHAPTERS 27–29 The cheerful behaviour of Socrates at his trial.

Chapter 27 *as he left:* presumably on his way to prison.

cheerful: cf. Plato's accounts of Socrates' cheerfulness in prison, *Cri.* 43c, *Phd.* 58e–59a *etc.*

Chapter 28 *Apollodorus:* for his devotion to Socrates *cf. Mem.* 3.17; he was present at Socrates' trial and willing to help with his fine, Plato *Ap.* 38c, and was with him on his last day, when he was particularly upset and tearful, *Phd.* 59a, 117d. He is also noteworthy as the narrator of the proceedings in Plato's *Smp.*

stroked...head: a gesture of affection; the phrase is in Herodotus 6.61. Plato in *Phd.* 89b has Socrates in prison stroking the head of Phaedo. Ollier 93 argues that this was a habit of Socrates and that Xenophon may be trusted on this point, but the possibility remains that Xenophon has been inaccurate in his use of material from Plato's *Phaedo*, or has adapted or distorted it. (Alternatively Xenophon's alleged informant Hermogenes, who was with Socrates in his last hours, Plato *Phd.* 59b, may have misinformed Xenophon or been misunderstood by Xenophon on this detail.)

simple: εὐηϑής, literally 'good-natured' is regularly used as a euphemism for 'simple', 'naïve'. Plato, however, makes Apollodorus the narrator of his *Smp.*, and his account is extremely sophisticated and far from feeble-minded. His nickname may have been μαλακός ('softie'), though an alternative manuscript reading is μανικός ('crazy'); see Plato *Smp.* 173d and Rowe's note.

*did you prefer: translating μᾶλλον ἐβούλου. But read μᾶλλον ἂν ἐβούλου, would you have preferred, as the apodosis of a past unfulfilled condition. Diogenes Laertius 2.35 has Socrates put a simpler question to his wife, Xanthippe, 'Did you wish me to die justly?'.

CHAPTERS 29–31 Socrates' remarks about Anytus and prophecy about his son.

Chapter 29 *on seeing Anytus passing:* Xenophon's vagueness about the precise time and place is suspicious.

Anytus was the most influential of Socrates' three accusers. He inherited a tannery from his father. The dates of his birth and death are uncertain. Plutarch's anecdotes, *Mor.* 762c and *Vit. Alc.* 4.4, 5, about him as a prosperous older man in love with a teenaged Alcibiades should be rejected on chronological grounds.

As a general in 409 he failed to save Pylos and was prosecuted but acquitted. Exiled by the thirty tyrants, he played a leading role with Thrasybulus in the seizure of Phyle and restoration of democracy in 403. He was still politically active in

397–6, *Hell. Ox.* 1.1.1–2, but need not have been the Anytus mentioned in Lysias 22 as a magistrate guarding the corn supply, *c.* 387, as several instances of the name are found in inscriptions of the period. Diogenes Laertius' statement, 2.43, that the Athenians quickly regretted the execution of Socrates and condemned Meletus to death and exiled Anytus and Lycon is unsubstantiated.

Anytus figures in Plato's *Meno* (dramatic date *c.* 403), a dialogue discussing whether ἀρετή, virtue, can be taught. In it, initially at least, he is favourably portrayed and addressed politely enough by Socrates. We learn that he had been well brought up and educated by a respectable father. However the mere mention of the word 'sophists' enrages him bitterly as he hates them, calling them λώβη καὶ διαφθορὰ τῶν συγγιγνομένων (the bane and ruin of his associates). When Socrates starts discussing the education of their sons by leading politicians, Anytus thinks Socrates is insulting them and departs in anger, telling Socrates he is too ready to speak ill of people, particularly in Athens. Plato's restrained attitude to Anytus can be explained, if he regarded him as an honourable but stupid politician labouring under the delusion engendered by *Clouds* that Socrates was a sophist, *cf.* Aeschines, *Tim.* 173, a mistake which Socrates is at pains to correct in Plato's *Apology*, but not in Xenophon's version. *Meno* is usually regarded as 'Socratic', *i.e.* as portraying the real Socrates, and from Plato's early, if not earliest period, *cf.* A. E. Taylor 130, Vlastos, 1991, 46–7; Bluck dates it *c.* 386–5. Probably Anytus was also influenced by political motives, regarding Socrates as μισόδημος (a hater of the common people), *cf.* Libanius, *Apologia Socratis* 54, because of his association with oligarchs like Critias and Charmides, *cf. Mem.* 1.2.12 ff., particularly 1.2.58 and his approval of Homer's attitude to Thersites in *Iliad* 2.

Chapter 30 *Homer attributed...foreknowledge:* to Patroclus *Il.* 16.891–4 and to Hector, *Il.* 22.358–60.

spirit: translating *psychê,* here, as often, of the non-physical, emotional and mental side of a living (usually human) creature, which gives it its personality.

servile occupation: this attitude to tanners seems Xenophontic rather than Socratic; *cf.* Aristophanes' sneers at the tanner Cleon in *Knights.*

Chapter 31 *enjoys a bad reputation:* *cf.* Plato *Ap.* 39c for Socrates' prophecy of the future punishment of the jurors who convicted him.

his father has arranged for him: it was normal for sons to be trained in their fathers' occupation in Socrates' time; earlier Solon had legislated that only fathers who had taught their sons a τέχνη (skill) should be maintained by them in their old age; *cf.* Plutarch, *Life of Solon* 22. Thus the Hippocratic Oath made doctors train their sons in medicine and they did so, as Lucian several times used παῖδες ἰατρῶν (sons of doctors) to mean 'doctors'; similarly Plato, *Laws* 769b had οἱ ζωγράφων παῖδες simply for 'painters'.

Chapters 29–31 may well be a Xenophontic fiction with the motif of Socrates prophesying when near to death suggested by Plato in *Apology* 39c and that of the future behaviour of Anytus' son from Socrates' instruction to the jurors to keep an eye on the behaviour of his own sons coming from *Apology* 41e; for the motif of education see note on c. 29.

Mentions of Anytus in Plato's *Apology* are few and brief, though they do include a reference to his powerful clique, to his representing the *demiourgoi* (he was a tanner) and politicians as accuser, and to his advocacy of the death penalty to stop Socrates' baneful influence on more young men. Even if this episode is fictitious, Xenophon deserves credit for using it to emphasise the importance of Anytus in the trial as the most formidable of the three accusers.

CHAPTERS 32–33 recapitulate the arguments of chapters 1–21.
Chapter 32 *glorifying himself:* cf. in particular μεγαληγορίας in c. 1, Xenophon's version of the Delphic response in chapter 14 and Socrates' substantiation of it.
to bring: the present participle, whether taken with the substantial neuter article and infinitive τὸ μεγαλύνειν, or with ἐποίησε, has a conative force = striving to bring; Cobet's conjecture of the aorist participle, assuming haplography, (see note on ch. 14) is, therefore, unnecessary.
Chapter 33 *put on ... display:* the middle of ἐπιδείκνυμι means 'show off', implying the pride which Xenophon attributes to Socrates throughout this work. The verb and the cognate noun ἐπίδειξις were often used of rhetoricians showing off their oratorical prowess in set speeches.
spirit: as in chapter 30 translating *psychê*. Plato's Socrates insisted, *Ap.* 29d, 30a, that one should care not for one's body or for money, but for one's *psychê*, making it as good as possible. See Guthrie (2) 147 ff. and notes on *Mem.* 1.24 *etc.*
duly saw it through: see note on chapter 6. Again I follow LSJ and take the literal meaning to be 'paid the debt of death'. Alternatively it could mean 'got it completed' as in Plato *Phlb.* 27c.
Chapter 34 Note Xenophon's switch from a simpler to a more exalted and rhetorical style in what is virtually a peroration in praise of his hero, culminating in the impressive, polysyllabic superlative of an adjective, not recorded elsewhere in Greek literature. He repeats in more emphatic manner his initial assertion that Socrates deserved to be remembered, after introducing a theme permeating *Mem.*, the benefits conferred upon his fellows by Socrates through his teachings and his example.
beneficial: useful, helpful, translating ὠφέλιμος, here of helpfulness to devotees of virtue as in *Mem.* 4.8.11, the much more detailed, rhetorical and elaborate character sketch and eulogy of Socrates, which brings *Mem.* to an impressive close; for a translation see p. 158.

INTRODUCTION TO *MEMORABILIA SOCRATIS*

The general purpose of *Mem.* is praise of Socrates as the perfect man and educator, whose virtues and lifestyle set an example for others to follow. It seems to fall into two main parts, Books 1 and 2, most of which was completed (though perhaps not published) some time after *Ap.*, and Books 3 and 4, maturer writings showing more thoughtfulness and variety and a little humour, completed after 371, as 3.5 seems to reflect the military situation between the battles of Leuctra and Mantinea.

Book 1. In 1.1–1.2.8 Xenophon, after giving the official charge against Socrates, makes his own defence for him against the accusation of religious non-conformity, explaining it as arising from his belief in his *daimonion* and stressing Socrates' piety. Next Xenophon rejects the charge of corrupting the young by emphasising the good example set by Socrates by his self-control, hardy life-style and lack of interest in money, and by encouraging his associates to become *kaloi kagathoi* (perfect men).

In 1.2.9–64 Xenophon rebuts the charges of Polycrates that Socrates encouraged his associates to depise the laws and that Critias and Alcibiades, who did such harm to Athens, were his associates, by insisting that they only joined him temporarily out of ambition to improve their political skills, illustrating his point with dialogues of Socrates with Critias and Charicles and of Pericles with the young Alcibiades.

From 1.3 onwards the material follows less closely any pre-arranged plan, with Xenophon from time to time making contributions towards the general vindication of Socrates, enumerating his various virtues, including his piety, thereby *en passant* rebutting the first of the two official charges, but putting his main emphasis on the ὠφέλιμος, useful and beneficial, influence of Socrates in word and deed, by the example of his personal life and by the wisdom of his teaching, not just upon the young but on all with whom he associated.

In 1.3 Xenophon describes Socrates' trust in Delphi and in sacrificing according to one's means, his frugal life-style and his self-control in sexual matters (including a rebuke to Xenophon himself for sympathising with Critobulus for kissing a handsome youth, which in my opinion may be Xenophon's later insertion into the original text). 1.4 contains a conversation with Aristodemus, a conspicuous despiser of sacrifice, divination and oracles, with Socrates elaborating on the providence of the divine creator of mankind; *cf.* 4.3.3 ff. 1.5 has a monologue of Socrates on self-control, while 1.6 consists of three conversations with Antiphon the sophist. Socrates counters the accusation that he is a 'teacher of misery' by claiming that his humble life-style ensures his self-sufficiency and happiness. When accused of folly in not charging his pupils, Socrates retorts by saying he is acting like a 'perfect man' instead of a 'prostituter of wisdom'. When criticised for avoiding politics, Socrates claims to do more good by trying to produce the greatest possible number of competent politicians. Finally 1.7 describes Socrates' discouragement of false pretences in his companions whether as musicians, generals, ships' pilots or politicians.

Book 2 has as its subjects self-control, behaviour within the family, and friendship, *cf.* Plato *Lysis*, in theory and practice. 2.1 reverts to the topic of 1.5, self-control, as Socrates recommends a more austere lifestyle to his hedonistic disciple, Aristippus, the founder of the Cyrenaic school, see Diogenes Laertius 2.65–104, leading up to a purple patch of *Mem.* as Socrates recites the fable of the sophist Prodicus, *The Choice of Heracles*. 2.2 and 2.3 contain Socrates' rebukes to his son Lamprocles for his treatment of Xanthippe and to two quarrelling brothers. 2.4, 5 and 6 have Socrates discussing the value of friendship and the qualities of a good friend and in 2.7 and 8 proving a friend in deed by offering sensible practical advice to two impoverished acquaintances on how to repair their fortunes.

Book 3 opens with seven chapters on related themes, as Socrates discusses military and political leadership with respectively a teacher of generalship, a newly elected general, a cavalry commander, (*cf. Eq. Mag.*), an unsuccessful candidate for the office of general, the younger Pericles as general in 406, Plato's brother Glaucon, and Charmides. Thereafter Book 3 becomes more disparate. In 3.8 Aristippus, *cf.* 2.1, is allowed by Socrates to cross-question him on various concepts while in 3.9 Socrates discusses various virtues and vices, and the conduct of kings and rulers. 3.10 recounts Socrates' conversations with a painter, sculptor and armour-maker. 3.11 introduces a touch of humour, *cf. Smp.*, as Xenophon elegantly recounts Socrates' light-hearted conversational exchanges with a high-class prostitute. The book ends with Socrates discoursing on the follies of neglecting one's physical condition, 3.12, or being unduly upset about trivial matters, 3.13, and Socrates offering various pieces of advice to symposiasts, 3.14.

Book 4. 4.1 notes Socrates' beneficial influence on his companions, both when serious and when jesting, *cf. Smp.* init.; he playfully claims to be in love, but it is not with bodies, but with souls well suited for virtue, and he emphasises the need for education for all, however clever or rich. 4.2 recounts Socrates' services to Euthydemus, a young man with political ambitions who prides himself on his wisdom gained from many books; Socrates seeks him out and by exercising his elenchus on him convinces him of his own ignorance, so that he becomes Socrates' regular companion, and is instructed by him. 4.3 records a conversation with Euthydemus on divine providence, *cf.* 1.4, illlustrating how Socrates promoted piety and *sôphrosynê* among his associates. In 4.4 Socrates, when asked by Hippias to define justice, *cf.* Plato *Republic*, says it's what he reveals by his conduct and is identical with *to nomimon* (what is lawful); 4.4.15 has a suspiciously Xenophontic reference to the Spartan Lycurgus, *cf. Ap.* 15.

Chapters 4.5 and 4.6 revert to Euthydemus as the beneficiary of Socrates' conversation, at first on the merits of self-control. 4.6 is perhaps the most interesting, revealing and typically Xenophontic chapter of *Mem.*, as Xenophon rightly stresses the importance of knowledge for Socrates and his insistence on definitions, but shrinks from a full account of Socrates' definitions as 'too laborious' and contents himself with illustrating Socrates' manner of investigation and with the help of Euthydemus *quickly* arrives at definitions of piety, justice, wisdom, the good, the beautiful, courage (*cf.* Plato *Euthphr.*, *R.*, *La.*), all depending explicitly or implicitly upon knowledge and its useful application. Kingship and tyranny are also discussed and Xenophon ends by praising Socrates' method of bringing the argument back to first principles and commending Socrates as a 'safe speaker', like Odysseus who gained general approval for his views. In 4.7 Socrates asserts that geometry, astronomy and arithmetic should only be studied as far as they are practically useful and deprecates being a *phrontistês* (student) of the heavenly bodies, *cf.* 1.1.11 and Aristophanes' *Clouds*. He also urges his companions to look after their health via a diet and life-style that suits them personally.

Chapter 8 rejects the view that Socrates' *daimonion* deserted him at the time of his trial, stressing, as in *Ap.*, that death was the best thing for an aged Socrates, and goes on to give a briefer version of the information about Socrates' last days he says was given to him by Hermogenes in *Apology* 2–27, covering the same ground, reporting the same arguments and even, as often in Xenophon, occasionally using identical words or phrases. The work is rounded off with an epilogue praising Socrates' piety, justice, self-control, wisdom and skill as a communicator, and typically of Xenophon, his usefulness to devotees of virtue. For a translation of this impressive, elaborate and carefully prepared epilogue, see p. 158.

TEXT OF *MEMORABILIA* OF SOCRATES

SIGLA

Π¹	P. Heid. 206, early 3rd century B.*C*.
Π²	P. Grenf. II I3 = P. Lit. Lond. I49, 3rd or 4th century A.D.
Π⁶	P. Berol. 2II08, 2nd century A.D.
A	Parisinus gr. I302, late 13th century
B	Parisinus gr. I740, late 13th century
M	Marcianus gr. 5II (coll. 590), late 14th century
Z	Vaticanus gr. I950, late 14th century
L	Laurentianus 80.13, late 14th century
W	Vindobonensis hist. gr. 95, late 15th century
Φ	MZLW in agreement
β	BΦ in agreement

Students of *Mem.* need no longer rely on the texts of Marchant or Hude, though still useful, thanks to the invaluable contribution of M. Bandini to the magnificent Budé edition of *Mem.* I published in 2000, providing an excellent text, a detailed and exhaustive apparatus criticus, and a wealth of information about many manuscripts and the textual tradition. As editor I must acknowledge my debt of gratitude to Bandini, my admiration of his scholarly expertise and chalcenteric diligence, and my complete reliance on him for details in preparing an apparatus more appropriate for this series.

There are three papyri containing extracts from *Mem.* I, many quotations by classical authors, and some extracts from the text, notably by Stobaeus of the fifth century A.D., but the earliest continuous text is provided in the late thirteenth century by A and B, the two most important manuscripts. According to Bandini, they are ultimately derived from the same source, perhaps a prestigious edition of the first or second century A.D. by a scholar from Alexandria or Pergamum, designated a by Bandini.

Whereas A is directly descended from a, B's descent is indirect via an intermediary β. Other important manuscripts are M, Z, L and W, akin to B, but via another intermediate exemplar Φ and its two copies φ^1, the source of M and Z, and φ^2, the source of L and W. For practical purposes M, Z, L and W are useful for two reasons, firstly as a check for the readings of B, and secondly as providing some alternative readings, coming from a revision of the text in the early fourteenth century by a Byzantine scholar, perhaps

Theodorus Metochites or more probably Nicephorus Gregoras, perhaps mainly erudite emendations but of some merit.

It is a pity that the papyri are so few, so short and so fragmentary, see 1.2.45–48, 56–59, 1.3.8, and 1.3.15–1.4.3, as they contain a few variant readings worth considering and even suggest some few words may have been lost here and there from the original text. Π^1 in particular deserves particular attention for its early date and for including a specially interesting passage, the sole dialogue between Socrates and Xenophon. Papyri should not be entirely disregarded as cheap hastily produced texts, and there must remain some doubt as to how faithfully and fully the edition a reproduced the original text of Xenophon.

I have tried to take full account of Bandini's fine text and critical notes in preparing the text, but as circumstances dictate a reproduction of Marchant's O.C.T. as the basis of the text, I have followed the same policy as for *Apologia Socratis*, described on p. 21, wherever possible, incorporating changes into the text or, where that has been impracticably difficult, printing Marchant's text with marginal asterisks and translating it, and explaining the reasons for the change in the Commentary. See also the list of changes on p. 163.

MEMORABILIA SOCRATIS

MEMORABILIA OF SOCRATES
BOOK I

ΑΠΟΜΝΗΜΟΝΕΥΜΑΤΩΝ Α

Πολλάκις ἐθαύμασα τίσι ποτὲ λόγοις Ἀθηναίους ἔπεισαν **I**
οἱ γραψάμενοι Σωκράτην ὡς ἄξιος εἴη θανάτου τῇ πόλει. ἡ
μὲν γὰρ γραφὴ κατ᾽ αὐτοῦ τοιάδε τις ἦν· ἀδικεῖ Σωκράτης
οὓς μὲν ἡ πόλις νομίζει θεοὺς οὐ νομίζων, ἕτερα δὲ καινὰ
5 δαιμόνια εἰσφέρων· ἀδικεῖ δὲ καὶ τοὺς νέους διαφθείρων.
Πρῶτον μὲν οὖν, ὡς οὐκ ἐνόμιζεν οὓς ἡ πόλις νομίζει **2**
θεούς, ποίῳ ποτ᾽ ἐχρήσαντο τεκμηρίῳ; θύων τε γὰρ φανερὸς
ἦν πολλάκις μὲν οἴκοι, πολλάκις δὲ ἐπὶ τῶν κοινῶν τῆς
πόλεως βωμῶν, καὶ μαντικῇ χρώμενος οὐκ ἀφανὴς ἦν.
10 διετεθρύλητο γὰρ ὡς φαίη Σωκράτης τὸ δαιμόνιον ἑαυτῷ
σημαίνειν· ὅθεν δὴ καὶ μάλιστά μοι δοκοῦσιν αὐτὸν αἰτιά-
σασθαι καινὰ δαιμόνια εἰσφέρειν. ὁ δ᾽ οὐδὲν καινότερον **3**
εἰσέφερε τῶν ἄλλων, ὅσοι μαντικὴν νομίζοντες οἰωνοῖς τε
χρῶνται καὶ φήμαις καὶ συμβόλοις καὶ θυσίαις. οὗτοί τε γὰρ
15 ὑπολαμβάνουσιν οὐ τοὺς ὄρνιθας οὐδὲ τοὺς ἀπαντῶντας εἰδέναι
τὰ συμφέροντα τοῖς μαντευομένοις, ἀλλὰ τοὺς θεοὺς διὰ
τούτων αὐτὰ σημαίνειν, κἀκεῖνος δὲ οὕτως ἐνόμιζεν. ἀλλ᾽ οἱ **4**
μὲν πλεῖστοί φασιν ὑπό τε τῶν ὀρνίθων καὶ τῶν ἀπαντώντων
ἀποτρέπεσθαί τε καὶ προτρέπεσθαι· Σωκράτης δ᾽ ὥσπερ
20 ἐγίγνωσκεν, οὕτως ἔλεγε· τὸ δαιμόνιον γὰρ ἔφη σημαίνειν.

MEMORABILIA OF SOCRATES
BOOK ONE

Chapter 1. I have often wondered what were the arguments used by Socrates' accusers to persuade the Athenians that he deserved a state execution. For the indictment against him was something like this: 'Socrates does wrong by not worshipping the gods worshipped by the state and by introducing other new divinities; he also does wrong by corrupting the young men.'
2. First then, what was the evidence they used to show that he did not worship the gods worshipped by the state? For he could often be seen sacrificing at home, and often too at the communal altars of the state and he was conspicuous in his use of divination; for it had become common talk that Socrates said that his divine sign communicated with him. This indeed is the particular reason why I think they accused him of introducing new divinities. 3. But he introduced nothing newer than do the others who practise augury and make use of birds, utterances, chance encounters and sacrifices. For they assume that it is not the birds or the people meeting them that know what is beneficial to those engaging in the divination, but that the gods use these means to signal this to them; and this was Socrates' opinion too.
4. But whereas most people say that they are both deterred and encouraged by the birds or the people meeting them, Socrates' words corresponded with his actual thought; for he said that it was his divine sign that gave signals

καὶ πολλοῖς τῶν συνόντων προηγόρευε τὰ μὲν ποιεῖν, τὰ δὲ
μὴ ποιεῖν, ὡς τοῦ δαιμονίου προσημαίνοντος· καὶ τοῖς μὲν
πειθομένοις αὐτῷ συνέφερε, τοῖς δὲ μὴ πειθομένοις μετέμελε.
5 καίτοι τίς οὐκ ἂν ὁμολογήσειεν αὐτὸν βούλεσθαι μήτ᾽ ἠλίθιον
μήτ᾽ ἀλαζόνα φαίνεσθαι τοῖς συνοῦσιν; ἐδόκει δ᾽ ἂν ἀμφό- 5
τερα ταῦτα, εἰ προαγορεύων ὡς ὑπὸ θεοῦ φαινόμενα καὶ
ψευδόμενος ἐφαίνετο. δῆλον οὖν ὅτι οὐκ ἂν προέλεγεν, εἰ
μὴ ἐπίστευεν ἀληθεύσειν. ταῦτα δὲ τίς ἂν ἄλλῳ πιστεύσειεν
ἢ θεῷ; πιστεύων δὲ θεοῖς πῶς οὐκ εἶναι θεοὺς ἐνόμιζεν;
6 ἀλλὰ μὴν ἐποίει καὶ τάδε πρὸς τοὺς ἐπιτηδείους. τὰ μὲν 10
γὰρ ἀναγκαῖα συνεβούλευε καὶ πράττειν ὡς ἐνόμιζεν ἄριστ᾽
ἂν πραχθῆναι· περὶ δὲ τῶν ἀδήλων ὅπως ἀποβήσοιτο μαν-
7 τευσομένους ἔπεμπεν, εἰ ποιητέα. καὶ τοὺς μέλλοντας οἴκους
τε καὶ πόλεις καλῶς οἰκήσειν μαντικῆς ἔφη προσδεῖσθαι·
τεκτονικὸν μὲν γὰρ ἢ χαλκευτικὸν ἢ γεωργικὸν ἢ ἀνθρώπων 15
ἀρχικὸν ἢ τῶν τοιούτων ἔργων ἐξεταστικὸν ἢ λογιστικὸν ἢ
οἰκονομικὸν ἢ στρατηγικὸν γενέσθαι, πάντα τὰ τοιαῦτα μαθή-
8 ματα καὶ ἀνθρώπου γνώμῃ αἱρετὰ ἐνόμιζεν εἶναι· τὰ δὲ
μέγιστα τῶν ἐν τούτοις ἔφη τοὺς θεοὺς ἑαυτοῖς καταλεί-
πεσθαι, ὧν οὐδὲν δῆλον εἶναι τοῖς ἀνθρώποις. οὔτε γὰρ 20
τῷ καλῶς ἀγρὸν φυτευσαμένῳ δῆλον ὅστις καρπώσεται, οὔτε
τῷ καλῶς οἰκίαν οἰκοδομησαμένῳ δῆλον ὅστις ἐνοικήσει,
οὔτε τῷ στρατηγικῷ δῆλον εἰ συμφέρει στρατηγεῖν, οὔτε τῷ
πολιτικῷ δῆλον εἰ συμφέρει τῆς πόλεως προστατεῖν, οὔτε
τῷ καλὴν γήμαντι, ἵν᾽ εὐφραίνηται, δῆλον εἰ διὰ ταύτην 25
ἀνιάσεται, οὔτε τῷ δυνατοὺς ἐν τῇ πόλει κηδεστὰς λαβόντι
9 δῆλον εἰ διὰ τούτους στερήσεται τῆς πόλεως. τοὺς δὲ μηδὲν
τῶν τοιούτων οἰομένους εἶναι δαιμόνιον, ἀλλὰ πάντα τῆς
ἀνθρωπίνης γνώμης, δαιμονᾶν ἔφη· δαιμονᾶν δὲ καὶ τοὺς
μαντευομένους ἃ τοῖς ἀνθρώποις ἔδωκαν οἱ θεοὶ μαθοῦσι 30

---

6   καὶ om. rec., Marchant in Loeb
8   ἀληθεύειν AB: corr. Φ
17–18 μαθητά Cobet
18   αἱρετέα ΑΦ
22   οἰκήσει Β¹Φ

to him. He would give many people early instructions to do some things or to avoid doing other things, claiming his divine sign was giving advance signals; and those who followed his advice prospered, but those who did not regretted it. 5. But who could fail to agree that he didn't wish to be shown up to his companions as a fool or an impostor? He would, however, have seemed both, if he could clearly be seen making forecasts purporting to come from divine revelation and mistaken in them. Obviously, therefore, he would not have made his forecasts, unless he was confident they were true. And whence could he derive this confidence except from a god? And if he had confidence in gods, how could he not believe in their existence?

6. Moreover he used the following procedure with his close friends. When a course of action was inevitable, he advised them to act as he thought would turn out best, but when the outcome was uncertain, he sent them to ask the oracle whether the course of action should be taken. 7. Furthermore he would say that those about to manage estates and cities well needed the extra help of divination. For to become skilled in carpentry or working in bronze or in farming or in ruling men or to be able to judge such activities or to be skilled in arithmetic or estate management or generalship, all such things he said were skills that could be learnt and grasped by human understanding. 8. But he said that the most important features of these concerns the gods retain for themselves, and that none of these things are clear to men. For it is not clear to the man, who has planted a field well, who will gather the crop, or to the man, who has had a house well built, who will live in it, or to the skilled general if being a general is to his advantage, or to the statesman whether it is advantageous to be head of state, or to the man, who has married a beautiful woman to bring him joy, whether she will cause him misery, nor is it clear to the man, who has acquired politically powerful relatives through marriage, whether he will be exiled because of them. 9. He said that those who think that none of these things depend upon the gods but all of them upon human understanding are themselves possessed and mad, as also are those who use divination for matters which the gods have

διακρίνειν (οἷον εἴ τις ἐπερωτῴη πότερον ἐπιστάμενον ἡνιοχεῖν
ἐπὶ ζεῦγος λαβεῖν κρεῖττον ἢ μὴ ἐπιστάμενον, ἢ πότερον
ἐπιστάμενον κυβερνᾶν ἐπὶ τὴν ναῦν κρεῖττον λαβεῖν ἢ μὴ
ἐπιστάμενον), ἢ ἃ ἔξεστιν ἀριθμήσαντας ἢ μετρήσαντας ἢ
5 στήσαντας εἰδέναι· τοὺς τὰ τοιαῦτα παρὰ τῶν θεῶν πυν-
θανομένους ἀθέμιτα ποιεῖν ἡγεῖτο. ἔφη δὲ δεῖν, ἃ μὲν
μαθόντας ποιεῖν ἔδωκαν οἱ θεοί, μανθάνειν, ἃ δὲ μὴ δῆλα
τοῖς ἀνθρώποις ἐστί, πειρᾶσθαι διὰ μαντικῆς παρὰ τῶν θεῶν
πυνθάνεσθαι· τοὺς θεοὺς γὰρ οἷς ἂν ὦσιν ἵλεῳ σημαίνειν.
10 Ἀλλὰ μὴν ἐκεῖνός γε ἀεὶ μὲν ἦν ἐν τῷ φανερῷ· πρῴ τε 10
γὰρ εἰς τοὺς περιπάτους καὶ τὰ γυμνάσια ᾔει καὶ πληθούσης
ἀγορᾶς ἐκεῖ φανερὸς ἦν, καὶ τὸ λοιπὸν ἀεὶ τῆς ἡμέρας ἦν
ὅπου πλείστοις μέλλοι συνέσεσθαι· καὶ ἔλεγε μὲν ὡς τὸ
πολύ, τοῖς δὲ βουλομένοις ἐξῆν ἀκούειν. οὐδεὶς δὲ πώποτε 11
15 Σωκράτους οὐδὲν ἀσεβὲς οὐδὲ ἀνόσιον οὔτε πράττοντος εἶδεν
οὔτε λέγοντος ἤκουσεν. οὐδὲ γὰρ περὶ τῆς τῶν πάντων
φύσεως, ᾗπερ τῶν ἄλλων οἱ πλεῖστοι, διελέγετο σκοπῶν
ὅπως ὁ καλούμενος ὑπὸ τῶν σοφιστῶν κόσμος ἔχει καὶ
τίσιν ἀνάγκαις ἕκαστα γίγνεται τῶν οὐρανίων, ἀλλὰ καὶ τοὺς
20 φροντίζοντας τὰ τοιαῦτα μωραίνοντας ἀπεδείκνυε. καὶ πρῶ- 12
τον μὲν αὐτῶν ἐσκόπει πότερά ποτε νομίσαντες ἱκανῶς ἤδη
τἀνθρώπινα εἰδέναι ἔρχονται ἐπὶ τὸ περὶ τῶν τοιούτων
φροντίζειν, ἢ τὰ μὲν ἀνθρώπινα παρέντες, τὰ δαιμόνια δὲ
σκοποῦντες ἡγοῦνται τὰ προσήκοντα πράττειν. ἐθαύμαζε δ' 13
25 εἰ μὴ φανερὸν αὐτοῖς ἐστιν, ὅτι ταῦτα οὐ δυνατόν ἐστιν
ἀνθρώποις εὑρεῖν· ἐπεὶ καὶ τοὺς μέγιστον φρονοῦντας ἐπὶ τῷ
περὶ τούτων λέγειν οὐ ταὐτὰ δοξάζειν ἀλλήλοις, ἀλλὰ τοῖς
μαινομένοις ὁμοίως διακεῖσθαι πρὸς ἀλλήλους. τῶν τε γὰρ 14
μαινομένων τοὺς μὲν οὐδὲ τὰ δεινὰ δεδιέναι, τοὺς δὲ καὶ τὰ
30 μὴ φοβερὰ φοβεῖσθαι, καὶ τοῖς μὲν οὐδ' ἐν ὄχλῳ δοκεῖν
αἰσχρὸν εἶναι λέγειν ἢ ποιεῖν ὁτιοῦν, τοῖς δὲ οὐδ' ἐξιτητέον

6   ἀθέμιτα Φ: ἀθέμιστα ΑΒ¹

allowed men to decide by use of knowledge. Suppose for example someone were to ask whether it is better to have a competent or incompetent driver for one's carriage, or a competent or incompetent steersman for one's ship, or to ask about things about which knowledge can be gained by calculating, measuring or weighing; he thought that those who inquire about such matters from the gods, are wrongful in their actions. He said the right course was for men to learn for themselves in areas where the gods have allowed men to learn and act, but only in matters obscured from humans to seek information from the gods by means of divination; for he said the gods send signals to those they favour. 10. Furthermore Socrates was always to be seen in public. For early in the morning he would go to the covered walks and the training areas, and in the forenoon, when the agora was full, he could be seen there, and for the rest of the day he would always be wherever he could expect most company; and generally he did the talking and those who wished could listen. 11. But no-one ever saw or heard Socrates doing or saying anything irreligious or impious. For unlike most of the others he did not discuss the nature of the universe or consider how what the sophists call 'The Universe' is constituted, or by what governing laws the heavenly phenomena come about, but he would prove that those who study such matters are fools. 12. The first thing he asked about them was whether it was because they thought they already had sufficient knowledge of human matters that they proceeded to the study of such subjects, or whether they thought they were acting properly in rejecting the affairs of men and studying divine matters. 13. He would express surprise that it wasn't evident to them that it was impossible for humans to discover these secrets, since even those priding themselves most as speakers on these subjects didn't have the same theories as one another but were like madmen in their attitude to each other. 14. For some of these madmen he would say did not fear even what was fearsome, while others were frightened of what was not frightening; some again were not ashamed of saying or doing anything at all in a crowd, while others did not

εἰς ἀνθρώπους εἶναι δοκεῖν, καὶ τοὺς μὲν οὔθ᾽ ἱερὸν οὔτε
βωμὸν οὔτ᾽ ἄλλο τῶν θείων οὐδὲν τιμᾶν, τοὺς δὲ καὶ λίθους
καὶ ξύλα τὰ τυχόντα καὶ θηρία σέβεσθαι· τῶν τε περὶ τῆς
τῶν πάντων φύσεως μεριμνώντων τοῖς μὲν δοκεῖν ἓν μόνον
τὸ ὂν εἶναι, τοῖς δ᾽ ἄπειρα τὸ πλῆθος, καὶ τοῖς μὲν ἀεὶ πάντα 5
κινεῖσθαι, τοῖς δ᾽ οὐδὲν ἄν ποτε κινηθῆναι, καὶ τοῖς μὲν πάντα
γίγνεσθαί τε καὶ ἀπόλλυσθαι, τοῖς δὲ οὔτ᾽ ἂν γενέσθαι ποτὲ
15 οὐδὲν οὔτε ἀπολεῖσθαι. ἐσκόπει δὲ περὶ αὐτῶν καὶ τάδε,
ἆρ᾽, ὥσπερ οἱ τἀνθρώπεια μανθάνοντες ἡγοῦνται τοῦθ᾽ ὅ τι
ἂν μάθωσιν ἑαυτοῖς τε καὶ τῶν ἄλλων ὅτῳ ἂν βούλωνται 10
ποιήσειν, οὕτω καὶ οἱ τὰ θεῖα ζητοῦντες νομίζουσιν, ἐπειδὰν
γνῶσιν αἷς ἀνάγκαις ἕκαστα γίγνεται, ποιήσειν, ὅταν βούλωνται, καὶ ἀνέμους καὶ ὕδατα καὶ ὥρας καὶ ὅτου ἂν ἄλλου
δέωνται τῶν τοιούτων, ἢ τοιοῦτον μὲν οὐδὲν οὐδ᾽ ἐλπίζουσιν,
ἀρκεῖ δ᾽ αὐτοῖς γνῶναι μόνον ᾗ τῶν τοιούτων ἕκαστα γίγνεται. 15
16 περὶ μὲν οὖν τῶν ταῦτα πραγματευομένων τοιαῦτα ἔλεγεν·
αὐτὸς δὲ περὶ τῶν ἀνθρωπείων ἀεὶ διελέγετο σκοπῶν τί
εὐσεβές, τί ἀσεβές, τί καλόν, τί αἰσχρόν, τί δίκαιον,
τί ἄδικον, τί σωφροσύνη, τί μανία, τί ἀνδρεία, τί δειλία, τί
πόλις, τί πολιτικός, τί ἀρχὴ ἀνθρώπων, τί ἀρχικὸς ἀνθρώ- 20
πων, καὶ περὶ τῶν ἄλλων, ἃ τοὺς μὲν εἰδότας ἡγεῖτο καλοὺς
κἀγαθοὺς εἶναι, τοὺς δ᾽ ἀγνοοῦντας ἀνδραποδώδεις ἂν δικαίως
κεκλῆσθαι.
17 Ὅσα μὲν οὖν μὴ φανερὸς ἦν ὅπως ἐγίγνωσκεν, οὐδὲν
θαυμαστὸν ὑπὲρ τούτων περὶ αὐτοῦ παραγνῶναι τοὺς δικα- 25
στάς· ὅσα δὲ πάντες ᾔδεσαν, οὐ θαυμαστὸν εἰ μὴ τούτων
18 ἐνεθυμήθησαν; βουλεύσας γάρ ποτε καὶ τὸν βουλευτικὸν
ὅρκον ὀμόσας, ἐν ᾧ ἦν κατὰ τοὺς νόμους βουλεύσειν, ἐπι-
στάτης ἐν τῷ δήμῳ γενόμενος, ἐπιθυμήσαντος τοῦ δήμου
παρὰ τοὺς νόμους ἐννέα στρατηγοὺς μιᾷ ψήφῳ τοὺς ἀμφὶ 30
Θράσυλλον καὶ Ἐρασινίδην ἀποκτεῖναι πάντας, οὐκ ἠθέλησεν

3–6   τῶν ... κινεῖσθαι om. A
4   τῶν Z, Stobaeus: om. B
7   ἀπολέσθαι Stob.
20   πολιτικόν...ἀρχικόν A
30   ἐννέα στρατηγοὺς del. Schenkl

think they should even go out in public; some too, he said, didn't honour any temple or altar or anything connected with the gods, while others revered stones or various pieces of wood or wild beasts. He said that to some of those who pondered on the nature of the universe reality consisted of one single entity, to others of infinitely many components, and some of them thought that all things were in perpetual motion, others that nothing could ever move; some again, he said, thought that all things come into being and pass away, other that nothing could ever have come into being or will perish. 15. He would add these further questions about those people: 'Is it the case that, just as students of human matters think they will use anything they learn for the benefit of themselves or anyone else of their choice, so too the investigators of divine affairs think that, whenever they know by what natural laws all things are brought into being, they will, whenever they wish, produce winds, waters, seasons of the year and anything else similar that they need, or do they not even expect anything of the sort, but are content merely to know how all things like that come into being?'
16. Well, that was what he had to say about those who busied themselves on *these* subjects. But he himself would always discuss human matters, investigating the nature of piety, impiety, beauty, ugliness, justice, injustice, prudence, madness, courage, cowardice, the state, the statesman, the ruling of men, the ruler of men, and all the other subjects, knowledge of which in his opinion identified perfect men, whereas those ignorant in these areas could justly be described as no better than slaves.
17. It is not surprising that on matters where his opinions were not obvious the jurors came to a wrong conclusion about him. But isn't it amazing that they didn't take account of what everyone knew about him? 18. For on one occasion, when he had become a member of the Council and taken the Councillors' Oath, which included a promise to carry out his office in accordance with the laws, and he had been president at a meeting of the Assembly, the people had conceived the desire to execute nine generals, Thrasyllus, Erasinides and their colleagues, one and all, by a single collective

ἐπιψηφίσαι, ὀργιζομένου μὲν αὐτῷ τοῦ δήμου, πολλῶν δὲ
καὶ δυνατῶν ἀπειλούντων· ἀλλὰ περὶ πλείονος ἐποιήσατο
εὐορκεῖν ἢ χαρίσασθαι τῷ δήμῳ παρὰ τὸ δίκαιον καὶ φυλάξασθαι τοὺς ἀπειλοῦντας.   καὶ γὰρ ἐπιμελεῖσθαι θεοὺς ἐνό- 19
5 μιζεν ἀνθρώπων οὐχ ὃν τρόπον οἱ πολλοὶ νομίζουσιν· οὗτοι
μὲν γὰρ οἴονται τοὺς θεοὺς τὰ μὲν εἰδέναι, τὰ δ' οὐκ εἰδέναι·
Σωκράτης δὲ πάντα μὲν ἡγεῖτο θεοὺς εἰδέναι, τά τε λεγόμενα καὶ πραττόμενα καὶ τὰ σιγῇ βουλευόμενα, πανταχοῦ δὲ
παρεῖναι καὶ σημαίνειν τοῖς ἀνθρώποις περὶ τῶν ἀνθρωπείων
10 πάντων.

    Θαυμάζω οὖν ὅπως ποτὲ ἐπείσθησαν Ἀθηναῖοι Σωκράτην 20
περὶ θεοὺς μὴ σωφρονεῖν, τὸν ἀσεβὲς μὲν οὐδέν ποτε περὶ
τοὺς θεοὺς οὔτ' εἰπόντα οὔτε πράξαντα, τοιαῦτα δὲ καὶ
λέγοντα καὶ πράττοντα περὶ θεῶν οἷά τις ἂν καὶ λέγων
15 καὶ πράττων εἴη τε καὶ νομίζοιτο εὐσεβέστατος.

    Θαυμαστὸν δὲ φαίνεταί μοι καὶ τὸ πεισθῆναί τινας ὡς II
Σωκράτης τοὺς νέους διέφθειρεν, ὃς πρὸς τοῖς εἰρημένοις
πρῶτον μὲν ἀφροδισίων καὶ γαστρὸς πάντων ἀνθρώπων
ἐγκρατέστατος ἦν, εἶτα πρὸς χειμῶνα καὶ θέρος καὶ πάντας
20 πόνους καρτερικώτατος, ἔτι δὲ πρὸς τὸ μετρίων δεῖσθαι
πεπαιδευμένος οὕτως, ὥστε πάνυ μικρὰ κεκτημένος πάνυ
ῥᾳδίως ἔχειν ἀρκοῦντα.   πῶς οὖν αὐτὸς ὢν τοιοῦτος ἄλλους 2
ἂν ἢ ἀσεβεῖς ἢ παρανόμους ἢ λίχνους ἢ ἀφροδισίων ἀκρατεῖς ἢ
πρὸς τὸ πονεῖν μαλακοὺς ἐποίησεν; ἀλλ' ἔπαυσε μὲν τούτων
25 πολλοὺς ἀρετῆς ποιήσας ἐπιθυμεῖν καὶ ἐλπίδας παρασχών,
ἂν ἑαυτῶν ἐπιμελῶνται, καλοὺς κἀγαθοὺς ἔσεσθαι· καίτοι 3
γε οὐδεπώποτε ὑπέσχετο διδάσκαλος εἶναι τούτου, ἀλλὰ τῷ
φανερὸς εἶναι τοιοῦτος ὢν ἐλπίζειν ἐποίει τοὺς συνδιατρί-
βοντας ἑαυτῷ μιμουμένους ἐκεῖνον τοιούτους γενήσεσθαι.
30 ἀλλὰ μὴν καὶ τοῦ σώματος αὐτός τε οὐκ ἠμέλει τούς τ' 4
ἀμελοῦντας οὐκ ἐπήνει· τὸ μὲν οὖν ὑπερεσθίοντα ὑπερπονεῖν

29   τοιούσδε β

vote in contravention of the laws. But Socrates refused to put it to the vote despite the anger of the people and the threats of many powerful men. No, he thought it more important to keep his oath than to gratify the people in their unjust wishes and to protect himself against his threateners. 19. For he thought that the gods look after humans but not in the way that most people think they do. For they suppose the gods to have knowledge of some things but to be ignorant of others, whereas Socrates thought the gods are omniscient, knowing men's words, deeds and unspoken designs, and are present everywhere and send signs to humans about all human affairs.

20. So it makes me wonder how the Athenians were ever persuaded to think that Socrates was a heretic, Socrates who never said anything irreverent about the gods or ever acted irreverently towards them, Socrates whose words and actions to the gods were such as would be the height of piety in anyone and recognised as such!

Chapter 2. It also seems amazing to me that some were convinced that Socrates was an evil influence on the young men; for quite apart from what I have already said, in the first place he was the strongest of all men in controlling his sexual appetites and his belly, and secondly the most steadfast in facing the cold of winter, the heat of summer and all manner of physical hardships, and moreover he had so schooled himself to moderate his needs that, though his possessions were minimal, he was very easily satisfied with them. 2. How then, if he was himself like that, could he have made others impious, criminal, gluttonous, sexually uncontrolled, or physically soft? No, he made many discontinue such behaviour, by making them eager to be virtuous and giving them hope that, if they looked after themselves, they would become perfect men. 3. However he never professed to teach how to achieve that, but, by making it obvious that he had those qualities, he made those who spent their time with him hope that by imitating him they would become like him. 4. Moreover he himself would never neglect his body and

ἀπεδοκίμαζε, τὸ δὲ ὅσα ἡδέως ἡ ψυχὴ δέχεται, ταῦτα ἱκανῶς
ἐκπονεῖν ἐδοκίμαζε· ταύτην γὰρ τὴν ἕξιν ὑγιεινήν τε ἱκανῶς
εἶναι καὶ τὴν τῆς ψυχῆς ἐπιμέλειαν οὐκ ἐμποδίζειν ἔφη.
5 ἀλλ' οὐ μὴν θρυπτικός γε οὐδὲ ἀλαζονικὸς ἦν οὔτ' ἀμπεχόνῃ
οὔθ' ὑποδέσει οὔτε τῇ ἄλλῃ διαίτῃ.   οὐ μὴν οὐδ' ἐρασιχρη- 5
μάτους γε τοὺς συνόντας ἐποίει.   τῶν μὲν γὰρ ἄλλων ἐπιθυμιῶν ἔπαυε, τοὺς δ' ἑαυτοῦ ἐπιθυμοῦντας οὐκ ἐπράττετο
6 χρήματα.   τούτου δ' ἀπεχόμενος ἐνόμιζεν ἐλευθερίας ἐπιμε-
λεῖσθαι· τοὺς δὲ λαμβάνοντας τῆς ὁμιλίας μισθὸν ἀνδρα-
ποδιστὰς ἑαυτῶν ἀπεκάλει διὰ τὸ ἀναγκαῖον αὐτοῖς εἶναι 10
7 διαλέγεσθαι παρ' ὧν ἂν λάβοιεν τὸν μισθόν.   ἐθαύμαζε δ'
εἴ τις ἀρετὴν ἐπαγγελλόμενος ἀργύριον πράττοιτο καὶ μὴ
νομίζοι τὸ μέγιστον κέρδος ἕξειν φίλον ἀγαθὸν κτησάμενος,
ἀλλὰ φοβοῖτο μὴ ὁ γενόμενος καλὸς κἀγαθὸς τῷ τὰ μέγιστα
8 εὐεργετήσαντι μὴ τὴν μεγίστην χάριν ἕξοι.   Σωκράτης δὲ 15
ἐπηγγείλατο μὲν οὐδενὶ πώποτε τοιοῦτον οὐδέν, ἐπίστευε
δὲ τῶν συνόντων ἑαυτῷ τοὺς ἀποδεξαμένους ἅπερ αὐτὸς
ἐδοκίμαζεν εἰς τὸν πάντα βίον ἑαυτῷ τε καὶ ἀλλήλοις φίλους
ἀγαθοὺς ἔσεσθαι.   πῶς ἂν οὖν ὁ τοιοῦτος ἀνὴρ διαφθείροι
τοὺς νέους; εἰ μὴ ἄρα ἡ τῆς ἀρετῆς ἐπιμέλεια διαφθορά 20
ἐστιν.

9   'Αλλὰ νὴ Δία, ὁ κατήγορος ἔφη, ὑπερορᾶν ἐποίει τῶν
καθεστώτων νόμων τοὺς συνόντας, λέγων ὡς μῶρον εἴη τοὺς
μὲν τῆς πόλεως ἄρχοντας ἀπὸ κυάμου καθιστάναι, κυβερνήτῃ
δὲ μηδένα θέλειν χρῆσθαι κυαμευτῷ μηδὲ τέκτονι μηδ' 25
αὐλητῇ μηδ' ἐπ' ἄλλα τοιαῦτα, ἃ πολλῷ ἐλάττονας βλάβας
ἁμαρτανόμενα ποιεῖ τῶν περὶ τὴν πόλιν ἁμαρτανομένων· τοὺς
δὲ τοιούτους λόγους ἐπαίρειν ἔφη τοὺς νέους καταφρονεῖν τῆς
10 καθεστώσης πολιτείας καὶ ποιεῖν βιαίους.   ἐγὼ δ' οἶμαι τοὺς
φρόνησιν ἀσκοῦντας καὶ νομίζοντας ἱκανοὺς ἔσεσθαι τὰ συμφέ- 30

would criticise those who did so. Furthermore he disapproved of overeating followed by overexertion, but approved of eating only as much as brings pleasure to the inner self and then taking sufficient exercise to work it off; for he said that that habit was healthy enough and didn't prevent looking after one's inner self. 5. But he wasn't foppish or pretentious in his clothing or footwear or his general way of life. Moreover he would discourage love of money in his associates; for he would make them renounce all other desires, but from those who desired *his* company he would expect no payment. 6. By abstaining from that he thought he was providing for his own independence, whereas those who took a fee for their company he would describe as 'self-enslavers', because they had to converse with those from whom they could take their fee. 7. He would express surprise that anyone who professed to teach virtue charged money and, instead of thinking he would gain the greatest of rewards in acquiring a good friend, was afraid that he who had become a perfect man wouldn't feel the greatest gratitude to his greatest benefactor. 8. Socrates never ever professed any such thing to anyone, but was confident that those of his companions who had adopted his own approved principles would throughout their whole lives be good friends to himself and to each other. How *could* such a man be a corrupter of the young? Unless in fact the pursuit of virtue is a corrupting influence!

9. 'But of course' said his accuser 'he made his associates scorn the established laws, by saying it was foolish to appoint the officials of the state by lot, whereas nobody was willing to resort to lottery when employing a steersman or carpenter or musician or anyone for any similar task, in which mistakes cause far less harm than mistakes in affairs of state.' Talk like that according to his accuser incited the young men to scorn the established constitution and made them violent. 10. But it is my personal opinion that those who

ροντα διδάσκειν τοὺς πολίτας ἥκιστα γίγνεσθαι βιαίους,
εἰδότας ὅτι τῇ μὲν βίᾳ πρόσεισιν ἔχθραι καὶ κίνδυνοι, διὰ
δὲ τοῦ πείθειν ἀκινδύνως τε καὶ μετὰ φιλίας ταὐτὰ γίγνεται.
οἱ μὲν γὰρ βιασθέντες ὡς ἀφαιρεθέντες μισοῦσιν, οἱ δὲ
5 πεισθέντες ὡς κεχαρισμένοι φιλοῦσιν.   οὔκουν τῶν φρόνησιν ἀσκούντων τὸ βιάζεσθαι, ἀλλὰ τῶν ἰσχὺν ἄνευ γνώμης
ἐχόντων τὰ τοιαῦτα πράττειν ἐστίν.   ἀλλὰ μὴν καὶ συμ-   11
μάχων ὁ μὲν βιάζεσθαι τολμῶν δέοιτ' ἂν οὐκ ὀλίγων, ὁ δὲ
πείθειν δυνάμενος οὐδενός· καὶ γὰρ μόνος ἡγοῖτ' ἂν δύνασθαι
10 πείθειν.   καὶ φονεύειν δὲ τοῖς τοιούτοις ἥκιστα συμβαίνει·
τίς γὰρ ἀποκτεῖναί τινα βούλοιτ' ἂν μᾶλλον ἢ ζῶντι πειθομένῳ
χρῆσθαι;
      'Αλλ' ἔφη γε ὁ κατήγορος, Σωκράτει ὁμιλητὰ γενομένω   12
Κριτίας τε καὶ 'Αλκιβιάδης πλεῖστα κακὰ τὴν πόλιν ἐποίη-
15 σάτην.   Κριτίας μὲν γὰρ τῶν ἐν τῇ ὀλιγαρχίᾳ πάντων
* πλεονεκτίστατός τε καὶ βιαιότατος. ἐγένετο, 'Αλκιβιάδης δὲ *
αὖ τῶν ἐν τῇ δημοκρατίᾳ πάντων ἀκρατέστατός τε καὶ
* ὑβριστότατος.   ἐγὼ δ', εἰ μέν τι κακὸν ἐκείνω τὴν πόλιν   13 *
ἐποιησάτην, οὐκ ἀπολογήσομαι· τὴν δὲ πρὸς Σωκράτην
20 συνουσίαν αὐτοῖν ὡς ἐγένετο διηγήσομαι.   ἐγενέσθην μὲν   14
γὰρ δὴ τὼ ἄνδρε τούτω φύσει φιλοτιμοτάτω πάντων 'Αθη-
ναίων, βουλομένω τε πάντα δι' ἑαυτῶν πράττεσθαι καὶ πάντων
ὀνομαστοτάτω γενέσθαι.   ᾔδεσαν δὲ Σωκράτην ἀπ' ἐλαχίστων
μὲν χρημάτων αὐταρκέστατα ζῶντα, τῶν ἡδονῶν δὲ πασῶν
25 ἐγκρατέστατον ὄντα, τοῖς δὲ διαλεγομένοις αὐτῷ πᾶσι χρώμενον ἐν τοῖς λόγοις ὅπως βούλοιτο.   ταῦτα δὲ ὁρῶντε καὶ   15
ὄντε οἵω προείρησθον, πότερόν τις αὐτὼ φῇ τοῦ βίου τοῦ
Σωκράτους ἐπιθυμήσαντε καὶ τῆς σωφροσύνης, ἣν ἐκεῖνος
εἶχεν, ὀρέξασθαι τῆς ὁμιλίας αὐτοῦ, ἢ νομίσαντε, εἰ ὁμιλη-
30 σαίτην ἐκείνῳ, γενέσθαι ἂν ἱκανωτάτω λέγειν τε καὶ πράττειν;
ἐγὼ μὲν γὰρ ἡγοῦμαι, θεοῦ διδόντος αὐτοῖν ἢ ζῆν ὅλον τὸν   16

---

3   ταῦτα nostri: τὰ αὐτὰ Stob.
7   τὰ] τὸ Schaefer
16   κλεπτίστατος A   *καὶ φονικώτατος ante ἐγένετο add. AB
18   ὑβριστικώτατος B   *καὶ βιαιότατος post ὑβριστικώτατος add. AB
20   αὐτῶν A
27   φήσει A

practise prudence and think they will be competent at showing their fellow citizens the expedient course of action are least likely to indulge in violence, because they know that violence is accompanied by enmities and dangers, but that the same results are accompanied by safe, friendly persuasion. For the victims of violence feel hatred through a sense of loss, whereas those who have been persuaded show affection for favours conferred. Violence, therefore, is the way not of those who practise prudence but to act like that is the way of those who have strength but lack understanding. 11. Moreover the man who dares to use violence would need numerous allies, whereas the man capable of persuasion would need nobody; for he would consider himself able to persuade alone and unaided. And such men are least likely to resort to bloodshed; for who would want to kill a man rather than to exercise persuasion on him and have the use of his living services?

12. 'But' said his accuser 'after becoming associates of Socrates, Critias and Alcibiades harmed Athens in countless ways. For, of all involved in the oligarchy, Critias proved the most rapacious and violent, while, of all involved in the democracy, Alcibiades showed himself the most dissolute and outrageous.' 13. For my part I shall not defend that pair for any harm they did to Athens, but shall explain how their association with Socrates came about. 14. For the pair proved the most naturally ambitious of all Athenians in their desire to have everything transacted through themselves and to become the most famous of men. They knew that Socrates enjoyed the most self-sufficient mode of life on the most meagre of resources, and showed the greatest self-control in dealing with all pleasures, but in verbal argument could do what he liked with all who conversed with him. 15. Since they saw this and were the sort of men I have just described, is anyone to say that their enthusiasm for Socrates' company sprang from eagerness to have his life-style and his self-control, rather than from a belief that if they kept his company, they would become supremely effective in both speech

βίον ὥσπερ ζῶντα Σωκράτην ἑώρων ἢ τεθνάναι, ἑλέσθαι
ἂν μᾶλλον αὐτῷ τεθνάναι. δῆλω δ' ἐγενέσθην ἐξ ὧν
ἐπραξάτην· ὡς γὰρ τάχιστα κρείττονε τῶν συγγιγνομένων
ἡγησάσθην εἶναι, εὐθὺς ἀποπηδήσαντε Σωκράτους ἐπραττέτην
τὰ πολιτικά, ὧνπερ ἕνεκα Σωκράτους ὠρεχθήτην.   5
17 Ἴσως οὖν εἴποι τις ἂν πρὸς ταῦτα ὅτι ἐχρῆν τὸν Σωκράτην
μὴ πρότερον τὰ πολιτικὰ διδάσκειν τοὺς συνόντας ἢ σωφρονεῖν. ἐγὼ δὲ πρὸς τοῦτο μὲν οὐκ ἀντιλέγω· πάντας δὲ τοὺς
διδάσκοντας ὁρῶ αὐτοὺς δεικνύντας τε τοῖς μανθάνουσιν ᾗπερ
αὐτοὶ ποιοῦσιν ἃ διδάσκουσι καὶ τῷ λόγῳ προσβιβάζοντας.   10
οἶδα δὲ καὶ Σωκράτην δεικνύντα τοῖς συνοῦσιν ἑαυτὸν καλὸν
κἀγαθὸν ὄντα καὶ διαλεγόμενον κάλλιστα περὶ ἀρετῆς καὶ
18 τῶν ἄλλων ἀνθρωπίνων. οἶδα δὲ κἀκείνω σωφρονοῦντε,
ἔστε Σωκράτει συνήστην, οὐ φοβουμένω μὴ ζημιοῖντο ἢ
παίοιντο ὑπὸ Σωκράτους, ἀλλ' οἰομένω τότε κράτιστον εἶναι 15
τοῦτο πράττειν.
19 Ἴσως οὖν εἴποιεν ἂν πολλοὶ τῶν φασκόντων φιλοσοφεῖν
ὅτι οὐκ ἄν ποτε ὁ δίκαιος ἄδικος γένοιτο, οὐδὲ ὁ σώφρων
ὑβριστής, οὐδὲ ἄλλο οὐδὲν ὧν μάθησίς ἐστιν ὁ μαθὼν ἀν-
επιστήμων ἄν ποτε γένοιτο. ἐγὼ δὲ περὶ τούτων οὐχ οὕτω 20
γιγνώσκω· ὁρῶ γὰρ ὥσπερ τὰ τοῦ σώματος ἔργα τοὺς μὴ τὰ
σώματα ἀσκοῦντας οὐ δυναμένους ποιεῖν, οὕτω καὶ τὰ τῆς
ψυχῆς ἔργα τοὺς μὴ τὴν ψυχὴν ἀσκοῦντας οὐ δυναμένους·
οὔτε γὰρ ἃ δεῖ πράττειν οὔτε ὧν δεῖ ἀπέχεσθαι δύνανται.
20 δι' ὃ καὶ τοὺς υἱεῖς οἱ πατέρες, κἂν ὦσι σώφρονες, ὅμως   25
ἀπὸ τῶν πονηρῶν ἀνθρώπων εἴργουσιν, ὡς τὴν μὲν τῶν
χρηστῶν ὁμιλίαν ἄσκησιν οὖσαν τῆς ἀρετῆς, τὴν δὲ τῶν
πονηρῶν κατάλυσιν. μαρτυρεῖ δὲ καὶ τῶν ποιητῶν ὅ τε
λέγων·

Ἐσθλῶν μὲν γὰρ ἄπ' ἐσθλὰ διδάξεαι· ἢν δὲ κακοῖσι   30
συμμίσγῃς, ἀπολεῖς καὶ τὸν ἐόντα νόον,

καὶ ὁ λέγων·

10   προβιβάζοντας ZL'W
30–31   Theognidea 34–35
30   διδάξεαι] μαθήσεαι Theognidea 35
31   ἐνόντα A

and action? 16. For it is my opinion that had God offered them the choice of living all their life in the way that they saw Socrates doing or of dying, they would have preferred death. They made that obvious by their actions; for as soon as they thought themselves superior to their companions, they immediately parted from Socrates and took to politics, that being the reason for their enthusiasm for Socrates.

17. Well, perhaps someone would make the retort to this that Socrates ought not to have taught his associates politics before he taught them self-restraint. I do not dispute that, but I *do* notice that all teachers manifest themselves to their students by the way they themselves practise what they preach and add persuasion by argument. 18. And I know that Socrates too manifested himself to his companions as being a perfect man and superlative in his discussions of virtue and all other human questions. I also know that these two did exercise self-restraint, as long as they were with Socrates, not because they were afraid of being punished or beaten by him, but because they thought it was the best thing to do.

19. Perhaps, therefore, many of those calling themselves philosophers would say that the just man never could become unjust or the sensible man wanton, or, in any area where knowledge is possible, could the knowledgeable man ever become ignorant. But *I* think differently on the matter; for I see that, just as those who don't train their bodies cannot perform their bodily functions, so too those who don't train their souls cannot perform the functions of the soul; for they cannot do what they ought to or avoid doing what they ought to avoid. 20. That is why fathers keep their sons away from bad company, even if they are sensibly behaved, realising that good company is a training in goodness, whereas bad company is its ruin. This is attested by the poet who says

> From noble men you'll learn nobility
> But lose your wits, if bad your company,

and by him who says

Αὐτὰρ ἀνὴρ ἀγαθὸς τοτὲ μὲν κακός, ἄλλοτε δ' ἐσθλός.

κἀγὼ δὲ μαρτυρῶ τούτοις· ὁρῶ γὰρ ὥσπερ τῶν ἐν μέτρῳ 21
πεποιημένων ἐπῶν τοὺς μὴ μελετῶντας ἐπιλανθανομένους,
οὕτω καὶ τῶν διδασκαλικῶν λόγων τοῖς ἀμελοῦσι λήθην
5 ἐγγιγνομένην. ὅταν δὲ τῶν νουθετικῶν λόγων ἐπιλάθηταί
τις, ἐπιλέλησται καὶ ὧν ἡ ψυχὴ πάσχουσα τῆς σωφροσύνης
ἐπεθύμει· τούτων δ' ἐπιλαθόμενον οὐδὲν θαυμαστὸν καὶ τῆς
σωφροσύνης ἐπιλαθέσθαι. ὁρῶ δὲ καὶ τοὺς εἰς φιλοποσίαν 22
προαχθέντας καὶ τοὺς εἰς ἔρωτας ἐγκυλισθέντας ἧττον δυνα-
10 μένους τῶν τε δεόντων ἐπιμελεῖσθαι καὶ τῶν μὴ δεόντων
ἀπέχεσθαι. πολλοὶ γὰρ καὶ χρημάτων δυνάμενοι φείδεσθαι,
πρὶν ἐρᾶν, ἐρασθέντες οὐκέτι δύνανται· καὶ τὰ χρήματα
καταναλώσαντες, ὧν πρόσθεν ἀπείχοντο κερδῶν, αἰσχρὰ
νομίζοντες εἶναι, τούτων οὐκ ἀπέχονται. πῶς οὖν οὐκ ἐν-23
15 δέχεται σωφρονήσαντας πρόσθεν αὖθις μὴ σωφρονεῖν καὶ
δίκαια δυνηθέντας πράττειν αὖθις ἀδυνατεῖν; πάντα μὲν οὖν
ἔμοιγε δοκεῖ τὰ καλὰ καὶ τἀγαθὰ ἀσκητὰ εἶναι, οὐχ ἥκιστα
δὲ σωφροσύνη. ἐν γὰρ τῷ αὐτῷ σώματι συμπεφυτευμέναι
τῇ ψυχῇ αἱ ἡδοναὶ πείθουσιν αὐτὴν μὴ σωφρονεῖν, ἀλλὰ τὴν
20 ταχίστην ἑαυταῖς τε καὶ τῷ σώματι χαρίζεσθαι.

Καὶ Κριτίας δὴ καὶ 'Αλκιβιάδης, ἕως μὲν Σωκράτει συν-24
ήστην, ἐδυνάσθην ἐκείνῳ χρωμένω συμμάχῳ τῶν μὴ καλῶν
ἐπιθυμιῶν κρατεῖν· ἐκείνου δ' ἀπαλλαγέντε, Κριτίας μὲν
φυγὼν εἰς Θετταλίαν ἐκεῖ συνῆν ἀνθρώποις ἀνομίᾳ μᾶλλον
25 ἢ δικαιοσύνῃ χρωμένοις, 'Αλκιβιάδης δ' αὖ διὰ μὲν κάλλος
ὑπὸ πολλῶν καὶ σεμνῶν γυναικῶν θηρώμενος, διὰ δύναμιν
δὲ τὴν ἐν τῇ πόλει καὶ τοῖς συμμάχοις ὑπὸ πολλῶν καὶ
δυνατῶν [κολακεύειν] ἀνθρώπων διαθρυπτόμενος, ὑπὸ δὲ τοῦ
δήμου τιμώμενος καὶ ῥᾳδίως πρωτεύων, ὥσπερ οἱ τῶν
30 γυμνικῶν ἀγώνων ἀθληταὶ ῥᾳδίως πρωτεύοντες ἀμελοῦσι

1 *Elegiaca Adespota*, Fr. 2, West
3 ἐπῶν del. Cobet
5 νουθετητικῶν β
9 παραχθέντας... ἐκκυλισθέντας Cobet
15, 16 σωφρονήσαντα... δυνηθέντα β
26–27 διὰ δὲ δύναμιν A
28 κολακεύειν del. Musurus

But he who's good sometimes is base,
Sometimes is noble in his ways.

21. I add my testimony to theirs; for I see that, just as verses of epic poetry are forgotten by those who don't keep in practice, so too those who neglect the words of their teachers become forgetful of them. Whenever anyone forgets words of advice, he has also forgotten the experiences which made his soul eager to be self-disciplined, and when he has forgotten these words, it is not surprising that he has also forgotten self-discipline. 22. I also see that those who have taken to drink or plunged into love-affairs are less able to attend to what is right and to avoid what is wrong. For many men, though able to be careful with money prior to being in love, can no longer be so after falling in love, and once they have spent all their money, no longer refrain from the profit-making practices they avoided previously because they thought them shameful. 23. How then is it impossible for the men, who previously have shown self-discipline, to fail to show it again later, and for those, who have been able to act justly, to be unable to act justly once again? For to me at least it seems that all things that are splendid and good come from practice and this is particularly true of self-discipline. For implanted in the same body along with the soul are the appetites for pleasure which persuade the soul not to discipline itself but to indulge them and the body as quickly as possible.

24. Indeed, as long as Critias and Alcibiades were associated with Socrates, they were able to use him as their ally and master their discreditable desires, but once they parted from him, Critias went into exile in Thessaly and there began to associate with men whose ways were lawless rather than just, while Alcibiades was pursued by many important women because of his personal beauty, pampered by many powerful people because of his influence at Athens and amongst her allies, and honoured by the common people, and he easily held first place among them, and so, just like the competitors at

25 τῆς ἀσκήσεως, οὕτω κἀκεῖνος ἠμέλησεν αὐτοῦ. τοιούτων
δὲ συμβάντων αὐτοῖν, καὶ ὠγκωμένω μὲν ἐπὶ γένει, ἐπηρμένω
δ' ἐπὶ πλούτω, πεφυσημένω δ' ἐπὶ δυνάμει, διατεθρυμμένω δὲ
ὑπὸ πολλῶν ἀνθρώπων, ἐπὶ δὲ πᾶσι τούτοις διεφθαρμένω καὶ
πολὺν χρόνον ἀπὸ Σωκράτους γεγονότε, τί θαυμαστὸν εἰ 5
26 ὑπερηφάνω ἐγενέσθην; εἶτα, εἰ μέν τι ἐπλημμελησάτην,
τούτου Σωκράτην ὁ κατήγορος αἰτιᾶται; ὅτι δὲ νέω ὄντε
αὐτώ, ἡνίκα καὶ ἀγνωμονεστάτω καὶ ἀκρατεστάτω εἰκὸς εἶναι,
Σωκράτης παρέσχε σώφρονε, οὐδενὸς ἐπαίνου δοκεῖ τῷ κατη-
27 γόρω ἄξιος εἶναι; οὐ μὴν τά γε ἄλλα οὕτω κρίνεται. τίς 10
μὲν γὰρ αὐλητής, τίς δὲ κιθαριστής, τίς δὲ ἄλλος διδάσκαλος
ἱκανοὺς ποιήσας τοὺς μαθητάς, ἐὰν πρὸς ἄλλους ἐλθόντες
χείρους φανῶσιν, αἰτίαν ἔχει τούτου; τίς δὲ πατήρ, ἐὰν ὁ
παῖς αὐτοῦ συνδιατρίβων τῳ σωφρονῇ, ὕστερον δὲ ἄλλῳ τῳ
συγγενόμενος πονηρὸς γένηται, τὸν πρόσθεν αἰτιᾶται, ἀλλ' 15
οὐχ ὅσῳ ἂν παρὰ τῷ ὑστέρῳ χείρων φαίνηται, τοσούτῳ
μᾶλλον ἐπαινεῖ τὸν πρότερον; ἀλλ' οἵ γε πατέρες αὐτοὶ
συνόντες τοῖς υἱέσι, τῶν παίδων πλημμελούντων, οὐκ αἰτίαν
28 ἔχουσιν, ἐὰν αὐτοὶ σωφρονῶσιν. οὕτω δὲ καὶ Σωκράτην
δίκαιον ἦν κρίνειν· εἰ μὲν αὐτὸς ἐποίει τι φαῦλον, εἰκότως 20
ἂν ἐδόκει πονηρὸς εἶναι· εἰ δ' αὐτὸς σωφρονῶν διετέλει,
πῶς ἂν δικαίως τῆς οὐκ ἐνούσης αὐτῷ κακίας αἰτίαν ἔχοι;
29 Ἀλλ' εἰ καὶ μηδὲν αὐτὸς πονηρὸν ποιῶν ἐκείνους φαῦλα
πράττοντας ὁρῶν ἐπῄνει, δικαίως ἂν ἐπιτιμῷτο. Κριτίαν
μὲν τοίνυν αἰσθανόμενος ἐρῶντα Εὐθυδήμου καὶ πειρῶντα 25
χρῆσθαι, καθάπερ οἱ πρὸς τἀφροδίσια τῶν σωμάτων ἀπο-
λαύοντες, ἀπέτρεπε φάσκων ἀνελεύθερόν τε εἶναι καὶ οὐ
πρέπον ἀνδρὶ καλῷ κἀγαθῷ τὸν ἐρώμενον, ᾧ βούλεται πολλοῦ ἄξιος φαίνεσθαι, προσαιτεῖν ὥσπερ τοὺς πτωχοὺς
ἱκετεύοντα καὶ δεόμενον προσδοῦναι, καὶ ταῦτα μηδενὸς 30

4   διεφθαρμένω del. Pluygers
9   σωφρονεῖν A

the athletic games who easily come first and neglect their training, so too he neglected himself. 25. Since such was the case with Alcibiades and Critias, and they were conceited about their birth, elated by their wealth, puffed up with pride about their power and pampered by many, and being corrupted for all reasons and since they had also been away from Socrates for a long time, how is it surprising that they became high-handed? 26. If then these two went wrong in any way, does Socrates' accuser blame *him* for that? Does his accuser think that Socrates deserves no credit at all for the fact that, though they were young and of an age when they could be expected to be utterly reckless and uncontrolled, he kept them behaving sensibly? That is certainly not how other cases are judged. 27. For what piper or lyre player or what other teacher is blamed, if after he has made his pupils capable, they show deterioration on going to other teachers? If a son, while spending his time with one teacher, is sensibly behaved, but later, after associating with someone else, becomes depraved, what father blames the earlier one? Is it not rather the case that the greater deterioration the son shows with the later teacher, the more his father praises the earlier teacher? Indeed, when fathers live themselves with their sons and the sons go wrong, the fathers are not blamed, if they themselves are sensibly behaved. 28. This would have been the fair way to judge Socrates also. If he himself had been acting discreditably in any way, he could reasonably have been thought to be vicious, but if he himself was consistently sensible in his conduct, how could he justly be blamed for the vice he did not have? 29. However, if he, though himself avoiding evil-doing, praised them when he saw them acting discreditably, he could justly be censured. Well, when he observed that Critias was in love with Euthydemus and trying to seduce him, he sought to deter him by saying that it was servile and unbecoming

ἀγαθοῦ. τοῦ δὲ Κριτίου τοῖς τοιούτοις οὐχ ὑπακούοντος οὐδὲ 30
ἀποτρεπομένου, λέγεται τὸν Σωκράτην ἄλλων τε πολλῶν
παρόντων καὶ τοῦ Εὐθυδήμου εἰπεῖν ὅτι ὑικὸν αὐτῷ δοκοίη
* πάσχειν ὁ Κριτίας, ἐπιθυμῶν Εὐθυδήμῳ προσκνῆσθαι ὥσπερ *
*5 τὰ ὕδια τοῖς λίθοις. ἐξ ὧν δὴ καὶ ἐμίσει τὸν Σωκράτην ὁ 31 *
Κριτίας, ὥστε καὶ ὅτε τῶν τριάκοντα ὢν νομοθέτης μετὰ
Χαρικλέους ἐγένετο, ἀπεμνημόνευσεν αὐτῷ καὶ ἐν τοῖς νόμοις
ἔγραψε λόγων τέχνην μὴ διδάσκειν, ἐπηρεάζων ἐκείνῳ καὶ
οὐκ ἔχων ὅπη ἐπιλάβοιτο, ἀλλὰ τὸ κοινῇ τοῖς φιλοσόφοις
10 ὑπὸ τῶν πολλῶν ἐπιτιμώμενον ἐπιφέρων αὐτῷ καὶ διαβάλλων
πρὸς τοὺς πολλούς· οὐδὲ γὰρ ἔγωγε οὔτ' αὐτὸς τοῦτο πώποτε
Σωκράτους ἤκουσα οὔτ' ἄλλου του φάσκοντος ἀκηκοέναι
ᾐσθόμην. ἐδήλωσε δέ· ἐπεὶ γὰρ οἱ τριάκοντα πολλοὺς μὲν 32
τῶν πολιτῶν καὶ οὐ τοὺς χειρίστους ἀπέκτεινον, πολλοὺς δὲ
15 προετρέποντο ἀδικεῖν, εἶπέ που ὁ Σωκράτης ὅτι θαυμαστόν
οἱ δοκοίη εἶναι, εἴ τις γενόμενος βοῶν ἀγέλης νομεὺς καὶ
τὰς βοῦς ἐλάττους τε καὶ χείρους ποιῶν μὴ ὁμολογοίη κακὸς
βουκόλος εἶναι, ἔτι δὲ θαυμαστότερον, εἴ τις προστάτης
γενόμενος πόλεως καὶ ποιῶν τοὺς πολίτας ἐλάττους τε καὶ
20 χείρους μὴ αἰσχύνεται μηδ' οἴεται κακὸς εἶναι προστάτης
τῆς πόλεως. ἀπαγγελθέντος δὲ αὐτοῖς τούτου, καλέσαντες 33
ὅ τε Κριτίας καὶ ὁ Χαρικλῆς τὸν Σωκράτην τόν τε νόμον
ἐδεικνύτην αὐτῷ καὶ τοῖς νέοις ἀπειπέτην μὴ διαλέγεσθαι.
ὁ δὲ Σωκράτης ἐπήρετο αὐτὼ εἰ ἐξείη πυνθάνεσθαι, εἴ τι
25 ἀγνοοῖτο τῶν προαγορευομένων. τὼ δ' ἐφάτην. Ἐγὼ 34
τοίνυν, ἔφη, παρεσκεύασμαι μὲν πείθεσθαι τοῖς νόμοις·
ὅπως δὲ μὴ δι' ἄγνοιαν λάθω τι παρανομήσας, τοῦτο βούλομαι σαφῶς μαθεῖν παρ' ὑμῶν, πότερον τὴν τῶν λόγων
τέχνην σὺν τοῖς ὀρθῶς λεγομένοις εἶναι νομίζοντες ἢ σὺν
30 τοῖς μὴ ὀρθῶς ἀπέχεσθαι κελεύετε αὐτῆς. εἰ μὲν γὰρ σὺν
τοῖς ὀρθῶς, δῆλον ὅτι ἀφεκτέον ⟨ἂν⟩ εἴη τοῦ ὀρθῶς λέγειν·

4   *προσκνῆσθαι Β: προσκνήσασθαι Α
5   *ὕδια Photius, edd.: ὑίδια codd.
11   οὐδὲ Weiske: οὔτε codd.
12   του om. β
14   ἀπέκτειναν Α
19   τε om. β
21   καλέσαντε Muretus
31   ἂν add. Dindorf

to a perfect man to solicit the loved one whose high esteem he desired, importuning as beggars do, and asking an extra favour and a vile one at that! 30. When Critias paid no attention to words like these and was undeterred by them, it is said that Socrates, in the presence of many including Euthydemus, said that Critias seemed to him to be behaving like a pig in his eagerness to rub against Euthydemus, just as piglets do against stones. 31. This also resulted in Socrates incurring the hatred of Critias, so that when, as one of the thirty tyrants, he became a legislator along with Charicles, he still harboured a grudge against Socrates and included in his laws a ban on the teaching of the art of words, out of spite against Socrates, when his sole means of attack was by directing against him the usual criticism of philosophers made by the general public and trying to discredit him with them. For I myself have never heard Socrates make this claim or heard anyone else say they have heard Socrates do so. 32. Socrates made the truth quite clear. For when the Thirty were putting many of the better citizens to death and inciting many also to unjust actions, Socrates said he thought it amazing that anyone, who had taken charge of a herd of cattle and had let their numbers decrease and their quality worsen, should fail to admit to being a bad herdsman, and still more amazing that anyone, who had become a civic leader and made his citizens fewer and worse, should neither feel any shame nor think himself a bad civic leader. 33. When this was reported to them, Critias and Charicles summoned Socrates, showed him the law and forbade him to converse with young men. But Socrates asked them if he was permitted to enquire about anything in the regulations that was not understood. They said he might.
34. 'Well then' he said 'I'm prepared to obey the laws, but in case I may inadvertently do anything unlawful out of ignorance, I want to be told clearly by you whether you think the art of words to involve rightness of speech or wrongness of speech when you ban it. For if it involves right speaking,

εἰ δὲ σὺν τοῖς μὴ ὀρθῶς, δῆλον ὅτι πειρατέον ὀρθῶς λέγειν.
35 καὶ ὁ Χαρικλῆς ὀργισθεὶς αὐτῷ, Ἐπειδή, ἔφη, ὦ Σώκρατες,
ἀγνοεῖς, τάδε σοι εὐμαθέστερα ὄντα προαγορεύομεν, τοῖς
νέοις ὅλως μὴ διαλέγεσθαι. καὶ ὁ Σωκράτης, Ἵνα τοίνυν,
ἔφη, μὴ ἀμφίβολον ᾖ ὡς ἄλλο τι ποιῶ ἢ τὰ προηγορευ- 5
μένα, ὁρίσατέ μοι μέχρι πόσων ἐτῶν δεῖ νομίζειν νέους
εἶναι τοὺς ἀνθρώπους. καὶ ὁ Χαρικλῆς, Ὅσουπερ, εἶπε,
χρόνου βουλεύειν οὐκ ἔξεστιν, ὡς οὔπω φρονίμοις οὖσι·
36 μηδὲ σὺ διαλέγου νεωτέροις τριάκοντα ἐτῶν. Μηδ' ἐάν τι
ὠνῶμαι, ἔφη, ἢν πωλῇ νεώτερος τριάκοντα ἐτῶν, ἔρωμαι 10
ὁπόσου πωλεῖ; Ναὶ τά γε τοιαῦτα, ἔφη ὁ Χαρικλῆς· ἀλλά
τοι σύγε, ὦ Σώκρατες, εἴωθας εἰδὼς πῶς ἔχει τὰ πλεῖστα
ἐρωτᾶν· ταῦτα οὖν μὴ ἐρώτα. Μηδ' ἀποκρίνωμαι οὖν, ἔφη,
ἄν τίς με ἐρωτᾷ νέος, ἐὰν εἰδῶ, οἷον ποῦ οἰκεῖ Χαρικλῆς ἢ
ποῦ ἐστι Κριτίας; Ναὶ τά γε τοιαῦτα, ἔφη ὁ Χαρικλῆς. 15
37 ὁ δὲ Κριτίας, Ἀλλὰ τῶνδέ τοί σε ἀπέχεσθαι, ἔφη, δεήσει,
ὦ Σώκρατες, τῶν σκυτέων καὶ τῶν τεκτόνων καὶ τῶν χαλ-
κέων· καὶ γὰρ οἶμαι αὐτοὺς ἤδη κατατετρῖφθαι διαθρυλου-
μένους ὑπὸ σοῦ. Οὐκοῦν, ἔφη ὁ Σωκράτης, καὶ τῶν ἐπο-
μένων τούτοις, τοῦ τε δικαίου καὶ τοῦ ὁσίου καὶ τῶν ἄλλων 20
τῶν τοιούτων; Ναὶ μὰ Δί', ἔφη ὁ Χαρικλῆς· καὶ τῶν
βουκόλων γε· εἰ δὲ μή, φυλάττου ὅπως μὴ καὶ σὺ ἐλάττους
38 τὰς βοῦς ποιήσῃς. ἔνθα καὶ δῆλον ἐγένετο ὅτι ἀπαγγελθέντος αὐτοῖς τοῦ περὶ τῶν βοῶν λόγου ὠργίζοντο τῷ
Σωκράτει. 25

Οἷα μὲν οὖν ἡ συνουσία ἐγεγόνει Κριτίᾳ πρὸς Σωκράτην
39 καὶ ὡς εἶχον πρὸς ἀλλήλους, εἴρηται. φαίην δ' ἂν ἔγωγε
μηδενὶ μηδεμίαν εἶναι παίδευσιν παρὰ τοῦ μὴ ἀρέσκοντος.
Κριτίας δὲ καὶ Ἀλκιβάδης οὐκ ἀρέσκοντος αὐτοῖς Σωκράτους
ὡμιλησάτην ὃν χρόνον ὡμιλείτην αὐτῷ, ἀλλ' εὐθὺς ἐξ 30
ἀρχῆς ὡρμηκότε προεστάναι τῆς πόλεως. ἔτι γὰρ Σωκράτει

---

5   ἀμφίλογον Β
5–6 ὡς... προηγορευμένα del. Cobet
14   τί Cobet

clearly one would have to avoid right speaking; but if wrong speaking is involved, obviously one must try to speak rightly.'

35. Charicles grew angry with him and said 'In view of your ignorance, Socrates, here are instructions to you that are easier to understand; you must not converse with young men in any way at all.'

'Well then,' said Socrates, 'so that there may be no doubt that I am contravening the edicts, give me your ruling on the age up to which men are to be considered young.'

'For as long' said Charicles 'as they are barred from being Councillors, as not yet being sensible. You must not converse with those younger than thirty.'

'Not even' asked Socrates 'if I am buying something, and someone younger than thirty is selling it? May I not even ask his price?'

'Yes, you may, in cases like that,' said Charicles 'but usually you, Socrates, already know the answer to most of the questions you ask. So you must not ask questions like that.'

'Well,' said Socrates 'suppose a young man asks me something like where does Charicles live or where is Critias, and I know, am I not even to answer them?'

'Yes,' said Charicles 'in such cases you may.'

37. 'But' said Critias 'I'll tell you what you'll have to avoid – cobblers, carpenters and smiths; for I think they are already completely worn out from your incessant talk about them.'

'Then' said Socrates 'must I also avoid the subjects which follow those – justice, piety and all other things like that?'

'Good heavens yes,' said Charicles 'and cowherds too! Otherwise you'd better take care that you too don't decrease the numbers of the herd.'

38. This clearly proved that Socrates' remark about the cattle had been reported to them and had angered them.

So much then for Critias' association with Socrates and their attitude to each other. 39. But for my part I'd say that nobody can ever learn anything from anyone they dislike. Critias and Alcibiades associated with Socrates as long as they did, not because they liked him, but because from the start

συνόντες οὐκ ἄλλοις τισὶ μᾶλλον ἐπεχείρουν διαλέγεσθαι
ἢ τοῖς μάλιστα πράττουσι τὰ πολιτικά. λέγεται γὰρ Ἀλκι- 40
βιάδην, πρὶν εἴκοσιν ἐτῶν εἶναι, Περικλεῖ ἐπιτρόπῳ μὲν
ὄντι αὑτοῦ, προστάτῃ δὲ τῆς πόλεως, τοιάδε διαλεχθῆναι
5 περὶ νόμων· Εἰπέ μοι, φάναι, ὦ Περίκλεις, ἔχοις ἄν με 41
διδάξαι τί ἐστι νόμος; Πάντως δήπου, φάναι τὸν Περικλέα.
Δίδαξον δὴ πρὸς τῶν θεῶν, φάναι τὸν Ἀλκιβιάδην· ὡς
ἐγὼ ἀκούων τινῶν ἐπαινουμένων, ὅτι νόμιμοι ἄνδρες εἰσίν,
οἶμαι μὴ ἂν δικαίως τούτου τυχεῖν τοῦ ἐπαίνου τὸν μὴ
10 εἰδότα τί ἐστι νόμος. Ἀλλ' οὐδέν τι χαλεποῦ πράγματος 42
ἐπιθυμεῖς, ὦ Ἀλκιβιάδη, φάναι τὸν Περικλέα, βουλόμενος
γνῶναι τί ἐστι νόμος· πάντες γὰρ οὗτοι νόμοι εἰσίν, οὓς τὸ
πλῆθος συνελθὸν καὶ δοκιμάσαν ἔγραψε, φράζον ἅ τε δεῖ
ποιεῖν καὶ ἃ μή. Πότερον δὲ τἀγαθὰ νομίσαν δεῖν ποιεῖν
15 ἢ τὰ κακά; Τἀγαθὰ νὴ Δία, φάναι, ὦ μειράκιον, τὰ δὲ
κακὰ οὔ. Ἐὰν δὲ μὴ τὸ πλῆθος, ἀλλ', ὥσπερ ὅπου 43
ὀλιγαρχία ἐστίν, ὀλίγοι συνελθόντες γράψωσιν ὅ τι χρὴ
ποιεῖν, ταῦτα τί ἐστι; Πάντα, φάναι, ὅσα ἂν τὸ κρατοῦν
τῆς πόλεως βουλευσάμενον, ἃ χρὴ ποιεῖν, γράψῃ, νόμος
20 καλεῖται. Κἂν τύραννος οὖν κρατῶν τῆς πόλεως γράψῃ
τοῖς πολίταις ἃ χρὴ ποιεῖν, καὶ ταῦτα νόμος ἐστί; Καὶ ὅσα
τύραννος ἄρχων, φάναι, γράφει, καὶ ταῦτα νόμος καλεῖται.
Βία δέ, φάναι, καὶ ἀνομία τί ἐστιν, ὦ Περίκλεις; ἆρ' οὐχ 44
ὅταν ὁ κρείττων τὸν ἥττω μὴ πείσας, ἀλλὰ βιασάμενος,
25 ἀναγκάσῃ ποιεῖν ὅ τι ἂν αὐτῷ δοκῇ; Ἔμοιγε δοκεῖ, φάναι
τὸν Περικλέα. Καὶ ὅσα ἄρα τύραννος μὴ πείσας τοὺς
πολίτας ἀναγκάζει ποιεῖν γράφων, ἀνομία ἐστί; Δοκεῖ μοι,
φάναι τὸν Περικλέα· ἀνατίθεμαι γὰρ τὸ ὅσα τύραννος μὴ
πείσας γράφει νόμον εἶναι. Ὅσα δὲ οἱ ὀλίγοι τοὺς πολ- 45
30 λοὺς μὴ πείσαντες, ἀλλὰ κρατοῦντες γράφουσι, πότερον
βίαν φῶμεν ἢ μὴ φῶμεν εἶναι; Πάντα μοι δοκεῖ, φάναι

14 ἐνόμισαν codd.: corr. Reiske
20 κρατῇ τῆς πόλεως καὶ A

they were set on political leadership. For while they still kept company with Socrates, they tried to converse in particular with those most involved in politics. 40. For it is said that Alcibiades, before he was twenty years old, had the following conversation about laws with Pericles, his guardian and Athens' leading statesman.

41. 'Tell me, Pericles,' he is said to have asked, 'could you inform me what law is?'

'By all means' said Pericles.

'Then, in heaven's name, please do so' said Alcibiades. 'For when I hear men being praised as law-abiding, I reflect that nobody could deserve that praise without knowing what law is.'

42. 'Well, Alcibiades,' said Pericles 'there's no great problem about obliging your desire to know what law is. Laws are without exception the approved enactments of most of the people, after assembling and declaring what ought and ought not to be done.'

'After first forming an opinion that good or that bad should be done?'

'Good, of course, young fellow, not bad.'

43. 'But if it is not most of the people, but, as happens where there is oligarchy, a few who have met and enacted what has to be done, what is that?'

'Everything enacted by the ruling power in the state, after deliberation over what must be done, is called law.'

'Then, even if it is a tyrant ruling over the state and enacting for the citizens what must be done, is that also law?'

'Yes, even the enactments of a tyrant in power are also called law.'

44. 'But, Pericles, what constitutes force and lawlessness? Is it not when the stronger man compels the weaker man to do what *he* wants not by persuasion but by force?'

'That's my personal opinion' said Pericles.

'Then whatever a tyrant compels his citizens to do by enactment without persuading them, is lawlessness?'

'Yes, that's my opinion,' said Pericles 'for I retract my statement that whatever a tyrant enacts without persuasion is law.'

45. 'And what the few enact without first persuading the many, but by use of their power, are we or are we not to call that force?'

τὸν Περικλέα, ὅσα τις μὴ πείσας ἀναγκάζει τινὰ ποιεῖν,
εἴτε γράφων εἴτε μή, βία μᾶλλον ἢ νόμος εἶναι. Καὶ ὅσα
ἄρα τὸ πᾶν πλῆθος κρατοῦν τῶν τὰ χρήματα ἐχόντων γράφει
46 μὴ πείσαν, βία μᾶλλον ἢ νόμος ἂν εἴη; Μάλα τοι, φάναι
τὸν Περικλέα, ὦ Ἀλκιβιάδη, καὶ ἡμεῖς τηλικοῦτοι ὄντες 5
δεινοὶ τὰ τοιαῦτα ἦμεν· τοιαῦτα γὰρ καὶ ἐμελετῶμεν καὶ
ἐσοφιζόμεθα οἷάπερ καὶ σὺ νῦν ἐμοὶ δοκεῖς μελετᾶν. τὸν
δὲ Ἀλκιβιάδην φάναι· Εἴθε σοι, ὦ Περίκλεις, τότε
συνεγενόμην ὅτε δεινότατος ἑαυτοῦ ταῦτα ἦσθα.

47 Ἐπεὶ τοίνυν τάχιστα τῶν πολιτευομένων ὑπέλαβον 10
κρείττονες εἶναι, Σωκράτει μὲν οὐκέτι προσῇσαν· οὔτε γὰρ
αὐτοῖς ἄλλως ἤρεσκεν, εἴ τε προσέλθοιεν, ὑπὲρ ὧν ἡμάρ-
τανον ἐλεγχόμενοι ἤχθοντο· τὰ δὲ τῆς πόλεως ἔπραττον,
48 ὧνπερ ἕνεκεν καὶ Σωκράτει προσῆλθον. ἀλλὰ Κρίτων τε
Σωκράτους ἦν ὁμιλητὴς καὶ Χαιρεφῶν καὶ Χαιρεκράτης καὶ 15
Ἑρμογένης καὶ Σιμίας καὶ Κέβης καὶ Φαιδώνδας καὶ ἄλλοι,
οἳ ἐκείνῳ συνῆσαν, οὐχ ἵνα δημηγορικοὶ ἢ δικανικοὶ γένοιντο,
ἀλλ᾽ ἵνα καλοί τε κἀγαθοὶ γενόμενοι καὶ οἴκῳ καὶ οἰκέταις
καὶ οἰκείοις καὶ φίλοις καὶ πόλει καὶ πολίταις δύναιντο
καλῶς χρῆσθαι. καὶ τούτων οὐδεὶς οὔτε νεώτερος οὔτε 20
πρεσβύτερος ὢν οὔτ᾽ ἐποίησε κακὸν οὐδὲν οὔτ᾽ αἰτίαν ἔσχεν.

49 Ἀλλὰ Σωκράτης γ᾽, ἔφη ὁ κατήγορος, τοὺς πατέρας
προπηλακίζειν ἐδίδασκε, πείθων μὲν τοὺς συνόντας αὐτῷ
σοφωτέρους ποιεῖν τῶν πατέρων, φάσκων δὲ κατὰ νόμον
ἐξεῖναι παρανοίας ἑλόντι καὶ τὸν πατέρα δῆσαι, τεκμηρίῳ 25
τούτῳ χρώμενος, ὡς τὸν ἀμαθέστερον ὑπὸ τοῦ σοφωτέρου
50 νόμιμον εἴη δεδέσθαι. Σωκράτης δὲ τὸν μὲν ἀμαθίας ἕνεκα
δεσμεύοντα δικαίως ἂν καὶ αὐτὸν ᾤετο δεδέσθαι ὑπὸ τῶν
ἐπισταμένων ἃ μὴ αὐτὸς ἐπίσταται· καὶ τῶν τοιούτων ἕνεκα
πολλάκις ἐσκόπει, τί διαφέρει μανίας ἀμαθία· καὶ τοὺς μὲν 30
μαινομένους ᾤετο συμφερόντως ἂν δεδέσθαι καὶ ἑαυτοῖς καὶ

5–19 Περικλέα... φίλοις partim praebet Π⁶
9   ἑαυτοῦ A: σαυτοῦ Π⁶Φ: om. B # ταῦτα Π⁶ MLW: περὶ ταῦτα B: om. AZ
14   ἕνεκα Π⁶
16   Ἑρμοκράτης Π⁶, codd.: corr. van Prinsterer # Φαιδώνδας B: Φαιδώνδης Φ: Φενδώνδης
A
19   post φίλοις deest Π⁶

'Everything, in my opinion,' said Pericles 'that anyone compels another to do whether by enactment or not, without first persuading him, is force rather than law.'

'Then what the whole populace enacts using its power over the owners of property instead of persuasion, would also be force rather than law?'

46. 'Yes, Alcibiades, very much so,' said Pericles, 'and when we were your age, we were clever at things like that; for the exercises we used to train our wits were of the sort I think you are using at present.'

Then Alcibiades said 'I wish I had been associated with you at the time when you were at your cleverest on these matters.'

47. Well, as soon as Alcibiades and Critias thought themselves superior to the politicians, they would no longer go near Socrates; for as well as a general aversion to him, they resented being cross-questioned over their wrongdoings, any time they went near him. Instead they engaged in politics, the very reason why they had gone to Socrates in the first place.

48. But Socrates' close companions were Crito, Chaerephon, Chaerecrates, Hermogenes, Simmias, Cebes, Phaedondas, and others who kept company with him, not to become good at public speaking or in the lawcourts, but so as to become perfect men, and to be able to do well by their household and its members, their relatives, friends, city and fellow citizens. And none of these men either in youth or in old age ever did anything evil or was blamed for it.

49. 'But' said his accuser, 'Socrates taught sons utter disrespect for their fathers, persuading them that he made his companions wiser than their fathers, and claiming that it was legally permissible to convict one's father of insanity and even to have him imprisoned, basing his evidence on the fact that it was lawful for the more ignorant man to be imprisoned by the wiser one.'

50. Socrates' real opinion was that the man, who had another chained up for ignorance, could himself also justly be imprisoned by those with extra knowledge, and reasoning like that often led him to consider how ignorance differs from madness. He also thought imprisoning the mad would benefit

τοῖς φίλοις, τοὺς δὲ μὴ ἐπισταμένους τὰ δέοντα δικαίως ἂν
μανθάνειν παρὰ τῶν ἐπισταμένων. ἀλλὰ Σωκράτης γε, 51
ἔφη ὁ κατήγορος, οὐ μόνον τοὺς πατέρας ἀλλὰ καὶ τοὺς
ἄλλους συγγενεῖς ἐποίει ἐν ἀτιμίᾳ εἶναι παρὰ τοῖς ἑαυτῷ
5 συνοῦσι, λέγων ὡς οὔτε τοὺς κάμνοντας οὔτε τοὺς δικαζο-
μένους οἱ συγγενεῖς ὠφελοῦσιν, ἀλλὰ τοὺς μὲν οἱ ἰατροί,
τοὺς δὲ οἱ συνδικεῖν ἐπιστάμενοι. ἔφη δὲ καὶ περὶ τῶν 52
φίλων αὐτὸν λέγειν ὡς οὐδὲν ὄφελος εὔνους εἶναι, εἰ μὴ
καὶ ὠφελεῖν δυνήσονται· μόνους δὲ φάσκειν αὐτὸν ἀξίους
10 εἶναι τιμῆς τοὺς εἰδότας τὰ δέοντα καὶ ἑρμηνεῦσαι δυνα-
μένους· ἀναπείθοντα οὖν τοὺς νέους αὐτόν, ὡς αὐτὸς εἴη
σοφώτατός τε καὶ ἄλλους ἱκανώτατος ποιῆσαι σοφούς, οὕτω
διατιθέναι τοὺς ἑαυτῷ συνόντας, ὥστε μηδαμοῦ παρ' αὐτοῖς
τοὺς ἄλλους εἶναι πρὸς ἑαυτόν. ἐγὼ δ' αὐτὸν οἶδα μὲν καὶ 53
15 περὶ πατέρων τε καὶ τῶν ἄλλων συγγενῶν [τε] καὶ περὶ
φίλων ταῦτα λέγοντα· καὶ πρὸς τούτοις γε δή, ὅτι τῆς
ψυχῆς ἐξελθούσης, ἐν ᾗ μόνῃ γίγνεται φρόνησις, τὸ σῶμα
τοῦ οἰκειοτάτου ἀνθρώπου τὴν ταχίστην ἐξενέγκαντες ἀφανί-
ζουσιν. ἔλεγε δ' ὅτι καὶ ζῶν ἕκαστος ἑαυτοῦ, ὃ πάντων 54
20 μάλιστα φιλεῖ, τοῦ σώματος ὅ τι ἂν ἀχρεῖον ᾖ καὶ ἀνωφελές,
αὐτός τε ἀφαιρεῖ καὶ ἄλλῳ παρέχει. αὐτοί τέ γε αὐτῶν
ὄνυχάς τε καὶ τρίχας καὶ τύλους ἀφαιροῦσι καὶ τοῖς ἰατροῖς
παρέχουσι μετὰ πόνων τε καὶ ἀλγηδόνων καὶ ἀποτέμνειν
καὶ ἀποκάειν, καὶ τούτων χάριν οἴονται δεῖν αὐτοῖς καὶ
25 μισθὸν τίνειν· καὶ τὸ σίαλον ἐκ τοῦ στόματος ἀποπτύουσιν
ὡς δύνανται πορρωτάτω, διότι ὠφελεῖ μὲν οὐδὲν αὐτοὺς ἐνόν,
βλάπτει δὲ πολὺ μᾶλλον. ταῦτ' οὖν ἔλεγεν οὐ τὸν μὲν 55
πατέρα ζῶντα κατορύττειν διδάσκων, ἑαυτὸν δὲ κατατέμνειν,
ἀλλ' ἐπιδεικνύων ὅτι τὸ ἄφρον ἄτιμόν ἐστι παρεκάλει
30 ἐπιμελεῖσθαι τοῦ ὡς φρονιμώτατον εἶναι καὶ ὠφελιμώτατον,

15 τε del. Morus
16 γε διότι codd.: corr. Weiske
18 ἄνθρωποι K. Schwartz
26 αὐτοῖς A

them and their friends, and that those without the proper knowledge could rightfully learn from those with it.

51. 'But' said his accuser 'Socrates caused his associates to disrespect not only their fathers but also their other relatives, by saying that neither invalids nor litigants are helped by their relatives, but the ones by their doctors and the others by those who know how to plead for them in court.' 52. According to his accuser Socrates also said on the subject of friends that their goodwill was of no benefit unless combined with ability to help, and that the only people deserving honour were those with the proper knowledge and the ability to communicate that knowledge to others, and that, by misleading the young into believing that he himself was the wisest of men and best able to impart wisdom to others, he had so strong an influence on his companions that all others ranked nowhere in their estimation compared with him.

53. Now I *do* know that was what he said about fathers and other relatives and friends, and furthermore that he said that, once the soul, the sole repository of intelligence, has departed, people carry out the body of their nearest and dearest with all haste and put it out of sight. 54. He would say that, though each man loves his own body more than anything else, even when still alive he himself removes any part of it that is useless and unserviceable, or lets someone else do so. People remove their own nails, hair and calluses themselves and let their doctors amputate and cauterise, causing them pain and suffering and feel obliged to offer thanks and payment for the service, and they spit saliva out of their mouths as far as they can, because its presence does no good, but rather great harm. 55. So that was what he said, not by way of instructing anyone to bury his father alive or cut up his own body, but rather to try to show that what lacked intelligence

ὅπως, ἐάν τε ὑπὸ πατρὸς ἐάν τε ὑπὸ ἀδελφοῦ ἐάν τε ὑπ᾽
ἄλλου τινὸς βούληται τιμᾶσθαι, μὴ τῷ οἰκεῖος εἶναι πιστεύων ἀμελῇ, ἀλλὰ πειρᾶται, ὑφ᾽ ὧν ἂν βούληται τιμᾶσθαι,
τούτοις ὠφέλιμος εἶναι.

56 Ἔφη δ᾽ αὐτὸν ὁ κατήγορος καὶ τῶν ἐνδοξοτάτων ποιητῶν 5
ἐκλεγόμενον τὰ πονηρότατα καὶ τούτοις μαρτυρίοις χρώμενον
διδάσκειν τοὺς συνόντας κακούργους τε εἶναι καὶ τυραννικούς,
Ἡσιόδου μὲν τὸ

Ἔργον δ᾽ οὐδὲν ὄνειδος, ἀεργίη δέ τ᾽ ὄνειδος·

τοῦτο δὴ λέγειν αὐτόν, ὡς ὁ ποιητὴς κελεύει μηδενὸς ἔργου 10
μήτ᾽ ἀδίκου μήτ᾽ αἰσχροῦ ἀπέχεσθαι, ἀλλὰ καὶ ταῦτα ποιεῖν
57 ἐπὶ τῷ κέρδει. Σωκράτης δ᾽ ἐπεὶ διομολογήσαιτο τὸ μὲν
ἐργάτην εἶναι ὠφέλιμόν τε ἀνθρώπῳ καὶ ἀγαθὸν εἶναι, τὸ
δὲ ἀργὸν βλαβερόν τε καὶ κακόν, καὶ τὸ μὲν ἐργάζεσθαι
ἀγαθόν, τὸ δ᾽ ἀργεῖν κακόν, τοὺς μὲν ἀγαθόν τι ποιοῦντας 15
ἐργάζεσθαί τε ἔφη καὶ ἐργάτας ἀγαθοὺς εἶναι, τοὺς δὲ
κυβεύοντας ἤ τι ἄλλο πονηρὸν καὶ ἐπιζήμιον ποιοῦντας
ἀργοὺς ἀπεκάλει. ἐκ δὲ τούτων ὀρθῶς ἂν ἔχοι τὸ

Ἔργον δ᾽ οὐδὲν ὄνειδος, ἀεργίη δέ τ᾽ ὄνειδος.

58 τὸ δὲ Ὁμήρου ἔφη ὁ κατήγορος πολλάκις αὐτὸν λέγειν, ὅτι 20
Ὀδυσσεὺς

Ὅντινα μὲν βασιλῆα καὶ ἔξοχον ἄνδρα κιχείη,
τὸν δ᾽ ἀγανοῖς ἐπέεσσιν ἐρητύσασκε παραστάς·
Δαιμόνι᾽, οὔ σε ἔοικε κακὸν ὡς δειδίσσεσθαι,
ἀλλ᾽ αὐτός τε κάθησο καὶ ἄλλους ἵδρυε λαούς.   25
ὅντινα δ᾽ αὖ δήμου τε ἴδοι βοόωντά τ᾽ ἐφεύροι,
τὸν σκήπτρῳ ἐλάσασκεν ὁμοκλήσασκέ τε μύθῳ·
Δαιμόνι᾽, ἀτρέμας ἧσο, καὶ ἄλλων μῦθον ἄκουε,
οἳ σέο φέρτεροί εἰσι· σὺ δ᾽ ἀπτόλεμος καὶ ἄναλκις,
οὔτε ποτ᾽ ἐν πολέμῳ ἐναρίθμιος οὔτ᾽ ἐνὶ βουλῇ.   30
ταῦτα δὴ αὐτὸν ἐξηγεῖσθαι, ὡς ὁ ποιητὴς ἐπαινοίη παίεσθαι

---

9   Op. 311
13   ὠφέλιμόν... 2.59 τούτῳ partim praebet Π⁶ # εἶναι om. Π⁶ Stob.
22–30 Il. 2.188–191, 198–202
26   ὅντινα... τε Π⁶: ὅντινα... τε ἄνδρα Αβ: ὅν... τ᾽ ἄνδρα Homerus

was worthless and he urged taking pains to be as intelligent and useful as possible, so that if one wished to be appreciated by father, brother or anyone else, one would not merely rely on kinship and be neglectful, but would try to be beneficial to all by whom he wished to be appreciated.

56. His accuser said that he chose out the most immoral passages, even of the most famous poets, and, using them as evidence, taught his companions to be evil-doers and tyrannical; this included Hesiod's line

'Work brings no shame, but working not *is* shame.'

Allegedly Socrates was saying that the poet instructed avoiding *no* work, whether unjust or shameful, but engaging even in such activities for gain. 57. But, whenever Socrates fully admitted that to be a worker was beneficial to a man and good, whereas to be idle was harmful and bad, and that working was good, idleness bad, he would say that those who did something good worked and were good workers, but those who played dice or did anything else depraved or criminal he would call idlers. Thus the saying would be right that

'Work brings no shame, but working not *is* shame.'

58. His accuser said that he often quoted the passage from Homer about Odysseus

'When king or man of eminence he did espy
With gentle words he'd him restrain, standing close by,
"Good sir, to fear like craven knave befits not thee,
Nay seat thyself, and bid the others seated be."
But any commoner he sighted shouting out
He'd smite with staff, berate with words and flout,
"Good sir, sit quiet and hear what others have to say,
Thy betters all, for feeble thou, useless in fray,
And art of no account in council or in war."

Socrates allegedly interpreted these lines as meaning that the poet approved of the beating of commoners and poor men.

τοὺς δημότας καὶ πένητας. Σωκράτης δ' οὐ ταῦτ' ἔλεγε· 59
καὶ γὰρ ἑαυτὸν οὕτω γ' ἂν ᾤετο δεῖν παίεσθαι· ἀλλ'
ἔφη δεῖν τοὺς μήτε λόγῳ μήτ' ἔργῳ ὠφελίμους ὄντας μήτε
στρατεύματι μήτε πόλει μήτε αὐτῷ τῷ δήμῳ, εἴ τι δέοι,
5 βοηθεῖν ἱκανούς, ἄλλως τε κἂν πρὸς τούτῳ καὶ θρασεῖς ὦσι,
πάντα τρόπον κωλύεσθαι, κἂν πάνυ πλούσιοι τυγχάνωσιν
ὄντες. ἀλλὰ Σωκράτης γε τἀναντία τούτων φανερὸς ἦν 60
καὶ δημοτικὸς καὶ φιλάνθρωπος ὤν. ἐκεῖνος γὰρ πολλοὺς
ἐπιθυμητὰς καὶ ἀστοὺς καὶ ξένους λαβὼν οὐδένα πώποτε
10 μισθὸν τῆς συνουσίας ἐπράξατο, ἀλλὰ πᾶσιν ἀφθόνως
ἐπήρκει τῶν ἑαυτοῦ· ὧν τινες μικρὰ μέρη παρ' ἐκείνου
προῖκα λαβόντες πολλοῦ τοῖς ἄλλοις ἐπώλουν, καὶ οὐκ
ἦσαν ὥσπερ ἐκεῖνος δημοτικοί· τοῖς γὰρ μὴ ἔχουσι χρήματα διδόναι οὐκ ἤθελον διαλέγεσθαι. ἀλλὰ Σωκράτης γε 61
15 καὶ πρὸς τοὺς ἄλλους ἀνθρώπους κόσμον τῇ πόλει παρεῖχε
πολλῷ μᾶλλον ἢ Λίχας τῇ Λακεδαιμονίων, ὃς ὀνομαστὸς
ἐπὶ τούτῳ γέγονε. Λίχας μὲν γὰρ ταῖς γυμνοπαιδίαις τοὺς
ἐπιδημοῦντας ἐν Λακεδαίμονι ξένους ἐδείπνιζε, Σωκράτης
δὲ διὰ παντὸς τοῦ βίου τὰ ἑαυτοῦ δαπανῶν τὰ μέγιστα
20 πάντας τοὺς βουλομένους ὠφέλει· βελτίους γὰρ ποιῶν τοὺς
συγγιγνομένους ἀπέπεμπεν.

Ἐμοὶ μὲν δὴ Σωκράτης τοιοῦτος ὢν ἐδόκει τιμῆς ἄξιος 62
εἶναι τῇ πόλει μᾶλλον ἢ θανάτου. καὶ κατὰ τοὺς νόμους
δὲ σκοπῶν ἄν τις τοῦθ' εὕροι. κατὰ γὰρ τοὺς νόμους, ἐάν
25 τις φανερὸς γένηται κλέπτων ἢ λωποδυτῶν ἢ βαλλαντιο-
τομῶν ἢ τοιχωρυχῶν ἢ ἀνδραποδιζόμενος ἢ ἱεροσυλῶν,
τούτοις θάνατός ἐστιν ἢ ζημία· ὧν ἐκεῖνος πάντων ἀνθρώπων
πλεῖστον ἀπεῖχεν. ἀλλὰ μὴν τῇ πόλει γε οὔτε πολέμου 63
κακῶς συμβάντος οὔτε στάσεως οὔτε προδοσίας οὔτε ἄλλου
30 κακοῦ οὐδενὸς πώποτε αἴτιος ἐγένετο· οὐδὲ μὴν ἰδίᾳ γε

---

5 τε ἂν codd.: corr. Ernesti
16 ὀνομαστότατος A

59. But that was not what Socrates said, for that would have meant he thought that he himself ought to be beaten, but what he said was that those useful neither in word nor deed and incapable of helping army, state or the people themselves in time of need, should be thwarted in every way, particularly if they added presumptuousness to these faults, no matter how rich they were. 60. But Socrates was the opposite of all that, clearly showing himself to be a man of the people and well disposed to all mankind. For though he acquired many eager disciples from Athens and elsewhere, he never charged any fee for his company, but was unsparing of his own resources in giving to all. Some of them, after receiving small items from him free, would sell them for a high price to others and were no friends of common men as he was; for they refused to talk with those unable to give them money.

61. But Socrates added distinction to his city in the eyes of all others also, far more than did Lichas for Sparta, though he has become famous for entertaining visitors to Sparta to dinner during the Gymnopaidiai, whereas Socrates, throughout all his life, would lavish what he had upon conferring the greatest benefits on all who wished for them, for he would try to make his associates better men before he let them go.

62. That was what Socrates was like, and in my opinion he deserved to be honoured by his city rather than executed, and anyone who considered the facts on the basis of the laws would find this to be the case; for according to the laws, if anyone is clearly shown to be a thief, footpad, cutpurse, housebreaker, kidnapper, or temple-robber, his punishment is death. 63. Furthermore Socrates was never responsible for causing a disastrous war, or sedition, or act of treason, or any other harm to Athens; moreover in private

οὐδένα πώποτε ἀνθρώπων οὔτε ἀγαθῶν ἀπεστέρησεν οὔτε
κακοῖς περιέβαλεν, ἀλλ᾽ οὐδ᾽ αἰτίαν τῶν εἰρημένων οὐδενὸς
64 πώποτ᾽ ἔσχε. πῶς οὖν ἔνοχος ἂν εἴη τῇ γραφῇ; ὃς ἀντὶ
μὲν τοῦ μὴ νομίζειν θεούς, ὡς ἐν τῇ γραφῇ ἐγέγραπτο,
φανερὸς ἦν θεραπεύων τοὺς θεοὺς μάλιστα τῶν ἄλλων 5
ἀνθρώπων, ἀντὶ δὲ τοῦ διαφθείρειν τοὺς νέους, ὃ δὴ ὁ
γραψάμενος αὐτὸν ᾐτιᾶτο, φανερὸς ἦν τῶν συνόντων τοὺς
πονηρὰς ἐπιθυμίας ἔχοντας τούτων μὲν παύων, τῆς δὲ καλ-
λίστης καὶ μεγαλοπρεπεστάτης ἀρετῆς, ᾗ πόλεις τε καὶ
οἶκοι εὖ οἰκοῦσι, προτρέπων ἐπιθυμεῖν· ταῦτα δὲ πράττων 10
πῶς οὐ μεγάλης ἄξιος ἦν τιμῆς τῇ πόλει;

III Οἷς δὲ δὴ καὶ ὠφελεῖν ἐδόκει μοι τοὺς συνόντας τὰ μὲν
ἔργῳ δεικνύων ἑαυτὸν οἷος ἦν, τὰ δὲ καὶ διαλεγόμενος,
τούτων δὴ γράψω ὁπόσα ἂν διαμνημονεύσω. τὰ μὲν τοίνυν
πρὸς τοὺς θεοὺς φανερὸς ἦν καὶ ποιῶν καὶ λέγων ᾗπερ ἡ 15
Πυθία ἀποκρίνεται τοῖς ἐρωτῶσι πῶς δεῖ ποιεῖν ἢ περὶ
θυσίας ἢ περὶ προγόνων θεραπείας ἢ περὶ ἄλλου τινὸς τῶν
τοιούτων· ἥ τε γὰρ Πυθία νόμῳ πόλεως ἀναιρεῖ ποιοῦντας
εὐσεβῶς ἂν ποιεῖν, Σωκράτης τε οὕτω καὶ αὐτὸς ἐποίει καὶ
τοῖς ἄλλοις παρῄνει, τοὺς δὲ ἄλλως πως ποιοῦντας περιέρ- 20
2 γους καὶ ματαίους ἐνόμιζεν εἶναι. καὶ ηὔχετο δὲ πρὸς τοὺς
θεοὺς ἁπλῶς τἀγαθὰ διδόναι, ὡς τοὺς θεοὺς κάλλιστα
εἰδότας ὁποῖα ἀγαθά ἐστι· τοὺς δ᾽ εὐχομένους χρυσίον ἢ
ἀργύριον ἢ τυραννίδα ἢ ἄλλο τι τῶν τοιούτων οὐδὲν διάφορον
ἐνόμιζεν εὔχεσθαι ἢ εἰ κυβείαν ἢ μάχην ἢ ἄλλο τι εὔχοιντο 25
3 τῶν φανερῶς ἀδήλων ὅπως ἀποβήσοιτο. θυσίας δὲ θύων
μικρὰς ἀπὸ μικρῶν οὐδὲν ἡγεῖτο μειοῦσθαι τῶν ἀπὸ πολλῶν
καὶ μεγάλων πολλὰ καὶ μεγάλα θυόντων. οὔτε γὰρ τοῖς
θεοῖς ἔφη καλῶς ἔχειν, εἰ ταῖς μεγάλαις θυσίαις μᾶλλον
ἢ ταῖς μικραῖς ἔχαιρον· πολλάκις γὰρ ἂν αὐτοῖς τὰ παρὰ 30
τῶν πονηρῶν μᾶλλον ἢ τὰ παρὰ τῶν χρηστῶν εἶναι κεχαρι-

5   τῶν ἄλλων ΒΦ: πάντων Α
10 οἴκους β
12 Οἷς Hartman: ὡς codd.
28 γὰρ] γὰρ ἂν Heindorf

life he never deprived anyone of good things or brought harm upon anyone, nor was he ever accused of any of the things I've mentioned. 64. How then could he be guilty of the charges? For instead of failing to acknowledge the gods, as specified in the indictment, he was the most conspicuous of all men in his service to the gods, and, instead of corrupting young men, as his prosecutor accused him of doing, he was conspicuous in stopping those of his companions with evil desires from indulging them, and in promoting in them an eager desire for virtue, the finest and most magnificent asset, whereby both states and households prosper. Since those were his activities, how could he fail to deserve great honour from his city?

Chapter 3. As for the ways by which, in my opinion, he did indeed benefit his companions, partly in practice by demonstrating his own character, and partly also by his conversation, I shall write down the examples I remember.

Well, as regards his attitude to the gods, he clearly showed that both his actions and his words corresponded with the answer the Delphic Priestess gives to those who ask how to act regarding sacrifice or homage to ancestors or any other such matter. For the answer of the Priestess is that those who act according to the custom of the state would act piously, and that was how Socrates himself always acted and urged others to act, whereas those who acted in any other way he thought futile and arrogant.

2. Moreover his prayers to the gods were simply to give what was good, since the gods know best what sort of things are good, whereas those who prayed for gold or silver or despotic power or any other such thing he thought to be no different from those playing a game of dice or a battle or anything else clearly of doubtful outcome. 3. He thought that, though offering small sacrifices from small resources, he was not at all inferior to those who offered many great sacrifices from many great resources. For he said it did not say much for the gods, if they took more pleasure in the great sacrifices than in the small ones, for in that case the offerings from the wicked would often be more pleasing to the gods than those from the good. On the contrary,

σμένα· οὔτ' ἂν τοῖς ἀνθρώποις ἄξιον εἶναι ζῆν, εἰ τὰ παρὰ
τῶν πονηρῶν μᾶλλον ἦν κεχαρισμένα τοῖς θεοῖς ἢ τὰ παρὰ
τῶν χρηστῶν· ἀλλ' ἐνόμιζε τοὺς θεοὺς ταῖς παρὰ τῶν
εὐσεβεστάτων τιμαῖς μάλιστα χαίρειν. ἐπαινέτης δ' ἦν καὶ
5 τοῦ ἔπους τούτου·

*   Καδδύναμιν δ' ἔρδειν ἱέρ' ἀθανάτοισι θεοῖσι,

καὶ πρὸς φίλους δὲ καὶ ξένους καὶ πρὸς τὴν ἄλλην δίαιταν
καλὴν ἔφη παραίνεσιν εἶναι τὴν Κὰδ δύναμιν δ' ἔρδειν. εἰ 4
δέ τι δόξειεν αὐτῷ σημαίνεσθαι παρὰ τῶν θεῶν, ἧττον ἂν
10 ἐπείσθη παρὰ τὰ σημαινόμενα ποιῆσαι ἢ εἴ τις αὐτὸν ἔπειθεν
ὁδοῦ λαβεῖν ἡγεμόνα τυφλὸν καὶ μὴ εἰδότα τὴν ὁδὸν ἀντὶ
βλέποντος καὶ εἰδότος· καὶ τῶν ἄλλων δὲ μωρίαν κατηγόρει,
οἵτινες παρὰ τὰ ὑπὸ τῶν θεῶν σημαινόμενα ποιοῦσί τι,
φυλαττόμενοι τὴν παρὰ τοῖς ἀνθρώποις ἀδοξίαν· αὐτὸς δὲ
15 πάντα τἀνθρώπινα ὑπερεώρα πρὸς τὴν παρὰ τῶν θεῶν
συμβουλίαν.

    Διαίτῃ δὲ τήν τε ψυχὴν ἐπαίδευσε καὶ τὸ σῶμα ᾗ 5
χρώμενος ἄν τις, εἰ μή τι δαιμόνιον εἴη, θαρραλέως καὶ
ἀσφαλῶς διάγοι καὶ οὐκ ἂν ἀπορήσειε τοσαύτης δαπάνης.
20 οὕτω γὰρ εὐτελὴς ἦν, ὥστ' οὐκ οἶδ' εἴ τις οὕτως ἂν
ὀλίγα ἐργάζοιτο ὥστε μὴ λαμβάνειν τὰ Σωκράτει ἀρκοῦντα.
σίτῳ μὲν γὰρ τοσούτῳ ἐχρῆτο, ὅσον ἡδέως ἤσθιε, καὶ ἐπὶ
τοῦτο οὕτω παρεσκευασμένος ᾔει ὥστε τὴν ἐπιθυμίαν τοῦ
σίτου ὄψον αὐτῷ εἶναι· ποτὸν δὲ πᾶν ἡδὺ ἦν αὐτῷ διὰ
25 τὸ μὴ πίνειν, εἰ μὴ διψῴη. εἰ δέ ποτε κληθεὶς ἐθε- 6
λήσειεν ἐπὶ δεῖπνον ἐλθεῖν, ὃ τοῖς πλείστοις ἐργωδέστατόν
ἐστιν, ὥστε φυλάξασθαι τὸ ὑπὲρ τὸν κόρον ἐμπίμπλασθαι,
τοῦτο ῥᾳδίως πάνυ ἐφυλάττετο. τοῖς δὲ μὴ δυναμένοις
τοῦτο ποιεῖν συνεβούλευε φυλάττεσθαι τὰ πείθοντα μὴ
30 πεινῶντας ἐσθίειν μηδὲ διψῶντας πίνειν· καὶ γὰρ τὰ λυμαι-

---

*6   Hes. Op. 336 # # Κὰδ δύναμιν Hes.: Καδδύναμιν nostri
*8   τὴν codd.: τό? vel delendum? # # Κὰδ δύναμιν legendum
11   ἀντὶ β: αὐτοῦ A
23   τούτῳ ABW: τοῦτο MZ: τοῦτον Stephanus
29   τὰ ἀναπείθοντα Plutarchus, Stobaeus

he thought the gods found more joy in the honours paid them by the most devout of men. He would express his approval of the following line:

'Thy utmost do in sacrifice to the deathless gods.'

And for dealing with friends and strangers and for manner of life generally, he acclaimed as excellent the advice 'Thy utmost do'. 4. If ever he thought a signal was being sent to him from the gods, he could no more have been persuaded to act against the signal than to choose as a guide for a journey a blind man ignorant of the way in preference to a man who could see and knew the way. He also criticised as fools all others who take any action contrary to the signals sent from the gods so as to avoid discredit with men. He himself despised all human considerations in comparison with the advice sent from the gods.

5. He trained his spirit and his body by a manner of life which would enable anyone, barring divine intervention, to live a confident, secure life and to have plenty for the expenses involved. For he was so frugal that I don't know if anyone could do so little work as not to earn enough for Socrates' needs. For he took only as much food as he could eat with enjoyment, and, when he went to eat, he was so ready for it that his hunger was his sauce, and any kind of drink was enjoyable to him, because he did not drink unless he was thirsty. 6. If ever he accepted an invitation to dinner, he found it very easy to do what most people find most difficult and to guard against overindulging his appetite. Those unable to do likewise he would advise to guard against things which encourage eating when not hungry and drinking when not thirsty. 7. For these things, he said, ruined stomachs, brains and

νόμενα γαστέρας καὶ κεφαλὰς καὶ ψυχὰς ταῦτ' ἔφη εἶναι.
7 οἴεσθαι δ' ἔφη ἐπισκώπτων καὶ τὴν Κίρκην ὗς ποιεῖν τοιούτοις πολλοῖς δειπνίζουσαν· τὸν δὲ Ὀδυσσέα Ἑρμοῦ τε
ὑποθημοσύνῃ καὶ αὐτὸν ἐγκρατῆ ὄντα καὶ ἀποσχόμενον
τοῦ ὑπὲρ τὸν κόρον τῶν τοιούτων ἅπτεσθαι, διὰ ταῦτα 5
8 οὐ γενέσθαι ὗν. τοιαῦτα μὲν περὶ τούτων ἔπαιζεν ἅμα
σπουδάζων.
   Ἀφροδισίων δὲ παρῄνει τῶν καλῶν ἰσχυρῶς ἀπέχεσθαι·
οὐ γὰρ ἔφη ῥᾴδιον εἶναι τῶν τοιούτων ἁπτόμενον σωφρο-
* νεῖν. ἀλλὰ καὶ Κριτόβουλόν ποτε τὸν Κρίτωνος πυθό- 10*
μενος ὅτι ἐφίλησε τὸν Ἀλκιβιάδου υἱὸν καλὸν ὄντα,
9 παρόντος τοῦ Κριτοβούλου ἤρετο Ξενοφῶντα· Εἰπέ μοι,
ἔφη, ὦ Ξενοφῶν, οὐ σὺ Κριτόβουλον ἐνόμιζες εἶναι τῶν
σωφρονικῶν ἀνθρώπων μᾶλλον ἢ τῶν θρασέων καὶ τῶν
προνοητικῶν μᾶλλον ἢ τῶν ἀνοήτων τε καὶ ῥιψοκινδύνων; 15
Πάνυ μὲν οὖν, ἔφη ὁ Ξενοφῶν. Νῦν τοίνυν νόμιζε αὐτὸν
θερμουργότατον εἶναι καὶ λεωργότατον· οὗτος κἂν εἰς μαχαί-
10 ρας κυβιστήσειε κἂν εἰς πῦρ ἅλοιτο. Καὶ τί δή, ἔφη ὁ
Ξενοφῶν, ἰδὼν ποιοῦντα τοιαῦτα κατέγνωκας αὐτοῦ; Οὐ γὰρ
οὗτος, ἔφη, ἐτόλμησε τὸν Ἀλκιβιάδου υἱὸν φιλῆσαι, ὄντα 20
εὐπροσωπότατον καὶ ὡραιότατον; Ἀλλ' εἰ μέντοι, ἔφη ὁ
Ξενοφῶν, τοιοῦτόν ἐστι τὸ ῥιψοκίνδυνον ἔργον, κἂν ἐγώ
11 μοι δοκῶ τὸν κίνδυνον τοῦτον ὑποστῆναι. Ὦ τλῆμον, ἔφη
ὁ Σωκράτης, καὶ τί ἂν οἴει παθεῖν καλὸν φιλήσας; ἆρ' οὐκ
ἂν αὐτίκα μάλα δοῦλος μὲν εἶναι ἀντ' ἐλευθέρου, πολλὰ δὲ 25
δαπανᾶν εἰς βλαβερὰς ἡδονάς, πολλὴν δὲ ἀσχολίαν ἔχειν
τοῦ ἐπιμεληθῆναί τινος καλοῦ κἀγαθοῦ, σπουδάζειν δ' ἀναγ-
12 κασθῆναι ἐφ' οἷς οὐδ' ἂν μαινόμενος σπουδάσειεν; Ὦ
* Ἡράκλεις, ἔφη ὁ Ξενοφῶν, ὡς δεινήν τινα λέγεις δύναμιν *
* τοῦ φιλήματος εἶναι. Καὶ τοῦτο, ἔφη ὁ Σωκράτης, θαυμά- 30*

6   μὲν... 3.13 πρόσωθεν partim praebet Π¹
10   ante ἀλλὰ c. iv litteras, dein ⟨δ⟩ὲ μᾶλλον, dein c. xx litteras dein ῃ κάεσθαι primo
     habebat Π¹; lacunam statuit Bandini
12   παρόντος τοῦ Κριτοβούλου om. Π¹
12–13 Εἰπέ... Ξενοφῶν om. Π¹
22–23 ἐγώ μοι δοκῶ Π¹ ZW: ἐγὼ δοκῶ μοι AB
23   ὑποστῆναι Π¹: Thuc. 2.61, 4.59 etc.: ὑπομεῖναι codd., cf. Cyr. 1.2.1:
28   οὐδ' codd., Stob.: οὐδεὶς? Π¹: οὐδεὶς οὐδ' Koraïs
*29–30 δύναμιν ante τοῦ codd., Stob.: ante εἶναι Π¹

characters. He would say in jest that he thought Circe made men into pigs, by feasting them on such things, whereas Odysseus, thanks to Hermes' advice, his own self-control and his avoidance of overindulgence in such foods, consequently escaped becoming a pig. Such were his remarks on the subject, made in jest, but also seriously meant.

8. He urged strenuous avoidance of sexual relations with beautiful people. For he said that merely touching such people made self-control difficult. Moreover on learning that Critobulus, the son of Crito, had kissed Alcibiades' handsome son, he questioned Xenophon in Critobulus' presence, saying: 9. 'Tell me, Xenophon, did you not think that Critobulus ranked among the self-controlled rather than the rash and among the cautious rather than the thoughtless and reckless?'

'Very much so' said Xenophon.

'Well now, you must consider him utterly hot-headed and unrestrained; he would somersault into a ring of knives and jump into fire.'

10. 'And what' asked Xenophon 'have you seen him doing that you have pronounced such a verdict against him?'

'Didn't he dare to kiss Alcibiades' superlatively handsome and attractive son?'

'Indeed,' said Xenophon 'if that's the sort of thing that's reckless, I think I too would offer to face the same risk.'

11. 'Then I'm sorry for you,' said Socrates 'and what do you think would happen to you after kissing someone handsome? Wouldn't you instantly be a slave instead of a free man, and spend vast sums on harmful pleasures, be much too busy for the concerns of a perfect man and be compelled to be serious about pursuits which not even a madman would take seriously?'

12. 'Lord almighty,' said Xenophon 'what fearful power you say a kiss has!'

'And are you surprised at that?' asked Socrates. 'Don't you know that

* ζεις; οὐκ οἶσθ' ὅτι τὰ φαλάγγια οὐδ' ἡμιωβελιαῖα τὸ μέγε- *
* θος ὄντα προσαψάμενα μόνον τῷ στόματι ταῖς τε ὀδύναις *
ἐπιτρίβει τοὺς ἀνθρώπους καὶ τοῦ φρονεῖν ἐξίστησι; Ναί
μὰ Δί', ἔφη ὁ Ξενοφῶν· ἐνίησι γάρ τι τὰ φαλάγγια κατὰ
5 τὸ δῆγμα. Ὦ μῶρε, ἔφη ὁ Σωκράτης, τοὺς δὲ καλοὺς οὐκ 13
οἴει φιλοῦντας ἐνιέναι τι, ὅτι σὺ οὐχ ὁρᾷς; οὐκ οἶσθ' ὅτι
τοῦτο τὸ θηρίον, ὃ καλοῦσι καλὸν καὶ ὡραῖον, τοσούτῳ
δεινότερόν ἐστι τῶν φαλαγγίων, ὅσῳ ἐκεῖνα μὲν ἁψάμενα,
τοῦτο δὲ οὐδ' ἁπτόμενον, ἐάν τις αὐτὸ θεᾶται, ἐνίησί τι καὶ
10 πάνυ πρόσωθεν τοιοῦτον ὥστε μαίνεσθαι ποιεῖν; [ἴσως δὲ
καὶ οἱ ἔρωτες τοξόται διὰ τοῦτο καλοῦνται, ὅτι καὶ πρόσωθεν οἱ καλοὶ τιτρώσκουσιν.] ἀλλὰ συμβουλεύω σοι, ὦ
Ξενοφῶν, ὁπόταν ἴδῃς τινὰ καλόν, φεύγειν προτροπάδην.
σοὶ δ', ὦ Κριτόβουλε, συμβουλεύω ἀπενιαυτίσαι· μόλις γὰρ
15 ἂν ἐν τοσούτῳ χρόνῳ τὸ δῆγμα ὑγιὴς γένοιο. οὕτω 14
δὴ καὶ ἀφροδισιάζειν τοὺς μὴ ἀσφαλῶς ἔχοντας πρὸς ἀφρο-
δίσια ᾤετο χρῆναι πρὸς τοιαῦτα, οἷα μὴ πάνυ μὲν δεομένου
τοῦ σώματος οὐκ ἂν προσδέξαιτο ἡ ψυχή, δεομένου δὲ οὐκ
ἂν πράγματα παρέχοι. αὐτὸς δὲ πρὸς ταῦτα φανερὸς ἦν
20 οὕτω παρεσκευασμένος ὥστε ῥᾷον ἀπέχεσθαι τῶν καλλίστων
καὶ ὡραιοτάτων ἢ οἱ ἄλλοι τῶν αἰσχίστων καὶ ἀωροτάτων.
περὶ μὲν δὴ βρώσεως καὶ πόσεως καὶ ἀφροδισίων οὕτω 15
κατεσκευασμένος ἦν καὶ ᾤετο οὐδὲν ἂν ἧττον ἀρκούντως
ἥδεσθαι τῶν πολλὰ ἐπὶ τούτοις πραγματευομένων, λυπεῖσθαι
25 δὲ πολὺ ἔλαττον.
* Εἰ δέ τινες Σωκράτην νομίζουσιν, οἷς ἔνιοι γράφουσί τε **IV** *
καὶ λέγουσι περὶ αὐτοῦ τεκμαιρόμενοι, προτρέψασθαι μὲν
ἀνθρώπους ἐπ' ἀρετὴν κράτιστον γεγονέναι, προαγαγεῖν

---

1 ὅτι Π¹ Stob.: ἔφη ABZLW # ἡμιωβελιαῖα Π¹ ex correctione: ἡμιωβολιαῖα B:
ἡμιοβελιμαῖα A
1–2 ὄντα post μέγεθος codd.: ante τὸ Π¹
2 *προσαψάμενα μόνον codd.: ὅσον μόνον ἁψάμενα Π¹ # ταῖς τε ὀδύναις codd. ὀδύναις τε
Π¹
3 τοῦ MZP Stob.: τὸ AB post πρόσωθεν deest Π¹
10–15 πρόσωθεν... τοσούτῳ partim praebet Π⁶
10–12 ἴσως... τιτρώσκουσιν del. Dindorf
15 ἂν ἴσως Stob.: ἂν Π⁶: ἴσως AB: ἂν πως Cobet # τὸ δῆγμα om. B # ὑγιὲς γένοιτο
Stob.
23 ἀρκούντως... 4.3 ἀνδριαντοποιίᾳ suppetit Π²
26 ὡς codd. Π²: οἷς Jacobs

poisonous spiders, though not even the size of a farthing, by the merest touch half-kill folk with pain and drive them out of their senses?'

'Good lord, yes,' said Xenophon 'for the spiders inject something with every bite.'

'Stupid fellow,' said Socrates 'don't you think that handsome kissers inject something invisible to you? Don't you know that this creature, the thing they call beautiful and blooming, is all the more to be feared than these spiders, because they must first touch, whereas this creature, without even touching, but if one merely looks at it, injects, even from a great distance, something to cause madness? [Perhaps that's also why Love-gods are called archers, because handsome youths wound even from far off.] No, Xenophon, I advise you, when you see any handsome youth, to take to your heels and flee, and you, Critobulus, to go away for a year; for you would perhaps find it difficult to recover [from the bite] even after all that time.'

14. He thought that those dangerously exposed to sexual passions should limit themselves to activities that the inner spirit would only accept in cases of urgent bodily need, and such as would not prove troublesome, when needed. His own approach to those matters clearly showed him to be so well prepared that he avoided the most handsome and attractive young people more easily than all others avoid the ugliest and most unattractive creatures. 15. Indeed that was how thoroughly he was prepared for dealing with food, drink and sex, and he thought that he would derive no less satisfying pleasure from them and suffer much less distress than did those busily engaged in these pursuits.

Chapter 4. If any base inferences on what several write or say about Socrates to think that, though his forte was encouraging folk to virtue, he

δ' ἐπ' αὐτὴν οὐχ ἱκανόν, σκεψάμενοι μὴ μόνον ἃ ἐκεῖνος
κολαστηρίου ἕνεκα τοὺς πάντ' οἰομένους εἰδέναι ἐρωτῶν
ἤλεγχεν, ἀλλὰ καὶ ἃ λέγων συνημέρευε τοῖς συνδιατρί-
βουσι, δοκιμαζόντων εἰ ἱκανὸς ἦν βελτίους ποιεῖν τοὺς
2 συνόντας. λέξω δὲ πρῶτον ἅ ποτε αὐτοῦ ἤκουσα περὶ τοῦ 5
δαιμονίου διαλεγομένου πρὸς Ἀριστόδημον τὸν μικρὸν ἐπικα-
λούμενον. καταμαθὼν γὰρ αὐτὸν οὔτε θύοντα τοῖς θεοῖς *
* οὔτε μαντικῇ χρώμενον, ἀλλὰ καὶ τῶν ποιούντων ταῦτα
καταγελῶντα, Εἰπέ μοι, ἔφη, ὦ Ἀριστόδημε, ἔστιν οὕσ-
τινας ἀνθρώπους τεθαύμακας ἐπὶ σοφίᾳ; Ἔγωγ', ἔφη. 10
3 καὶ ὅς, Λέξον ἡμῖν, ἔφη, τὰ ὀνόματα αὐτῶν. Ἐπὶ μὲν
τοίνυν ἐπῶν ποιήσει Ὅμηρον ἔγωγε μάλιστα τεθαύμακα,
ἐπὶ δὲ διθυράμβῳ Μελανιππίδην, ἐπὶ δὲ τραγῳδίᾳ Σοφοκλέα,
ἐπὶ δὲ ἀνδριαντοποιίᾳ Πολύκλειτον, ἐπὶ δὲ ζωγραφίᾳ Ζεῦξιν.
4 Πότερά σοι δοκοῦσιν οἱ ἀπεργαζόμενοι εἴδωλα ἄφρονά τε 15
καὶ ἀκίνητα ἀξιοθαυμαστότεροι εἶναι ἢ οἱ ζῷα ἔμφρονά τε
καὶ ἐνεργά; Πολὺ νὴ Δία οἱ ζῷα, εἴπερ γε μὴ τύχῃ τινί,
ἀλλ' ὑπὸ γνώμης ταῦτα γίγνεται. Τῶν δὲ ἀτεκμάρτως
ἐχόντων ὅτου ἕνεκα ἔστι καὶ τῶν φανερῶς ἐπ' ὠφελείᾳ
ὄντων πότερα τύχης καὶ πότερα γνώμης ἔργα κρίνεις; Πρέπει 20
5 μὲν τὰ ἐπ' ὠφελείᾳ γιγνόμενα γνώμης εἶναι ἔργα. Οὔκουν
δοκεῖ σοι ὁ ἐξ ἀρχῆς ποιῶν ἀνθρώπους ἐπ' ὠφελείᾳ προσ-
θεῖναι αὐτοῖς δι' ὧν αἰσθάνονται ἕκαστα, ὀφθαλμοὺς μὲν
ὥσθ' ὁρᾶν τὰ ὁρατά, ὦτα δὲ ὥστ' ἀκούειν τὰ ἀκουστά;
ὀσμῶν γε μήν, εἰ μὴ ῥῖνες προσετέθησαν, τί ἂν ἡμῖν ὄφελος 25
ἦν; τίς δ' ἂν αἴσθησις ἦν γλυκέων καὶ δριμέων καὶ πάντων
τῶν διὰ στόματος ἡδέων, εἰ μὴ γλῶττα τούτων γνώμων
6 ἐνειργάσθη; πρὸς δὲ τούτοις οὐ δοκεῖ σοι καὶ τάδε προνοίας
ἔργοις ἐοικέναι, τὸ ἐπεὶ ἀσθενὴς μέν ἐστιν ἡ ὄψις, βλεφά-
ροις αὐτὴν θυρῶσαι, ἅ, ὅταν μὲν αὐτῇ χρῆσθαί τι δέῃ, ἀνα- 30

1   δὲ ταύτην A
7–8 post θεοῖς add. μὴ μαχόμενον AB: ...... χομεν ...... τα Π²: οὔτ' εὐχόμενον F. Portus:
     οὔτ' εὐχόμενον δῆλον ὄντα Marchant
10   ἐπὶ σοφίᾳ] σοφίας vel σοφίᾳ? Π²
14   ante Πολύκλειτον deficit Π²
18   ἀπὸ A
21   οὐκοῦν codd.: corr. Bornemann

was incapable of guiding them to it, let them consider not only his searching questions to chastise and show up those who thought themselves omniscient, but also what he said in daylong conversation with his close companions and then let them decide whether he was capable of making his associates better men.

2. First I shall recount what I heard him say about the divinity in conversation with Aristodemus nicknamed 'The Dwarf'; for on learning that he did not sacrifice to the gods .... or use divination but would even mock those who did so, Socrates said 'Tell me, Aristodemus, are there any men you have admired for their cleverness?'

'Yes, indeed' he said.

3. 'Tell us their names' said Socrates.

'Well, in epic poetry I personally have most admired Homer, in dithyramb Melanippides, in tragedy Sophocles, in sculpture Polyclitus, and in painting Zeuxis.'

4. 'Do you consider the creators of likenesses, which are unable to think or move, more admirable than the creators of living creatures able to think and act?'

'Good lord, I far prefer the creators of living creatures, provided at least they are produced not by some chance but by design.'

'As between creatures whose purpose cannot be surmised and those that clearly serve a useful one, which of them do you judge to be works of chance and which of design?'

'Those that serve a useful purpose ought to be works of design.'

5. 'Then don't you think that it was for their benefit that the original creator of men also provided them with all the means of perception, eyes to see visible objects, and ears to hear audible things? And as for smells too, what good would they be to us, if we had not also been given noses? And what perception would we have of things sweet and bitter and all the pleasures of the palate but for the incorporation of a tongue to distinguish between them? 6. In addition to these, don't other things too seem like the products of forethought? The supplying of a protective door for the eyes, weak as they

πετάννυται, ἐν δὲ τῷ ὕπνῳ συγκλείεται, ὡς δ' ἂν μηδὲ
ἄνεμοι βλάπτωσιν, ἠθμὸν βλεφαρίδας ἐμφῦσαι, ὀφρύσι τε
ἀπογεισῶσαι τὰ ὑπὲρ τῶν ὀμμάτων, ὡς μηδ' ὁ ἐκ τῆς
κεφαλῆς ἱδρὼς κακουργῇ· τὸ δὲ τὴν ἀκοὴν δέχεσθαι μὲν
5 πάσας φωνάς, ἐμπίμπλασθαι δὲ μήποτε· καὶ τοὺς μὲν πρόσθεν ὀδόντας πᾶσι ζῴοις οἵους τέμνειν εἶναι, τοὺς δὲ γομφίους οἵους παρὰ τούτων δεξαμένους λεαίνειν· καὶ στόμα
μέν, δι' οὗ ὧν ἐπιθυμεῖ τὰ ζῷα εἰσπέμπεται, πλησίον ὀφθαλ-
μῶν καὶ ῥινῶν καταθεῖναι· ἐπεὶ δὲ τὰ ἀποχωροῦντα δυσχερῆ,
10 ἀποστρέψαι τοὺς τούτων ὀχετοὺς καὶ ἀπενεγκεῖν ᾗ δυνατὸν
προσωτάτω ἀπὸ τῶν αἰσθήσεων· ταῦτα οὕτω προνοητικῶς
πεπραγμένα ἀπορεῖς πότερα τύχης ἢ γνώμης ἔργα ἐστίν;
Οὐ μὰ τὸν Δί', ἔφη, ἀλλ' οὕτω γε σκοπουμένῳ πάνυ ἔοικε 7
ταῦτα σοφοῦ τινος δημιουργοῦ καὶ φιλοζῴου τεχνήμασι. Τὸ
15 δὲ ἐμφῦσαι μὲν ἔρωτα τῆς τεκνοποιίας, ἐμφῦσαι δὲ ταῖς
γειναμέναις ἔρωτα τοῦ ἐκτρέφειν, τοῖς δὲ τραφεῖσι μέγιστον
μὲν πόθον τοῦ ζῆν, μέγιστον δὲ φόβον τοῦ θανάτου; Ἀμέλει
καὶ ταῦτα ἔοικε μηχανήμασί τινος ζῷα εἶναι βουλευσαμένου.
Σὺ δὲ σαυτῷ δοκεῖς τι φρόνιμον ἔχειν; Ἐρώτα γοῦν καὶ 8
20 ἀποκρινοῦμαι. Ἄλλοθι δὲ οὐδαμοῦ οὐδὲν οἴει φρόνιμον
εἶναι; καὶ ταῦτ' εἰδὼς ὅτι γῆς τε μικρὸν μέρος ἐν τῷ σώματι
πολλῆς οὔσης ἔχεις καὶ ὑγροῦ βραχὺ πολλοῦ ὄντος καὶ τῶν
ἄλλων δήπου μεγάλων ὄντων ἑκάστου μικρὸν μέρος λαβόντι
τὸ σῶμα συνήρμοσταί σοι· νοῦν δὲ μόνον ἄρα οὐδαμοῦ ὄντα
25 σε εὐτυχῶς πως δοκεῖς συναρπάσαι, καὶ τάδε τὰ ὑπερμεγέθη
* καὶ πλῆθος ἄπειρα δι' ἀφροσύνην τινά, ὡς οἴει, εὐτάκτως *
ἔχειν; Μὰ Δί' οὐ γὰρ ὁρῶ τοὺς κυρίους, ὥσπερ τῶν ἐνθάδε 9
γιγνομένων τοὺς δημιουργούς. Οὐδὲ γὰρ τὴν σαυτοῦ σύγε
ψυχὴν ὁρᾷς, ἣ τοῦ σώματος κυρία ἐστίν· ὥστε κατά γε
30 τοῦτο ἔξεστί σοι λέγειν, ὅτι οὐδὲν γνώμῃ, ἀλλὰ τύχῃ πάντα

7   καταλεαίνειν A
9   ἐπεὶ A: ἐπὶ β
14   τεχνήματι AMLW
19–20   Ἐρώτα... ἀποκρινοῦμαι del. Muretus
25   σὺ Bandini
*26   ὡς A β: οὕτως Leonclavius
30   οὐδὲ codd.: corr. Vossius

are, in which eyelids open, when the eyes need to be used, and close during sleep? The provision of eyelashes growing like filters, so that not even the winds may do any harm? The eyebrows like cornices covering the area above the eyes, so that even the sweat from the head may do no damage? The ears receiving all manner of sounds, but never blocked up by them? The front teeth of all creatures suited to act as incisors? The back teeth to receive the food from them and act as molars? The placing of the mouth, through which the food desired by all creatures is introduced, near the eyes and the nose? And since excrement is disagreeable, its channels have been directed away and removed as far as possible from the senses. When all these things have been executed with such forethought, can you be in any doubt whether they are the products of chance or design?'

7. 'Good lord, no.' he said. 'When thought of in that way, they do look very much like the handiwork of a clever craftsman who loves living creatures.'

'What about the implanting of the eager desire to procreate children and the implanting in new mothers of the eager desire to nurture their young, and in the children of an intense craving for life and an intense fear of death?'

'Certainly these things too *do* look like the contrivances of one who has planned the existence of living creatures.'

8. 'What about yourself? Do *you* think you have any intelligence?'

'Just ask and I'll give you your answer.'

'Do you think that intelligence exists nowhere else, although you know that you have in your body but a tiny portion of the vast earth and but a tiny drop of the vast quantities of moisture and that only a tiny scrap of all the other presumably mighty elements was incorporated in you when you received your body? And do you think that, though mind alone exists nowhere else, you have by a stroke of luck got hold of it? And that in your opinion these elemental materials, vast in size and infinite in number, owe good order to some lack of intelligence?'

9. 'Good lord, yes I do; for I don't see those in control, in the way I see the craftsmen who make things in this world.'

'Neither do you see your own soul which controls your body; so by that

10 πράττεις. καὶ ὁ Ἀριστόδημος, Οὗτοι, ἔφη, ἐγώ, ὦ Σώκρατες, ὑπερορῶ τὸ δαιμόνιον, ἀλλ᾽ ἐκεῖνο μεγαλοπρεπέστερον ἡγοῦμαι ἢ ὡς τῆς ἐμῆς θεραπείας προσδεῖσθαι.
Οὐκοῦν, ἔφη, ὅσῳ μεγαλοπρεπέστερον ὂν ἀξιοῖ σε θερα-
11 πεύειν, τοσούτῳ μᾶλλον τιμητέον αὐτό. Εὖ ἴσθι, ἔφη, ὅτι, 5
εἰ νομίζοιμι θεοὺς ἀνθρώπων τι φροντίζειν, οὐκ ἂν ἀμελοίην
αὐτῶν. Ἔπειτ᾽ οὐκ οἴει φροντίζειν; οἳ πρῶτον μὲν μόνον
τῶν ζῴων ἄνθρωπον ὀρθὸν ἀνέστησαν· ἡ δὲ ὀρθότης καὶ
προορᾶν πλέον ποιεῖ δύνασθαι καὶ τὰ ὕπερθεν μᾶλλον θεᾶ-
σθαι καὶ ἧττον κακοπαθεῖν [καὶ ὄψιν καὶ ἀκοὴν καὶ στόμα 10
ἐνεποίησαν] ἔπειτα τοῖς μὲν ἄλλοις ἑρπετοῖς πόδας ἔδωκαν,
οἳ τὸ πορεύεσθαι μόνον παρέχουσιν, ἀνθρώπῳ δὲ καὶ χεῖρας
προσέθεσαν, αἳ τὰ πλεῖστα οἷς εὐδαιμονέστεροι ἐκείνων
12 ἐσμὲν ἐξεργάζονται. καὶ μὴν γλῶττάν γε πάντων τῶν
ζῴων ἐχόντων, μόνην τὴν τῶν ἀνθρώπων ἐποίησαν οἵαν 15
ἄλλοτε ἀλλαχῇ ψαύουσαν τοῦ στόματος ἀρθροῦν τε τὴν
φωνὴν καὶ σημαίνειν πάντα ἀλλήλοις ἃ βουλόμεθα. τὸ δὲ
καὶ τὰς τῶν ἀφροδισίων ἡδονὰς τοῖς μὲν ἄλλοις ζῴοις δοῦναι
περιγράψαντας τοῦ ἔτους χρόνον, ἡμῖν δὲ συνεχῶς μέχρι
13 γήρως ταῦτα παρέχειν. οὐ τοίνυν μόνον ἤρκεσε τῷ θεῷ τοῦ 20
σώματος ἐπιμεληθῆναι, ἀλλ᾽, ὅπερ μέγιστόν ἐστι, καὶ τὴν
ψυχὴν κρατίστην τῷ ἀνθρώπῳ ἐνέφυσε. τίνος γὰρ ἄλλου
ζῴου ψυχὴ πρῶτα μὲν θεῶν τῶν τὰ μέγιστα καὶ κάλλιστα
συνταξάντων ᾔσθηται ὅτι εἰσί; τί δὲ φῦλον ἄλλο ἢ ἄνθρωποι θεοὺς θεραπεύουσι; ποία δὲ ψυχὴ τῆς ἀνθρωπίνης 25
ἱκανωτέρα προφυλάττεσθαι ἢ λιμὸν ἢ δίψος ἢ ψύχη ἢ
θάλπη, ἢ νόσοις ἐπικουρῆσαι, ἢ ῥώμην ἀσκῆσαι, ἢ πρὸς
μάθησιν ἐκπονῆσαι, ἢ ὅσα ἂν ἀκούσῃ ἢ ἴδῃ ἢ μάθῃ ἱκανω-
14 τέρα ἐστὶ διαμεμνῆσθαι; οὐ γὰρ πάνυ σοι κατάδηλον ὅτι

3   ἢ supra lineam add. Laur. C. S. 110: om. cett.
4   ὂν M²: om. cett.
10–11 καὶ ὄψιν ... ἐνεποίησαν del. Dindorf
11   ἐνεποίησαν β: ἐποίησαν A: ἄνω ἐποίησαν Heindorf
20   ταύτας MZ
24   οἱ ἄνϑρωποι A

argument you could say that you do nothing by design and everything by chance.'

10. 'Indeed,' said Aristodemus 'I don't disregard the divinity, but I think it too magnificent to need extra service from me.'

'Then' said Socrates 'the more magnificent the power that deigns to serve you, the greater the honour it should have.'

11. 'You can be quite sure' said Aristodemus 'that, if I considered the gods were at all concerned about men, I would not neglect them.'

'Then do you really think them unconcerned? In the first place they made man alone of all creatures stand upright, and the upright position allows him to see further ahead, have a better view of things above him and be less prone to injury [and they have provided him with vision, hearing and a mouth]. In the second place, though they have given all other terrestrial animals feet which merely provide locomotion, to men they have also given hands whereby they accomplish most of the things which make us more fortunate than all other creatures. 12. Moreover, though all creatures have a tongue, it is only the human tongue they have made of a sort to touch various parts of the mouth at various times, enabling it to articulate the voice and to communicate everything we wish to each other. Again, though they have given all other creatures the delights of sex for a limited time of the year, they provide them to us continuously till our old age.

13. Well, God wasn't merely satisfied with caring about the human body, but the most important thing is that he also implanted in man his inner spirit and made it supreme. For what other creature has a spirit that in the first place has realised the existence of the gods who have organised the world in its vastness and great beauty? What race other than man worships gods? What spirit is more capable than the human one of taking precautions against hunger, thirst, cold or heat, or of ministering to ailments, developing strength, toiling for knowledge or remembering in detail all it hears, sees or

παρὰ τἆλλα ζῷα ὥσπερ θεοὶ ἄνθρωποι βιοτεύουσι, φύσει
καὶ τῷ σώματι καὶ τῇ ψυχῇ κρατιστεύοντες; οὔτε γὰρ βοὸς
ἂν ἔχων σῶμα, ἀνθρώπου δὲ γνώμην ἐδύνατ' ἂν πράττειν ἃ
ἐβούλετο, οὔθ' ὅσα χεῖρας ἔχει, ἄφρονα δ' ἐστί, πλέον οὐδὲν
5 ἔχει. σὺ δ' ἀμφοτέρων τῶν πλείστου ἀξίων τετυχηκὼς
οὐκ οἴει σοῦ θεοὺς ἐπιμελεῖσθαι; ἀλλ' ὅταν τί ποιήσωσι,
νομιεῖς αὐτοὺς σοῦ φροντίζειν; "Οταν πέμπωσιν, ὥσπερ σοὶ 15
φῇς πέμπειν αὐτούς, συμβούλους ὅ τι χρὴ ποιεῖν καὶ μὴ
ποιεῖν. "Οταν δὲ 'Αθηναίοις, ἔφη, πυνθανομένοις τι διὰ
10 μαντικῆς φράζωσιν, οὐ καὶ σοὶ δοκεῖς φράζειν αὐτούς, οὐδ'
ὅταν τοῖς "Ελλησι τέρατα πέμποντες προσημαίνωσιν, οὐδ'
ὅταν πᾶσιν ἀνθρώποις, ἀλλὰ μόνον σὲ ἐξαιροῦντες ἐν ἀμε-
λείᾳ κατατίθενται; οἴει δ' ἂν τοὺς θεοὺς τοῖς ἀνθρώποις 16
δόξαν ἐμφῦσαι ὡς ἱκανοί εἰσιν εὖ καὶ κακῶς ποιεῖν, εἰ μὴ
15 δυνατοὶ ἦσαν, καὶ ἀνθρώπους ἐξαπατωμένους τὸν πάντα
χρόνον οὐδέποτ' ἂν αἰσθέσθαι; οὐχ ὁρᾷς ὅτι τὰ πολυχρο-
νιώτατα καὶ σοφώτατα τῶν ἀνθρωπίνων, πόλεις καὶ ἔθνη,
θεοσεβέστατά ἐστι, καὶ αἱ φρονιμώταται ἡλικίαι θεῶν ἐπι-
μελέσταται; ὠγαθέ, ἔφη, κατάμαθε ὅτι καὶ ὁ σὸς νοῦς ἐνὼν 17
20 τὸ σὸν σῶμα ὅπως βούλεται μεταχειρίζεται. οἴεσθαι οὖν
χρὴ καὶ τὴν ἐν ⟨τῷ⟩ παντὶ φρόνησιν τὰ πάντα, ὅπως ἂν
αὐτῇ ἡδὺ ᾖ, οὕτω τίθεσθαι, καὶ μὴ τὸ σὸν μὲν ὄμμα δύνασθαι
ἐπὶ πολλὰ στάδια ἐξικνεῖσθαι, τὸν δὲ τοῦ θεοῦ ὀφθαλμὸν
ἀδύνατον εἶναι ἅμα πάντα ὁρᾶν, μηδὲ τὴν σὴν μὲν ψυχὴν
25 καὶ περὶ τῶν ἐνθάδε καὶ περὶ τῶν ἐν Αἰγύπτῳ καὶ ἐν Σικε-
λίᾳ δύνασθαι φροντίζειν, τὴν δὲ τοῦ θεοῦ φρόνησιν μὴ
ἱκανὴν εἶναι ἅμα πάντων ἐπιμελεῖσθαι. ἂν μέντοι, ὥσπερ 18
ἀνθρώπους θεραπεύων γιγνώσκεις τοὺς ἀντιθεραπεύειν ἐθέ-
λοντας καὶ χαριζόμενος τοὺς ἀντιχαριζομένους καὶ συμβου-
30 λευόμενος καταμανθάνεις τοὺς φρονίμους, οὕτω καὶ τῶν
θεῶν πεῖραν λαμβάνῃς θεραπεύων, εἴ τί σοι θελήσουσι περὶ

7 σοὶ Cobet: σὺ β: σοῦ σοὶ A: σοὶ σὺ Dindorf
21 τῷ add. Hindenburg

learns? 14. Is it not abundantly clear to you that, compared with any other creatures, men live like gods, naturally supreme both in body and spirit? For if he had the body of an ox along with a human mind, a man could not do what he wanted; nor do creatures with hands but lacking reason have any advantages. But since you enjoy both these priceless gifts, do you not think the gods care for *you*? What will they have to do to make you think they are concerned for *you*?'

15. 'When they send advisers, as you say they do to you, to tell you what to do and what not to do.'

'But' said Socrates 'when the Athenians make an enquiry by divination and the gods tell them something, don't you think they are telling *you* too, or when, by sending omens, they give warnings to the Greeks, or when they do so to all mankind? Do they, however, make *you* their sole exception and decide to neglect *you*? 16. Do you think the gods would have implanted in men a belief in divine capability of doing good and harm, if they did not have that power, and that men have been deceived for all eternity and would never have realised it? Don't you see that the most enduring and enlightened of human establishments, I mean cities and nations, are the most reverent and that the most intelligent generations are those most devoted to the gods? 17. You must realise, my good friend,' he continued, 'that your mind within you directs your body as it wishes; so you must also think that the intelligence in the universe arranges everything as it pleases; nor must you believe that, though your eye can see for several miles, the eye of God cannot see everything simultaneously, and that, though your spirit can reflect upon matters here and in Egypt and in Sicily, the intelligence of God is incapable of taking care of all matters simultaneously. 18. Suppose, however, that you test out the gods by serving them to see whether they will consent to advise you on matters obscure to mankind, just as by serving humans you discover those willing to serve you in return and by favourable

τῶν ἀδήλων ἀνθρώποις συμβουλεύειν, γνώσει τὸ θεῖον ὅτι
τοσοῦτον καὶ τοιοῦτόν ἐστιν ὥσθ' ἅμα πάντα ὁρᾶν καὶ πάντα
ἀκούειν καὶ πανταχοῦ παρεῖναι καὶ ἅμα πάντων ἐπιμελεῖ-
19 σθαι [αὐτούς]. ἐμοὶ μὲν οὖν ταῦτα λέγων οὐ μόνον τοὺς
συνόντας ἐδόκει ποιεῖν ὁπότε ὑπὸ τῶν ἀνθρώπων ὁρῷντο, 5
ἀπέχεσθαι τῶν ἀνοσίων τε καὶ ἀδίκων καὶ αἰσχρῶν, ἀλλὰ
καὶ ὁπότε ἐν ἐρημίᾳ εἶεν, ἐπείπερ ἡγήσαιντο μηδὲν ἄν ποτε
ὧν πράττοιεν θεοὺς διαλαθεῖν.

V Εἰ δὲ δὴ καὶ ἐγκράτεια καλόν τε κἀγαθὸν ἀνδρὶ κτῆμά
ἐστιν, ἐπισκεψώμεθα εἴ τι προυβίβαζε λέγων εἰς ταύτην 10
τοιάδε· Ὦ ἄνδρες, εἰ πολέμου ἡμῖν γενομένου βουλοίμεθα
ἑλέσθαι ἄνδρα, ὑφ' οὗ μάλιστ' ἂν αὐτοὶ μὲν σῳζοίμεθα,
τοὺς δὲ πολεμίους χειροίμεθα, ἆρ' ὅντινα ἂν αἰσθανοίμεθα
ἥττω γαστρὸς ἢ οἴνου ἢ ἀφροδισίων ἢ πόνου ἢ ὕπνου, τοῦτον ἂν αἱροίμεθα; καὶ πῶς ἂν οἰηθείημεν τὸν τοιοῦτον ἢ 15
2 ἡμᾶς σῶσαι ἢ τοὺς πολεμίους κρατῆσαι; εἰ δ' ἐπὶ τελευτῇ
τοῦ βίου γενόμενοι βουλοίμεθά τῳ ἐπιτρέψαι ἢ παῖδας ἄρρε-
νας παιδεῦσαι ἢ θυγατέρας παρθένους διαφυλάξαι ἢ χρήματα
* διασῶσαι, ἆρ' ἀξιόπιστον εἰς ταῦθ' ἡγησόμεθα τὸν ἀκρατῆ; *
δούλῳ δ' ἀκρατεῖ ἐπιτρέψαιμεν ἂν ἢ βοσκήματα ἢ ταμιεῖα ἢ 20
* ἔργων ἐπίστασιν; διάκονον δὲ καὶ ἀγοραστὴν τοιοῦτον *
3 ἐθελήσαιμεν ἂν προῖκα λαβεῖν; ἀλλὰ μὴν εἴ γε μηδὲ δοῦλον
ἀκρατῆ δεξαίμεθ' ἄν, πῶς οὐκ ἄξιον αὐτόν γε φυλάξασθαι
τοιοῦτον γενέσθαι; καὶ γὰρ οὐχ ὥσπερ οἱ πλεονέκται τῶν
ἄλλων ἀφαιρούμενοι χρήματα ἑαυτοὺς δοκοῦσι πλουτίζειν, 25
οὕτως ὁ ἀκρατὴς τοῖς μὲν ἄλλοις βλαβερός, ἑαυτῷ δ' ὠφέλιμος, ἀλλὰ κακοῦργος μὲν τῶν ἄλλων, ἑαυτοῦ δὲ πολὺ
κακουργότερος, εἴ γε κακουργότατόν ἐστι μὴ μόνον τὸν οἶκον

---

4   αὐτοὺς β: αὐτὸ: del. Hindenburg
10   τι] πῃ Stob.
*19   ἡγησόμεθα nostri: ἡγησαίμεθ' ἂν Stob.
*21   ἐπιστασιν nostri: ἐπιστασίαν Stob.:   *τὸν τοιοῦτον Ath., Stob.
21–22 διάκονον … λαβεῖν citat Athenaeus, 171a

treatment those who repay favours, and by asking advice you recognise the man with intelligence; then, by so doing, you'll learn that the divine is so mighty and its nature such that it sees and hears all things simultaneously, is present everywhere and takes care of all things simultaneously.'
19. Therefore it was my personal opinion that, by talking like that, Socrates made his companions refrain from impious, unjust and base conduct, not only when they were in human view, but also when they were alone, because they thought that none of their actions could escape the notice of the gods.

Chapter 5. If indeed self-control is something fine and good for a man to possess, let us consider whether Socrates brought people closer to it by conversation of the following sort:
'Gentlemen, if we were to be at war and wanted to choose a man best able to save ourselves and subdue the enemy, would we choose any man we could see to be unable to resist gluttony, drunkenness, lechery, toil or sleep? How could we imagine that such a fellow would save us or conquer the enemy?
2. If we were to be at death's door and wanted to entrust someone with the education of our sons, the safeguarding of our unmarried daughters, or the preservation of our property, would we consider the man lacking self-control trustworthy for these purposes? Would we entrust a slave lacking self-control with livestock, stores or the supervision of work in progress? Would we accept even as a free gift a fellow like that to serve us and buy for us? 3. Indeed, if we would reject a mere slave lacking self-control, surely it is proper to guard against becoming like that oneself. For, unlike unscrupulous money-grubbers who seem to enrich themselves by depriving others of their property, the man lacking self-control, though harming others, does not benefit himself; rather does he combine damage to others with much greater damage to himself, if at least the most harmful thing of all is to destroy not

τὸν ἑαυτοῦ φθείρειν, ἀλλὰ καὶ τὸ σῶμα καὶ τὴν ψυχήν· ἐν 4
συνουσίᾳ δὲ τίς ἂν ἡσθείη τῷ τοιούτῳ, ὃν εἰδείη τῷ ὄψῳ τε
καὶ τῷ οἴνῳ χαίροντα μᾶλλον ἢ τοῖς φίλοις καὶ τὰς πόρνας
ἀγαπῶντα μᾶλλον ἢ τοὺς ἑταίρους; ἆρά γε οὐ χρὴ πάντα
5 ἄνδρα, ἡγησάμενον τὴν ἐγκράτειαν ἀρετῆς εἶναι κρηπῖδα,
ταύτην πρῶτον ἐν τῇ ψυχῇ κατασκευάσασθαι; τίς γὰρ ἄνευ 5
ταύτης ἢ μάθοι τι ἂν ἀγαθὸν ἢ μελετήσειεν ἀξιολόγως; ἢ
τίς οὐκ ἂν ταῖς ἡδοναῖς δουλεύων αἰσχρῶς διατεθείη καὶ τὸ
σῶμα καὶ τὴν ψυχήν; ἐμοὶ μὲν δοκεῖ νὴ τὴν "Ηραν ἐλευ-
10 θέρῳ μὲν ἀνδρὶ εὐκτὸν εἶναι μὴ τυχεῖν δούλου τοιούτου,
δουλεύοντι δὲ ταῖς τοιαύταις ἡδοναῖς ἱκετευτέον τοὺς θεοὺς
δεσποτῶν ἀγαθῶν τυχεῖν· οὕτω γὰρ ἂν μόνως ὁ τοιοῦτος
σωθείη. τοιαῦτα δὲ λέγων ἔτι ἐγκρατέστερον τοῖς ἔργοις 6
ἢ τοῖς λόγοις ἑαυτὸν ἐπεδείκνυεν· οὐ γὰρ μόνον τῶν διὰ
15 τοῦ σώματος ἡδονῶν ἐκράτει, ἀλλὰ καὶ τῆς διὰ τῶν χρημάτων, νομίζων τὸν παρὰ τοῦ τυχόντος χρήματα λαμβάνοντα
δεσπότην ἑαυτοῦ καθιστάναι καὶ δουλεύειν δουλείαν οὐδεμιᾶς
ἧττον αἰσχράν.

Ἄξιον δ' αὐτοῦ καὶ ἃ πρὸς Ἀντιφῶντα τὸν σοφιστὴν VI
20 διελέχθη μὴ παραλιπεῖν. ὁ γὰρ Ἀντιφῶν ποτε βουλόμενος
τοὺς συνουσιαστὰς αὐτοῦ παρελέσθαι προσελθὼν τῷ Σωκράτει παρόντων αὐτῶν ἔλεξε τάδε· Ὦ Σώκρατες, ἐγὼ μὲν 2
ᾤμην τοὺς φιλοσοφοῦντας εὐδαιμονεστέρους χρῆναι γίγνε-
σθαι· σὺ δέ μοι δοκεῖς τἀναντία τῆς φιλοσοφίας ἀπολελαυ-
25 κέναι. ζῇς γοῦν οὕτως ὡς οὐδ' ἂν εἷς δοῦλος ὑπὸ δεσπότῃ
διαιτώμενος μείνειε· σιτία τε σιτῇ καὶ ποτὰ πίνεις τὰ φαυ-
λότατα, καὶ ἱμάτιον ἠμφίεσαι οὐ μόνον φαῦλον, ἀλλὰ τὸ
αὐτὸ θέρους τε καὶ χειμῶνος, ἀνυπόδητός τε καὶ ἀχίτων
διατελεῖς. καὶ μὴν χρήματά γε οὐ λαμβάνεις, ἃ καὶ κτω- 3
30 μένους εὐφραίνει καὶ κεκτημένους ἐλευθεριώτερόν τε καὶ

---

6   πρώτην Stob.
7   ἂν om. AB Stob.: ante ἄνευ trs. Cobet
11   δουλεύοντι B Stob.: δουλεύοντα ΑΦ # ἱκετευτέον Stob.: ἱκετεύειν β: ἱκέτευον A
14   ἀπεδείκνυεν B
26   σῖτά A

only one's household but also one's body and soul. 4. Who in his associations would find pleasure in men like that, whom he knew to take more delight in his food and drink than in his friends and have more affection for the harlots than his companions? Ought not everyone to consider self-control the basis of virtue and before anything else to establish it in his soul? 5. For who without this could learn anything good or practise it creditably? Or what man enslaved by his pleasures would not suffer degradation of body and soul? In my opinion, by Hera, a free man ought to pray not to land up with a slave like that and anyone enslaved by such pleasures should entreat the gods that he may find good masters; for only in that way would such a man achieve salvation.' 6. Though he talked like that, he showed himself to have even more self-control in his actions than in his words. For not only did he have mastery over the pleasures that come from the body but also over the one that comes from money, for he thought that the man who takes money from anyone who comes along sets up a master over himself and is subjected to the most disgraceful sort of slavery.

Chapter 6. It is also fair to Socrates not to omit his conversations with Antiphon the Sophist; for on one occasion Antiphon, wishing to steal Socrates' companions for himself, approached Socrates in their presence, and had this to say:

2. 'Socrates, my opinion was that those who are philosophers ought thereby to become happier, but you seem to me to have derived the very opposite benefits from philosophy; at any rate you seem to have a life-style that no slave living in subjection to a master would put up with and stay; your food and drink are of the poorest quality, your cloak is not only poor but unchanged summer and winter and you never wear shoes or a tunic. 3. Moreover, you don't accept money, something that gladdens its recipients and ensures its

ἥδιον ποιεῖ ζῆν. εἰ οὖν ὥσπερ καὶ τῶν ἄλλων ἔργων οἱ
διδάσκαλοι τοὺς μαθητὰς μιμητὰς ἑαυτῶν ἀποδεικνύουσιν,
οὕτω καὶ σὺ τοὺς συνόντας διαθήσεις, νόμιζε κακοδαιμονίας
4 διδάσκαλος εἶναι. καὶ ὁ Σωκράτης πρὸς ταῦτα εἶπε· Δοκεῖς
μοι, ὦ 'Αντιφῶν, ὑπειληφέναι με οὕτως ἀνιαρῶς ζῆν, ὥστε 5
πέπεισμαι σὲ μᾶλλον ἀποθανεῖν ἂν ἑλέσθαι ἢ ζῆν ὥσπερ
ἐγώ. ἴθι οὖν ἐπισκεψώμεθα τί χαλεπὸν ᾔσθησαι τοῦ ἐμοῦ
5 βίου. πότερον ὅτι τοῖς μὲν λαμβάνουσιν ἀργύριον ἀναγ-
καῖόν ἐστιν ἀπεργάζεσθαι τοῦτο ἐφ' ᾧ ἂν μισθὸν λάβωσιν,
ἐμοὶ δὲ μὴ λαμβάνοντι οὐκ ἀνάγκη διαλέγεσθαι ᾧ ἂν μὴ 10
βούλωμαι; ἢ τὴν δίαιτάν μου φαυλίζεις ὡς ἧττον μὲν ὑγιεινὰ
ἐσθίοντος ἐμοῦ ἢ σοῦ, ἧττον δὲ ἰσχὺν παρέχοντα; ἢ ὡς
χαλεπώτερα πορίσασθαι τὰ ἐμὰ διαιτήματα τῶν σῶν διὰ τὸ
σπανιώτερά τε καὶ πολυτελέστερα εἶναι; ἢ ὡς ἡδίω σοι ἃ
σὺ παρασκευάζῃ ὄντα ἢ ἐμοὶ ἃ ἐγώ; οὐκ οἶσθ' ὅτι ὁ μὲν 15
ἥδιστα ἐσθίων ἥκιστα ὄψου δεῖται, ὁ δὲ ἥδιστα πίνων ἥκιστα
6 τοῦ μὴ παρόντος ἐπιθυμεῖ ποτοῦ; τά γε μὴν ἱμάτια οἶσθ' ὅτι
οἱ μεταβαλλόμενοι ψύχους καὶ θάλπους ἕνεκα μεταβάλλον-
ται, καὶ ὑποδήματα ὑποδοῦνται, ὅπως μὴ διὰ τὰ λυποῦντα
τοὺς πόδας κωλύωνται πορεύεσθαι· ἤδη οὖν ποτε ᾔσθου 20
ἐμὲ ἢ διὰ ψῦχος μᾶλλόν του ἔνδον μένοντα, ἢ διὰ θάλπος
μαχόμενόν τῳ περὶ σκιᾶς, ἢ διὰ τὸ ἀλγεῖν τοὺς πόδας οὐ
7 βαδίζοντα ὅπου ἂν βούλωμαι; οὐκ οἶσθ' ὅτι οἱ φύσει ἀσθε-
νέστατοι τῷ σώματι μελετήσαντες τῶν ἰσχυροτάτων ἀμελη-
σάντων κρείττους τε γίγνονται πρὸς ἃ ἂν μελετῶσι καὶ ῥᾷον 25
αὐτὰ φέρουσιν; ἐμὲ δὲ ἄρα οὐκ οἴει, τῷ σώματι ἀεὶ τὰ
συντυγχάνοντα μελετῶντα καρτερεῖν, πάντα ῥᾷον φέρειν σοῦ
8 μὴ μελετῶντος; τοῦ δὲ μὴ δουλεύειν γαστρὶ μηδ' ὕπνῳ καὶ
λαγνείᾳ οἴει τι ἄλλο αἰτιώτερον εἶναι ἢ τὸ ἕτερα ἔχειν τούτων ἡδίω, ἃ οὐ μόνον ἐν χρείᾳ ὄντα εὐφραίνει, ἀλλὰ καὶ 30

17   οὐκ οἶσθ' ...; A
23   ὅποι Dindorf

possessors a more independent and pleasant life. If, therefore, you follow the practice of teachers of other occupations who make their disciples copy themselves and have a similar effect on your companions, you must consider yourself a teacher of misery.'

4. In reply to this Socrates said: 'You seem to me, Antiphon, to have assumed my life is so miserable that I am convinced you would rather die than live as I do. So come now, let us consider what hardship you have observed in my life. 5. Is it because, whereas those who receive money must complete any work for which they are paid, I, as I don't receive money, am under no compulsion to talk with anyone against my will? Or do you disparage my life-style on the grounds that my food is less healthy and nutritious than yours? Or on the grounds that my victuals are harder to come by than yours, as being rarer and more expensive? Or because you think that your provisions are pleasanter to you than mine to me? Don't you know that the person who most enjoys his food is in least need of a relish, and that the one most enjoying his drink has the least desire for drink that isn't there? 6. Furthermore, you are well aware that those who change their cloaks do so because of cold or heat, and that they wear shoes so as not to be impeded in their progress by things that hurt their feet. Well, have you ever to this day seen me remain indoors because of cold more than anyone else or because of heat fight with anyone for shade or be stopped by sore feet from going anywhere I want? 7. Don't you know that those, who are weakest naturally, by physical training become better at any exercises they practise in training and find them easier to undergo than the strongest of men, if they have neglected to train? Doesn't that, then, apply to me? Don't you think that I who am always training my body to endure whatever befalls me can bear anything at all more easily than you, if you don't train? 8. Do you think there is anything better for avoiding slavery to gluttony, sleepiness and lust than having more enjoyable alternatives which give pleasure not only by being available for use but also by providing hopes

ἐλπίδας παρέχοντα ὠφελήσειν ἀεί; καὶ μὴν τοῦτό γε οἶσθα,
ὅτι οἱ μὲν οἰόμενοι μηδὲν εὖ πράττειν οὐκ εὐφραίνονται, οἱ
δὲ ἡγούμενοι καλῶς προχωρεῖν ἑαυτοῖς ἢ γεωργίαν ἢ ναυκλη-
ρίαν ἢ ἄλλ᾽ ὅ τι ἂν τυγχάνωσιν ἐργαζόμενοι ὡς εὖ πράτ-
5 τοντες εὐφραίνονται. οἴει οὖν ἀπὸ πάντων τούτων τοσαύτην 9
ἡδονὴν εἶναι ὅσην ἀπὸ τοῦ ἑαυτόν τε ἡγεῖσθαι βελτίω
γίγνεσθαι καὶ φίλους ἀμείνους κτᾶσθαι; ἐγὼ τοίνυν διατελῶ
ταῦτα νομίζων. ἐὰν δὲ δὴ φίλους ἢ πόλιν ὠφελεῖν δέῃ,
ποτέρῳ ἡ πλείων σχολὴ τούτων ἐπιμελεῖσθαι, τῷ ὡς ἐγὼ
10 νῦν ἢ τῷ ὡς σὺ μακαρίζεις διαιτωμένῳ; στρατεύοιτο δὲ
πότερος ἂν ῥᾷον, ὁ μὴ δυνάμενος ἄνευ πολυτελοῦς διαίτης
ζῆν ἢ ᾧ τὸ παρὸν ἀρκοίη; ἐκπολιορκηθείη δὲ πότερος ἂν
θᾶττον, ὁ τῶν χαλεπωτάτων εὑρεῖν δεόμενος ἢ ὁ τοῖς
ῥᾴστοις ἐντυγχάνειν ἀρκούντως χρώμενος; ἔοικας, ὦ ᾽Αντι- 10
15 φῶν, τὴν εὐδαιμονίαν οἰομένῳ τρυφὴν καὶ πολυτέλειαν εἶναι·
ἐγὼ δὲ νομίζω τὸ μὲν μηδενὸς δεῖσθαι θεῖον εἶναι, τὸ δ᾽ ὡς
ἐλαχίστων ἐγγυτάτω τοῦ θείου, καὶ τὸ μὲν θεῖον κράτιστον,
τὸ δ᾽ ἐγγυτάτω τοῦ θείου ἐγγυτάτω τοῦ κρατίστου.

Πάλιν δέ ποτε ὁ ᾽Αντιφῶν διαλεγόμενος τῷ Σωκράτει 11
20 εἶπεν· ῏Ω Σώκρατες, ἐγώ τοί σε δίκαιον μὲν νομίζω, σοφὸν
δὲ οὐδ᾽ ὁπωστιοῦν· δοκεῖς δέ μοι καὶ αὐτὸς τοῦτο γιγνώσκειν·
οὐδένα γοῦν τῆς συνουσίας ἀργύριον πράττῃ. καίτοι τό γε
ἱμάτιον ἢ τὴν οἰκίαν ἢ ἄλλο τι ὧν κέκτησαι νομίζων ἀργυρίου ἄξιον εἶναι οὐδενὶ ἂν μὴ ὅτι προῖκα δοίης, ἀλλ᾽ οὐδ᾽
25 ἔλαττον τῆς ἀξίας λαβών. δῆλον δὴ ὅτι εἰ καὶ τὴν συνου- 12
σίαν ᾤου τινὸς ἀξίαν εἶναι, καὶ ταύτης ἂν οὐκ ἔλαττον τῆς
ἀξίας ἀργύριον ἐπράττου. δίκαιος μὲν οὖν ἂν εἴης, ὅτι οὐκ
ἐξαπατᾷς ἐπὶ πλεονεξίᾳ, σοφὸς δὲ οὐκ ἄν, μηδενός γε ἄξια
ἐπιστάμενος. ὁ δὲ Σωκράτης πρὸς ταῦτα εἶπεν· ῏Ω ᾽Αν- 13
30 τιφῶν, παρ᾽ ἡμῖν νομίζεται τὴν ὥραν καὶ τὴν σοφίαν ὁμοίως
μὲν καλόν, ὁμοίως δὲ αἰσχρὸν διατίθεσθαι εἶναι. τήν τε

9   ἢ om. Stob.
16   δὲ νομίζω Φ Stob.: δ᾽ ἐνόμιζον AB
22   γοῦν β: γὰρ A

that they will always be of benefit? Moreover, you *do* know that those who think themselves failures in everything they tackle are miserable, whereas those who think they are doing well in farming or shipping or any other activity, take pleasure from being successful in their work. 9. So do you think the pleasures gained from all those activities as great as that coming from thinking oneself to be improving and acquiring better friends? Well, that's what I for my part go on thinking.

Indeed, if friends or city must be helped, which of the two has more leisure to look after them – someone whose lifestyle is like mine today or someone enjoying your imagined bliss? Which of us would have less difficulty with military service – the one who cannot live without an expensive diet or the one satisfied with what's there? Which of us would more quickly succumb to a siege – the one needing the hardest things to find, or the one who does well enough with what's easiest to obtain? 10. You seem to think, Antiphon, that happiness consists in luxury and an expensive lifestyle, but I think that needing nothing is godlike, that needing as little as possible is closest to the godlike, that the godlike is best of all, and that the closest to the godlike is closest to the best of all.'

11. On another occasion in conversation with Socrates, Antiphon said: 'Socrates, I think you are just, but not at all wise, and I think you realise that yourself; for you don't charge anyone money for your company. However, if you thought your cloak or house or any other of your possessions to be worth money, far from giving them to anyone for nothing, you would not even do so for less than their value. 12. Indeed it's obvious that if you thought your company too to be worth anything, you'd charge the full monetary value for that also. So that would make you a just man for not deceiving for a profit, but not a wise one, seeing that your knowledge is worthless.' 13. In reply to this Socrates said: 'Antiphon, amongst us the same views are usually held about the bestowal upon others both of one's beauty and of one's wisdom, when judging whether it be honourable or disgraceful. For, if anyone sells

γὰρ ὥραν ἐὰν μέν τις ἀργυρίου πωλῇ τῷ βουλομένῳ, πόρνον
αὐτὸν ἀποκαλοῦσιν, ἐὰν δέ τις, ὃν ἂν γνῷ καλόν τε κἀγαθὸν
ἐραστὴν ὄντα, τοῦτον φίλον ἑαυτῷ ποιῆται, σώφρονα νομί-
ζομεν· καὶ τὴν σοφίαν ὡσαύτως τοὺς μὲν ἀργυρίου τῷ
βουλομένῳ πωλοῦντας σοφιστὰς [ὥσπερ πόρνους] ἀποκα- 5
λοῦσιν, ὅστις δὲ ὃν ἂν γνῷ εὐφυᾶ ὄντα διδάσκων ὅ τι ἂν
ἔχῃ ἀγαθὸν φίλον ποιεῖται, τοῦτον νομίζομεν, ἃ τῷ καλῷ
14 κἀγαθῷ πολίτῃ προσήκει, ταῦτα ποιεῖν. ἐγὼ δ' οὖν καὶ
αὐτός, ὦ 'Αντιφῶν, ὥσπερ ἄλλος τις ἢ ἵππῳ ἀγαθῷ ἢ κυνὶ
ἢ ὄρνιθι ἥδεται, οὕτω καὶ ἔτι μᾶλλον ἥδομαι φίλοις ἀγαθοῖς, 10
καὶ ἐάν τι ἔχω ἀγαθόν, διδάσκω, καὶ ἄλλοις συνίστημι παρ'
ὧν ἂν ἡγῶμαι ὠφελήσεσθαί τι αὐτοὺς εἰς ἀρετήν· καὶ τοὺς
θησαυροὺς τῶν πάλαι σοφῶν ἀνδρῶν, οὓς ἐκεῖνοι κατέλιπον
ἐν βιβλίοις γράψαντες, ἀνελίττων κοινῇ σὺν τοῖς φίλοις
διέρχομαι, καὶ ἄν τι ὁρῶμεν ἀγαθὸν ἐκλεγόμεθα· καὶ μέγα 15
νομίζομεν κέρδος, ἐὰν ἀλλήλοις φίλοι γιγνώμεθα. ἐμοὶ
μὲν δὴ ταῦτα ἀκούοντι ἐδόκει αὐτός τε μακάριος εἶναι καὶ
τοὺς ἀκούοντας ἐπὶ καλοκἀγαθίαν ἄγειν.

15 Καὶ πάλιν ποτὲ τοῦ 'Αντιφῶντος ἐρομένου αὐτόν, πῶς
ἄλλους μὲν ἡγεῖται πολιτικοὺς ποιεῖν, αὐτὸς δ' οὐ πράττει 20
τὰ πολιτικά, εἴπερ ἐπίσταται· Ποτέρως δ' ἄν, ἔφη, ὦ 'Αντιφῶν, μᾶλλον τὰ πολιτικὰ πράττοιμι, εἰ μόνος αὐτὰ πράττοιμι ἢ εἰ ἐπιμελοίμην τοῦ ὡς πλείστους ἱκανοὺς εἶναι
πράττειν αὐτά;

VII Ἐπισκεψώμεθα δὲ εἰ καὶ ἀλαζονείας ἀποτρέπων τοὺς 25
συνόντας ἀρετῆς ἐπιμελεῖσθαι προέτρεπεν· ἀεὶ γὰρ ἔλεγεν
ὡς οὐκ εἴη καλλίων ὁδὸς ἐπ' εὐδοξίαν ἢ δι' ἧς ἄν τις
ἀγαθὸς τοῦτο γένοιτο, ⟨ὃ⟩ καὶ δοκεῖν βούλοιτο. ὅτι δ'
2 ἀληθῆ ἔλεγεν, ὧδ' ἐδίδασκεν· Ἐνθυμώμεθα γάρ, ἔφη, εἰ

5   ὥσπερ πόρνους del. Ruhnken
12 ὠφεληθήσεσθαι A
28 ὃ add. Brodaeus

his beauty for money to a willing purchaser, they call him a prostitute, but, if someone makes a personal friend of anyone he knows to be a perfect man in love with him, we think him a man of character. It's the same with wisdom; those who sell it for money to a willing buyer, they call sophists, whereas the person who befriends anyone he discovers to be naturally gifted, by teaching him everything good he can, we think to be acting as the perfect man and citizen should. 14. In any case for my own part, Antiphon, just as anyone else delights in a good horse or hound or bird, I take still more delight in good friends, and teach them anything of benefit at my disposal and introduce them to others from whom I think they will gain help towards virtuous conduct; and along with my friends I unroll and go through the treasure stores of the sages of old, which they have written down and left in books, and we pick out anything good we see and think it great gain, if we prove helpful to one another.'

As I listened to these words, it seemed to me that he was really fortunate himself and was guiding his listeners towards becoming perfect men.
15. On another occasion, when Antiphon asked him how he could think he was making others into politicians, though himself avoiding politics, if indeed he had any knowledge of the subject, Socrates said: 'In which way, Antiphon, could I be more active in politics – by taking part on my own or by trying to produce the greatest possible number of competent politicians?'

Chapter 7. Let us consider whether by discouraging his companions from imposture he also encouraged them to pursue goodness. For he would always say there was no better route to a fine reputation than that by which one would become good in the area in which one wished to be thought good. This is how he would teach the truth of his words:
2. 'Let us consider what would have to be done by anyone wishing to be

τις μὴ ὢν ἀγαθὸς αὐλητὴς δοκεῖν βούλοιτο, τί ἂν αὐτῷ
ποιητέον εἴη. ἆρ' οὐ τὰ ἔξω τῆς τέχνης μιμητέον τοὺς
ἀγαθοὺς αὐλητάς; καὶ πρῶτον μέν, ὅτι ἐκεῖνοι σκεύη τε
καλὰ κέκτηνται καὶ ἀκολούθους πολλοὺς περιάγονται, καὶ
5 τούτῳ ταῦτα ποιητέον· ἔπειτα, ὅτι ἐκείνους πολλοὶ ἐπαι-
νοῦσι, καὶ τούτῳ πολλοὺς ἐπαινέτας παρασκευαστέον. ἀλλὰ
μὴν ἔργον γε οὐδαμοῦ ληπτέον, ἢ εὐθὺς ἐλεγχθήσεται γε-
λοῖος ὢν καὶ οὐ μόνον αὐλητὴς κακός, ἀλλὰ καὶ ἄνθρωπος
ἀλαζών. καίτοι πολλὰ μὲν δαπανῶν, μηδὲν δ' ὠφελούμενος,
10 πρὸς δὲ τούτοις κακοδοξῶν, πῶς οὐκ ἐπιπόνως τε καὶ ἀλυ-
σιτελῶς καὶ καταγελάστως βιώσεται; ὡς δ' αὔτως εἴ τις 3
βούλοιτο στρατηγὸς ἀγαθὸς μὴ ὢν φαίνεσθαι ἢ κυβερνήτης,
ἐννοῶμεν τί ἂν αὐτῷ συμβαίνοι. ἆρ' οὐκ ἄν, εἰ μὲν
ἐπιθυμῶν τοῦ δοκεῖν ἱκανὸς εἶναι ταῦτα πράττειν μὴ δύναιτο
15 πείθειν, τοῦτ' εἴη λυπηρόν, εἰ δὲ πείσειεν, ἔτι ἀθλιώτερον;
δῆλον γὰρ ὅτι κυβερνᾶν κατασταθεὶς ὁ μὴ ἐπιστάμενος ἢ
στρατηγεῖν ἀπολέσειεν ἂν οὓς ἥκιστα βούλοιτο καὶ αὐτὸς
αἰσχρῶς ἂν καὶ κακῶς ἀπαλλάξειεν. ὡσαύτως δὲ καὶ τὸ 4
πλούσιον καὶ τὸ ἀνδρεῖον καὶ τὸ ἰσχυρὸν μὴ ὄντα δοκεῖν
20 ἀλυσιτελὲς ἀπέφαινε· προστάττεσθαι γὰρ αὐτοῖς ἔφη μείζω
ἢ κατὰ δύναμιν, καὶ μὴ δυναμένους ταῦτα ποιεῖν, δοκοῦντας
ἱκανοὺς εἶναι, συγγνώμης οὐκ ἂν τυγχάνειν. ἀπατεῶνα δ' 5
ἐκάλει οὐ μικρὸν μὲν οὐδ' εἴ τις ἀργύριον ἢ σκεῦος παρά
του πειθοῖ λαβὼν ἀποστεροίη, πολὺ δὲ μέγιστον ὅστις
25 μηδενὸς ἄξιος ὢν ἐξηπατήκοι πείθων ὡς ἱκανὸς εἴη τῆς
πόλεως ἡγεῖσθαι. ἐμοὶ μὲν οὖν ἐδόκει καὶ τοῦ ἀλαζονεύεσθαι
ἀποτρέπειν τοὺς συνόντας τοιάδε διαλεγόμενος.

3–4   σκευήν τε καλήν Cobet
15   τοῦτ' εἴη Heindorf: ταύτῃ codd.
23   οὐδ' del. Ruhnken
25   ἐξαπατήκει codd.: corr. Weiske

thought a good pipe-player, though a bad one. Would he not have to copy the good players in the details external to the art? In the first place, because they have acquired fine equipment and travel with a large entourage, he must do the same; secondly, because they are applauded by many, he too must lay on for himself a large claque. He must, however, not accept any engagement anywhere or he will immediately be exposed as ridiculous and not only as a bad player, but also a charlatan. Nevertheless, if he incurs great expense but gains no benefit and a poor reputation to boot, won't his life be laborious, profitless and utterly ridiculous? 3. Similarly let us consider what would happen to anyone wanting to appear to be a good general or helmsman, though a bad one. Wouldn't he suffer misery, if, though eager to be thought competent in the activity, he couldn't persuade others of his competence? And wouldn't he be even more miserable, if he *could* convince them of that? For clearly the man who didn't know how to pilot a ship or to command an army, though appointed to do so, would bring ruin upon those for whom he least wished it, and also incur personal disgrace and misfortune.'

4. Likewise he would prove that there was no profit in being thought rich or brave or strong, if one wasn't so. For he would say that tasks beyond their powers were being given to such people and if they could not perform them, though apparently competent, they would not be forgiven. 5. The man who persuaded anyone to part with money or goods and deprived him of either he would call no small cheat; but to him far the greatest cheat was the man who, though worthless, had practised deception by persuading others he was competent to direct the state.

Therefore my opinion was that, by talking like that, he also discouraged false pretensions in his companions.

COMMENTARY ON *MEMORABILIA SOCRATIS* BOOK I

TITLE As the Latin word *Memorabilia* is now part of the English language, it seems a better translation than *Memoirs of Socrates*, which tends to suggest autobiography. An alternative title in English might be *Memories of Socrates*. Note the similarity of the title *apomnêmoneumata*, with *axion... memnêsthai, Ap.* 1 and *axiomnêmoneuta, Smp.* 1.; see note on *Ap.* 1. This time Xenophon doesn't start by justifying his choice of subject, though he does immediately use the adjective *axios* in protesting that Socrates was not deserving of death.

CHAPTERS 1, 2.1–2.7
Xenophon's personal rejection of the charges against Socrates, often using or adapting what in his *Ap.* he reports Socrates as saying in his own defence.

Chapter 1.1 *I have often wondered: cf. Ap.* 11 where Socrates expresses surprise at the accusations. Xenophon often expresses his own surprise at things of which he disapproves.

something like this: Xenophon's version of the charges is in fact almost identical with the officially recorded one; see note on *Ap.* 10.

worshipping: on the meaning of *nomizô* see note on *Ap.* 10.

new: translating *καινὰ*, see note on *Ap.* 10.

divinities: translating *δαιμόνια*, which the accusers took as a neuter plural noun, whereas Xenophon's Socrates in *Ap.* and Xenophon here and elsewhere in *Mem.* probably took *daimonion* as a neuter adjective; see note on 'my divine sign' in *Ap.* 4.

2–4 See notes on *Ap.* 11–13, where we have very similar material and arguments, though there they are ascribed to Socrates himself.

2 *his divine sign communicated with him:* a more literal translation of τὸ δαιμόνιον ... σημαίνειν might be 'his divine thing gave him signals'; see notes on 'divinities' just above and on σημεῖον *Ap.* 4.

3 *practise:* translating νομίζοντες practise or regard as customary in accordance with *nomos*; see note on *Ap.* 10. An alternative translation might be 'respect'.

4 *to do some things:* here and elsewhere Xenophon differs from Plato in suggesting that the *daimonion* could give positive instructions, but he gives no specific examples.

5 *and mistaken:* Marchant in his Loeb deletes καὶ on poor ms. authority, taking only ψευδόμενος with ἐφαίνετο.

an impostor: Socrates and Chaerephon had been called *alazonas* (impostors) by Pheidippides in Aristophanes *Clouds* 102. See note on imposture at 1.7.1.

believe in their existence: irrelevant; Socrates was not being accused of atheism.

7 *estates:* οἶκοι could simply refer to urban households or be used in a wider sense of rural estates, undoubtedly Xenophon's meaning here, in view of his upbringing at Erchia and his own estate at Scillous, and the subject of his later work *Oeconomicus*.

the extra help of divination: cf. the similar arguments of *Oec.* 5. 19–20 (presumably a later passage re-using material from here) where Xenophon makes Socrates say that sensible farmers use sacrifices and omens for divine guidance as to what to do and what not to do. Probably Xenophon ascribes to Socrates rather more of his own interest in οἰκονομία, managing a household or estate, than he actually had. *Cf.* Plato, *Ap.* 35b.

9 *possessed and mad:* translating δαιμονᾶν = 'to be under the influence of an evil spirit'; *cf.* κακοδαιμονῶντος, 2.1.5., where the implied meaning is to be utterly mad.

10 *covered walks...training areas:* thus of Plato's Socratic dialogues, *Euthyphro* is set in a stoa, and *Charmides*, *Laches*, and *Lysis* in *palaistrai*, wrestling grounds.

11 *he did not discuss the nature of the universe...heavenly phenomena:* Xenophon agrees with Plato, *Ap.* 18b, 19c in expressly rejecting the portrayal of Socrates in *Clouds* as a *ta meteôra phrontistês*, a student of the heavenly bodies, and interested in cosmology, the workings of nature and causation. In *Mem.* 4.7.5 Xenophon's Socrates admits he had heard about these things, or, if Marchant's interpretation is right, had attended lectures on these subjects. In *Phaedo* 96a ff. Plato's Socrates recalls how once he had been a tremendously enthusiastic inquirer into nature, causation and *ta peri ton ouranon kai tên gên pathê*, the phenomena involving heaven and the earth, but finally realised he was unsuited for such studies, and goes on to describe his initial eagerness to hear Anaxagoras' explanations of such matters and his disappointment with them. Cicero, *Tusc.* 5.4.10 and Diogenes Laertius, 2.16, say that Socrates was a pupil of the natural philosopher Archelaus, himself a pupil of Anaxagoras. Moreover the representation of Socrates in *Clouds* as a student of *ta meteôra* would need to contain some grains of truth to achieve comic effect with the audience, even if by 423, the date of the original *Clouds*, Socrates' interest in natural history was already over. Xenophon's 'he did not discuss' and the assertions of Plato's Socrates in *Ap.* 18b, 19c should be rejected as basically unhistorical; the two philosophers merely made Socrates talk, as they remembered him, viz. in his later years. Socrates had indeed once been something of a *physiologos*, a student of natural history, but these days were past. See Guthrie (2) 100–105.

the sophists: from the late fifth century onwards the term 'sophists' was particularly applied to Greeks from other cities who came to Athens to earn huge fees by public lectures and teaching politically ambitious young men many subjects but particularly rhetoric and the art of persuasion; see *Cyn.* 13 in this series, with Willcock's notes, for Xenophon's views on sophists of his day; I agree with Willcock that *Cyn.* (dated by him to *c.* 390) is indeed by Xenophon; note *e.g.*, how *Cyn.* starts with the typical Xenophontic expression of surprise, see note on *Mem.* 1.1.1, and stresses how sophists *oudena ouden ôphelousin*, are not of the slightest help or benefit to anyone; in other words they are the complete opposites of Xenophon's Socrates. The relevance of this chapter to *Cyn.* is that to Xenophon the sophists are hunters with rich young men as their quarries.

As, however, the leading sophists, with the possible exceptions of Prodikos and the polymath Hippias, showed little interest in cosmology *etc.*, Xenophon presumably here uses 'sophists' in a wider sense to include clever new thinkers such as Diogenes of Apollonia whose theories provided Aristophanes with material for *Clouds*, and Anaxagoras.

14 *didn't honour...anything connected with the gods:* Protagoras was an agnostic and Gorgias' assertion that nothing existed presumably included the gods. The most notorious atheist was Diagoras of Melos. Even the tragedian Euripides was portrayed by Aristophanes as an atheist, rather unfairly, though some of his characters talk like sceptical sophists. Theological rationalists included Critias, whose association with Socrates Xenophon is soon to play down in *Mem.*, and Prodikos, though he was approved of by both Xenophon, *Mem.* 2.1.21 ff. and Socrates himself, see Guthrie 1971(1) 275.

consisted of one single entity: the belief of the Eleatics, Parmenides, Zeno and Melissus, as by Xenophanes before them, *cf.* Plato *Sph.* 242d.

of infinitely many components: this refers particularly to the belief of the atomists, Democritus and Leucippus.

thought that all things were in perpetual motion: perhaps referring to Heraclitus of an earlier generation, to the more recent Empedocles, and more loosely to the atomists.

that nothing could ever move: again referring more particularly to the Eleatics.

that all things come into being and pass away: again referring mainly to Heraclitus and Empedocles.

nothing could ever be born or perish: again referring mainly to the Eleatics.

16 In this section Xenophon stresses a vital Socratic feature, his interest in definitions, *cf.* Aristotle, *Metaph.* 1078 b 27, particularly of moral concepts; thereby he counters the subjectivity of sophists like Protagoras, though Plato was to go further with his Ideal Theory, giving his Forms independent and unchanging existence. In *Mem.* 4.6 Xenophon reworks this chapter, elaborating on its material.

would always discuss human matters: Cicero, who greatly admired Xenophon, goes further and says, *Tusc.* 5.4.10, *cf. Acad.* 1.4.15, that Socrates was the *first* to call philosophy 'down from the skies'; by and large this is acceptable, though Protagoras had made man 'the measure' and, if we accept Diogenes Laertius 2.16, Socrates' teacher Archelaus was interested in ethics as well as natural philosophy.

piety: *cf.* 4.6.2–4, and Plato *Euthyphro.*

beauty...ugliness: *kalos* means 'beautiful', whether physically of morally or both, whereas *aischros* combines the connotations of physical ugliness and moral baseness; *cf.* 4.6.5, 9 and Plato *Smp.* 183d.

justice...injustice: *cf.* 4.6.5–6 and Plato *Republic* Book I (with perhaps Book 2 up to 368c) containing a Socratic examination of the nature of justice: the rest of *Republic* discussing justice on a larger scale, in a state, is to be regarded as Platonic rather than Socratic.

prudence...madness: *sôphrosynê* is the quality of being *sôphrôn*, literally 'safe-' (or 'sound-') 'minded'. Though here opposed to *mania*, madness, for Xenophon it includes, in addition to the meaning of 'wisdom' or 'good sense', the connotation of prudent moderation in controlling the pleasures of the flesh by being *enkratês* and having *enkrateia*, as discussed in 1.2 etc. *Sôphrosynê* is also the focal point of study in Plato *Charmides*. Xenophon, however, in his reworking of this chapter in 4.6.7, discusses not *sôphrosynê* but *sophia*, on which see notes on 1.4.2, 7.

the state...the ruler of men: cf. 4.6.12.

knowledge of which: for the importance to Xenophon's Socrates of knowledge as a factor in piety, justice and courage see 4.6.3–4, 6, 11. This agrees well with Plato's view of Socrates; see *e.g. Laches* 199d on the necessity of knowledge for *aretê* as a whole and for courage, *sôphrosynê*, justice and piety.

perfect men: *kaloskagathos* and *kalokagathia* are used passim by Xenophon in a highly complimentary sense for the qualities of the ideal man. On *kalos* see previous page. *Agathos* suggests possessing *aretê*, the admirable qualities that befit a proper man.

The combination of *kalos* and *agathos* in adjectival or noun form or in a verb occurs first in Herodotus, and is used by most writers including Plato, being mainly applied to upper class men, *cf.* Aristotle *Pol.* 1293 b 39. For Xenophon the essential components were piety, morality, courage, self-control, fortitude, prudence, wisdom, knowledge and the behaviour and generosity of spirit befitting a free man, the qualities possessed by the Socrates of *Mem.* and carefully described in elaborate detail in 4.8.11 by Xenophon in a final eulogy: see pp. 156*ff.* and Waterfield 2004. Ischomachos is also praised as a perfect man by Socrates in *Oec.* vi.12, see Pomeroy's note. Plato's Socrates, however, claims, *Ap.* 21d, to know nothing καλὸν κἀγαθὸν. For fuller treatment see H. Wankel, *Kalos kai agathos*, Würzburg, 1951.

18 on one occasion: at a meeting of the assembly in Athens in 406 B.*C.*, which resulted in one of its most outrageous and foolish decisions and a damning indictment of the whole Athenian democratic system, the decision to execute by a block vote all the generals, who had just won a great naval victory over the Peloponnesians at the battle of the Arginusae Islands off Lesbos, obtained during a desperate crisis for Athens by a scratch fleet, partly manned by slaves and metics. Unfortunately a storm blew up after the battle and most of the crew members of 25 crippled Athenian ships were lost. The task of picking up survivors may have been delegated by the generals to the trierarchs Theramenes and Thrasyllus on whom see below (*cf.* Xenophon *HG* 1.35 and a different account in Diodorus Siculus, 13.98 ff.), but in any case the generals were blamed in the assembly by many speakers including Theramenes. The matter, however, was deferred to the next meeting of the assembly after celebration of the Apaturia, a festival involving family reunions, so that emotions engendered by the loss of loved ones would have run even higher and exacerbated the anger against the generals for their use of a block vote. For Xenophon's account of the battle and its aftermath see *HG* 1.6–7 with Krentz's notes.

become a member of the Council: had been elected by lot to be one of the fifty men of his tribe to serve on the *boulê*, the council, the executive organ of the democracy, for the tenth part of the year allotted to his tribe; see note on 1.2.35.

become president: sc. just for that day. Here, as in *Mem.* 4.4.2, Xenophon expressly states that Socrates was president, whereas Plato in *Ap.* 32b makes Socrates simply refer to himself as the only one of the *prytaneis* (the fifty presiding Councillors) to oppose the bloc vote. Similarly in *HG* 1.7.15 Xenophon merely says that Socrates was the only *prytanis* to oppose a block vote. Cawkwell, 1979, 88–89 argues convincingly that Socrates was indeed president, but that Xenophon felt no need to say so, because readers knew that the president was in charge of putting the matter to the vote and that the uproar of Plato *Ap.* 32b only arose because Socrates was the only *prytanis* who really mattered then; *cf.* Plato *Grg.* 473e where, with a typical piece of irony, Socrates portrays himself as not knowing how to put the matter to the vote. Cawkwell further follows Pseudo-Plato *Axiochus* 368d in believing that the debate and decision were deferred to the day after Socrates' presidency.

all nine generals: the tenth general Conon was excluded, because he was elsewhere, being blockaded with his fleet in the harbour of Mytilene. Only eight generals in fact had been at Arginusae, *cf.* Xenophon *HG* 1.7.30, because one of them, Archestratus, had been with Conon at Mytilene and had died there; see Krentz on *HG* 1.5.16. Two of the eight were sensible enough not to return to Athens, but the other six including Thrasyllus and the younger Pericles were executed.

TEXT. I see no need to delete ἐννέα στρατηγούς with Schenkl or correct nine to ten or eight with Bandini. Generals must be mentioned and the numerical error may be due to Xenophon, despite *HG* 1.34, or more probably to the implied hotheadedness and ignorance of the assembly.

Thrasyllus: a prominent democrat, with Thrasybulus one of the leading opponents of the oligarchical revolution of 411.

Erasinides: probably a friend of the recently exiled Alcibiades; he had already been convicted by an Athenian jury for embezzlement and misconduct as a general and sent to prison even before the decision for his execution.

the gods are omniscient: *cf.* 1.4.18, *Cyr.* 1.6.46 *etc.*

send signs: *cf. Ap.* 13, *Mem.* 1.4.15, 4.3.12.

Chapter 1.2.1 **strongest... in controlling:** translating the superlative of the adjective ἐγκρατής, which means having power (κράτος) or control over oneself and the temptations of the flesh (food, drink, sexual urges *etc.*). Xenophon returns to the topic of Socrates' own *enkrateia* and his views on it in 1.3.5–15, 1.5, and in the long conversation with the hedonist Aristippus in 2.1. For Xenophon's views on the importance of *enkrateia* see note on 1.5.4.

steadfast in facing...winter: *cf.* Plato *Smp.* 219e ff. for Alcibiades' praise of Socrates' endurance when on campaign at Potidaea. The comic poet, Ameipsias, also called Socrates *karterikos* (hardy), though mocking his lack of shoes and a proper cloak, Diogenes Laertius 2.28.

was...satisfied with them: literally 'had what was sufficient'. In support of Reiske's conjecture, *cf. Cyr.* 8.2.21, *Smp.* 4.35.

2 perfect men: see note on 1.1.10.

4 the inner self: translating *psychê*.

5 *he would exact no payment:* see Plato *Ap.* 19e for Socrates' express rejection of this feature of the sophists and of his own caricatures in *Clouds.* See also Socrates' encounters with Antiphon the sophist, 1.6.3 ff.

6 *self-enslavers: cf. Ap.* 14, 16 for Xenophon's version of a Delphic tribute to his freedom of spirit and Socrates' own substantiation of the verdict.

those from whom they could take: ἂν λάβοιεν could be taken as potential, *cf.* Goodwin, § 557. There seems no need to follow Dindorf in deleting ἂν to restore the more normal indefinite construction in a relative clause in past sequence.

7 *a good friend:* for Socrates' views on friendship see 2.4–8 and Plato *Lysis.*

CHAPTER 2.9–2.61

Having rejected the charge made by Meletus, Anytus and Lycon at the actual trial, Xenophon now answers the charges made by a single, unnamed accuser, ὁ κατήγορος, that, 9–12, Socrates made his associates despise the laws, that, 12–48, he had been a bad influence on Critias and Alcibiades, that, 49–55, he had taught young men to have no respect for fathers, relatives and friends, and that, 56–61, he approved of immoral or antidemocratic passages in Homer and Hesiod. This individual is to be differentiated from any one of the three accusers at the actual trial, Meletus, Anytus or Lycon, and has been identified as the rhetorician Polycrates, who composed a rhetorical exercise accusing Socrates after the rebuilding of the Long Walls of Athens in 393, see Diogenes Laertius 2.39, and after the publication of Isocrates *Busiris,* see p. 13; for Polycrates see also Dodds, *Plato's Gorgias,* 28 ff.

9 *appoint the officials of the state by lot:* apart from the *stratēgoi* (the ten generals with military, naval and political duties), a few other top military men, and the *Hellēnotamiai* (Athenians chosen to control the finances of the Delian League), all magistrates were chosen by lot. Socrates disapproved because he believed that politics and civic administration needed knowledge and specialised skills, just as much as any other art or craft, *cf.* 3.6, where Socrates reproves Plato's brother Glaucon for having political ambitions without the necessary knowledge. In much the same way Socrates in Plato *Protagoras* 319d,e objects to the assembly's habit of listening to the political advice of anyone at all whatever his trade or profession.

12 *becoming associates...harmed:* note the dual forms referring to the pair of Critias and Alcibiades. The plural equivalents are ὁμιληταὶ γενόμενοι... ἐποίησαν. This is one of the rare passages in Greek literature with an extended use of the dual form. Whether Polycrates used the dual cannot be decided; more probably these are Xenophon's own words, as he goes on to show his expertise in duals throughout this passage. Perhaps the idea was suggested to Xenophon by Plato, *Euthydemus,* 271c ff., referring to Euthydemus and Dionysodorus, a dialogue with which Xenophon may show some familiarity in both *Smp.* and *Mem.* 1 (see notes on *Mem.* 1.3.8, 10, 1.4.1), even if he may disagree with Plato on who was the father of the beautiful young Clinias.

Critias, c. 460–403, a rich aristocrat with strong oligarchical and pro-Spartan sympathies, who achieved notoriety as one of the 'thirty tyrants' of 404–403, though previously he had been comparatively uninvolved in politics. Plato's *Protagoras* has him as a teenaged companion of Alcibiades. In 415 he was accused of mutilating the Hermai but released on the evidence of a kinsman, Andocides. After the revolution of the 400, he proposed the recall of Alcibiades, but after the battle of Notium in 406 and Alcibiades' renewed exile, he retired to Thessaly till the defeat of Athens in 404, when he became one, if not the chief, of the leaders of the hated 'thirty tyrants', but died in 403 in battle against the popular democrat, Thrasybulus, who shared with Anytus most of the kudos for the restoration of the democracy.

Critias was a talented writer and thinker. His poetry included elegiac poems and tragedies, and fragments have also survived of two *Politeiai* (*Constitutions*), one in prose, the other in verse. Sextus Empiricus, a reputable source on philosophy, writing perhaps *c.* A.D. 200, records a passage in tragic metre, in which Sisyphus, the mythological villain, called by Homer 'the craftiest of men', claims the gods were invented by a clever man to stop lawlessness by frightening humans. Sextus says this came from *Sisyphus* by Critias, but other ancients thought that the play was by Euripides. As later generations certainly regarded Critias as an atheist, Critias was probably the author and put his own ideas into Sisyphus' mouth. Though strictly speaking he was not a sophist, as he did not teach or perform for money, he thought like one, so that Guthrie was fully justified in the place he found for him and the attention he paid him in *The Sophists*; see Guthrie (1) pp. 63, 69, 243–4 and 298–304.

Critias was a cousin of Plato's mother Periktione, and Plato was not deterred by Critias' notoriety in fourth century democratic Athens from according to him a role in four dialogues. Plato was not yet alive at the dramatic dates, late 430s, of *Protagoras*, in which he is briefly mentioned, and *Charmides*, where Critias has a prominent and not unfavourable role as a confident young man with a genuine interest in philosophy. In the late work *Timaeus* Critias is merely a listener, but in the incomplete sequel, which bears his name, *Critias*, he takes over as the main speaker to describe primeval Attica and the island of Atlantis.

Critias was the most notorious and bloodthirsty of the thirty tyrants, *cf.* Xenophon *HG* 2.3.15 ff. where Xenophon describes at great length how Critias engineered the condemnation and death of his much more humane and moderate colleague and erstwhile friend, Theramenes. Critias' unpopularity was undoubtedly a major factor in the condemnation of Socrates; thus 54 years later Aeschines, *In Timarchum* 173, could tell Athenians that they had killed 'Socrates, **the sophist**, because he had been proved to be (or 'was obviously') 'the teacher of Critias'.

Alcibiades, who lived *c.* 450 to 404 B.C., was by 399 less unpopular with the Athenians than Critias, because of his services to Athens in the last few years of the Peloponnesian War, but his activities in the decade following the Peace of Nicias of 421 had on balance done far greater harm to Athens.

He was supremely fortunate in coming from a rich family, being a relative and protégé of Pericles, and possessing outstanding personal beauty, a charismatic personality, a brilliant mind and great eloquence. He suffered, however, from excessive political ambition and was utterly unscrupulous in its pursuit, while in his private life he was notoriously debauched and unrestrained. At first he was able to manipulate the Athenian assembly for his own purposes, but Thucydides well illustrates his attitude to the Athenian democracy when he makes Alcibiades call it 'acknowledged folly', 6.89. For further details see Thucydides Books 5–8, Xenophon, *HG* 1, and Plutarch's *Life* and *Comparison with Coriolanus*.

Early in his political career Alcibiades played a leading part in encouraging Athens to reject the Peace of Nicias and to form an anti-Spartan alliance with Argos and other Greek cities, precipitating in 418 the first battle of Mantinea with its Spartan victory. Next he persuaded the Athenians, against the advice of Nicias, to launch the Sicilian Expedition under the leadership of himself, Nicias and Lamachus. Just before the fleet sailed, the *Hermai* (busts of Hermes) were found to have been mutilated, whether by Alcibiades and his friends or by enemies wishing to discredit him. Alcibiades was accused of this and of holding profane parodies of the Eleusinian Mysteries in his house, but could not get himself tried before he had to set sail for Sicily. Rather than face an uncertain future he defected to Sparta, where he gave the Spartans two pieces of advice highly damaging to Athens, first to establish a permanent fortress at Decelea, between Athens and Laurium, thereby cutting off land access to the silver mines, and secondly sending a Spartan military man to organise the Sicilians' resistance to Athens, something which Gylippus did most effectively.

After the disastrous end to the Athenian expedition to Sicily in 413, Alcibiades continued to help the Spartans by participating in their naval and military activities in the eastern Aegean with the support of the Persian satrap Tissaphernes, whose friendship he had cultivated. But by 411 Alcibiades had incurred the enmity of the Spartan King Agis by seducing his wife and had to flee to Tissaphernes, whom he now urged to limit his help to the Peloponnesians so that both Greek sides could wear themselves out; see the speech that Thucydides 8.46 attributes to Alcibiades. This policy, whether the product of Alcibiades' fertile brain or formulated by Tissaphernes himself from the outset, did irreparable harm to Athens and indeed to Sparta also. In 411 came the short-lived oligarchical revolution at Athens, but Alcibiades, despite his blatantly oligarchical sympathies, shrewdly joined the more democratic Athenian forces in Samos, where he was welcomed not only for the prospects of Persian help from Tissaphernes which he dangled before them, but also for his new found sensibly moderate political policy. He was elected general by the forces at Samos and played a leading part in several notable Athenian victories in the Hellespont area over Spartan forces which were supported by a rival Persian satrap, Pharnabazus. He returned to Athens in a blaze of glory, and as *stratêgos* took charge of operations in the Aegean, but when at Notion in 406 one of his subordinates lost a naval battle, Alcibiades was unjustly blamed and instead of returning to Athens he retired to a castle he had acquired on the Hellespont. Despite a naval victory off Arginusae in the same year Athens' fortunes were at such a low ebb that in January 405 in *The Frogs* Aristophanes could suggest among other desperate solutions to the crisis the recall of Alcibiades. He remained, however, at the Hellespont and did his best to warn the Athenian generals of their dangerous situation at Aegospotamoi before their final utter and humiliating defeat. He was again formally banished from Athens and remained in Asia Minor till his murder in 404, which seems to have been carried out on the orders of Lysander or Pharnabazus or both. According to Plutarch his murder was also recommended to Lysander by his former friend Critias, when one of the 'thirty tyrants'. Perhaps he had become a true patriot in the end, but he had done Athens great damage over the years, something which contributed greatly to Socrates' fate in view of their great friendship.

The relationship of Alcibiades and Socrates is notably illustrated in Plato *Smp.* 215 ff. in Alcibiades' speech in praise of Socrates, where he admits his love for Socrates and the spellbinding effect of Socrates' words on himself and describes how Socrates, despite his love, remained impervious to his physical charms. That Alcibiades was for a time at least Socrates' admirer, companion, *cf.* Plato *Gorgias* 519a, and disciple is indisputable; Aeschines Sphettius and Antisthenes wrote lost works entitled *Alcibiades*. Two dialogues entitled *Alcibiades* and ascribed to Plato have, however, survived. *Alcibiades* 1 seems to be Platonic enough with Socrates crossquestioning and instructing a teenaged, but already politically ambitious Alcibiades; *Alcibiades* 2 is generally rejected as the work of a later imitator.

12 *Text. Read the additions καὶ φονικώτατος (and most bloodthirsty) and καὶ βιαιότατος ('and most violent') with AB; see notes on p 76.

18 virtue: for Socrates *aretê* depended on knowledge and meant moral virtue, embracing courage, temperance, justice, piety and wisdom, see Vlastos 1994, 200; previously *aretê* was used, like the adjective *agathos*, basically to refer to competitive goodness or excellence rather than to co-operative qualities; thus, when the sophists claimed that *aretê* was teachable and they could teach it, morality didn't come into it, as they were claiming merely how to succeed in life.

20 realising that good company is: ὡς τὴν... ἄσκησιν οὖσαν is the accusative absolute construction, which is normally used instead of the genitive absolute only with impersonal verbs or when introduced by ὡς, as here, or by ὥσπερ, as in *An.* 3.14.

attested: the basic meaning of the verb μαρτυρῶ is 'bear witness', 'testify', but Xenophon uses it here to refer to the support of a quotation, as does Plato's Socrates in *Protagoras* 344d.

the poet: Theognis, 35–36. Theognis of Megara was a moralising elegiac poet, active probably about 540 B.C., though some of the lines attributed to him are later additions.

Here Xenophon quotes for himself, whereas in *Smp.* 2.4 he has Socrates quoting the same couplet, while in *Meno* 95d,e Plato's Socrates quotes the preceding couplet along with this one. Manuscripts of both Plato and Xenophon read διδάξαι for Theognis' μαθήσεαι. J. Mitscherling, *CQ* XXXII 1982, 468–9, convincingly suggests that Plato adapted the quotation for his own purposes in the context, and that Xenophon used the quotation via *Meno*.

him who says: unknown. Plato's Socrates quotes the same hexameter in *Protagoras*

344d, introducing it by use of the verb μαϱτυϱῶ, see previous note. It therefore seems probable that Xenophon has used both *Meno* and *Protagoras* in writing this passage.

1.2.21 to theirs: *toutois* is masculine; the dative is of advantage with *marturô*.

23 splendid and good: the qualities of the perfect man; see note on 1.1.16.

self-discipline: translating *sôphrosynê*; *cf. Cyr.* 7.5.77 where Xenophon makes Cyrus say that *sôphrosynê* and self-control, *enkrateia*, see note on 1.2.1, degenerate into vice, *ponêria*, unless kept in practice.

1.2.24 went into exile in Thessaly: presumably after Alcibiades' undeserved fall from favour at Athens after the battle of Notion in 406; see note on Alcibiades p. 124. For Critias' activities in Thessaly see *HG* 2.3.36, where Xenophon makes Theramenes say that Critias was trying to establish democracy and arming the serfs against their masters. See Krentz's note with its convincing suggestion that Critias' aim may have been tyranny, not democracy.

men whose ways were lawless: perhaps *penestai*, members of the depressed Thessalian labourer class, for whom Xenophon would have little sympathy.

personal beauty: see Plutarch, *Alc.* 1.3, Plato *Smp.* passim.

powerful people: editors seem justified in deleting *kolakeuein*; it could have intruded into the text from being an explanatory gloss on the meaning of *diathruptomenos*; *dunatôn kolakeuein* could be translated as 'able to flatter' but its inclusion reads unnaturally. *Anthrôpôn* here and in the next chapter could include women, though here one would have expected *andrôn*, in contrast to the preceding *gunaikôn*, but Xenophon may have thought that word too complimentary to use.

1.2.27 piper: player of the *aulos*, the double pipe.

1.2.29 Euthydemus: not the quibbling sophist, the eponym of Plato's dialogue, or the brother of the orator, Lysias, mentioned as present in Plato, *R.* 328b, but the handsome son of Diocles, named in Plato, *Smp.* 22b along with the famous young beauty, Charmides, by Alcibiades in drunken jest as two of many victims deceived by Socrates' pretence of being their lover, though really he was their beloved one. According to Xenophon he became a devoted disciple after the conversational exchanges recorded in 4.2; 4.3, 5, 6 also describe Socrates' conversations with him; at one of these, 4.3, Xenophon says he himself was present.

seduce: literally translated 'use him as do those who enjoy the bodies for sex', *i.e.* 'use men like women' the phrase of Virtue in *Mem.* 2.1.30 in the Prodicus fable as recounted by Xenophon's Socrates in referring to homosexual copulation, in condemning it, as did the Socrates of both Xenophon and Plato. On the whole subject see K. J. Dover, *Greek Homosexuality*, London 1978.

servile: translating *aneleutheron*, literally 'not free'; *cf.* Socrates' remarks in 1.3.11 ff. in admonishing Xenophon for his approval of displays of male homosexual affection.

1.2.30 *Text: read προσκνήσασϑαι (instantaneous aorist middle infinitive) with B and ὑΐδια, diminutive of ὗς, pig, with mss.

1.2.31 Charicles: one of the 'thirty tyrants'. Previously he had been involved in

the investigations into the mutilation of the *Hermai*, and in 413 had commanded
Athenian naval raids on Laconia.

1.2.32 *many ... many also:* for the anaphora see note on *Ap.* 17.

the usual criticism of philosophers: presumably that made in Aristophanes' *Clouds*,
'making the inferior argument the superior one', as claimed by Protagoras; *cf.* Plato
Ap. 19b, Xenophon *Oec.* 11, 25.

herdsman...civic leader: cf. Cyr. 8.2.13, where Xenophon attributes to Cyrus the Great
this same view, presumably of Socrates himself, that the duties of the good herdsman
and of the good king were similar; Homer called Odysseus 'shepherd of the people'.
Xenophon a natural hero-worshipper, retained an admiration for Cyrus the Pretender,
even after his discreditable death. His chief heroes were Socrates, Cyrus the Great, and
Agesilaus, whom he made into idealised composite figures, each of them possessing
features and views of the others and also of Xenophon himself.

1.2.33 *forbade him to converse with young men: cf.* 4.4.3 for Xenophon's assertion
that Socrates disobeyed them in this respect, and also by failing to arrest Leon of
Salamis, *cf.* Plato *Ap.* 32c, d.

1.2.35 *Councillors:* Athenian citizens aged at least 30 who had been chosen by lot
to serve for a year of the *boulê*; that age limit for councillors and other magistrates
had already been ordained by the legislator Dracon according to Aristotle *Ath.* 4.3.

1.2.36 *already know the answer:* acting with his usual irony.

1.2.37 *cobblers, carpenters and smiths:* for Socrates' fondness for the topic of skilled
artisans *cf.* 1.2.9 with note and Plato *Prt.* 319d, where these three craftsmen head
Socrates' list of workmen with expert knowledge who can be trusted in their own
fields, but not for the advice they give in the assembly, *cf.* 3.7.6. Socrates believed
that political leadership needed expert knowledge; thus Xenophon depicts Socrates
making this clear to the young, politically ambitious Glaucon in 3.6. Perhaps Critias
is here to be understood as resenting the implication that he lacked the expertise in
politics that the craftsman possessed in their own fields.

justice: as discussed in the *Republic*, of which at least the initial section with its
concentration on a definition may be regarded as Socratic.

piety: the subject of Plato's 'Socratic' dialogue, *Euthyphro*.

1.2.38 *before he was twenty years old:* see note on 1.2.12. Alcibiades could hardly
have been born much before 450 B.C., though an anecdote in Plutarch, *Alc.* 7.2
has him as a *meirakion* (a youth, stripling) serving at Potidaea (besieged 432–430).
Xenophon's own anecdote here, whether fictitious or historical, will also have to be
dated to this time, just before the outbreak of the Peloponnesian War or early in it,
as Pericles died in 429.

1.2.41 *inform me what law is:* note how Socrates' young protégé here reproduces
his master's own habit of asking others for definitions and using elenchus on them
to prove them wrong and make them retract their opinions. In *Ap.* 21c–23b Plato's
Socrates describes the unpopularity he acquired from his continual cross-questioning
of others and proving their ignorance, and in 23c ff. accounts for the charge against
him of corrupting the young from his imitation by rich young men with time on

their hands who take it on themselves to 'examine' others. Aristophanes parodies this exercise of 'Socratic' argumentative skills by a young man at the end of *Clouds*, where Pheidippides 'proves' to his father that it is just for him to beat up his own father and so exasperates Strepsiades that he sets fire to Socrates' 'Thinkery'.

1.2.42 *young fellow:* the mention of his ward's age implies a mild reproof.

1.2.43 *even the enactments of a tyrant are also called law:* a surprising admission extracted by Alcibiades' tricky questioning from Pericles, the most famous leader and most eloquent spokesman of, and for, Athenian democracy. Tyranny was particularly hateful to Athens because of the behaviour of Hippias, elder son and successor of Peisistratus. Hippias ruled Athens for 17 years till his expulsion in 510, and even 20 years later hoped to be reinstated by the Persians, if they won the battle of Marathon. Moreover, Harmodius and Aristogeiton were still in Socrates' time held in the utmost veneration as 'tyrannicides' for their killing of Hippias' younger brother, Hipparchus.

1.2.44 *without first persuading them:* translating μὴ πείσας. Throughout this passage the verb πείθειν is used, but one thinks of the cognate noun πειθώ and the compliment paid to Pericles by the comic poet, Eupolis, that 'a sort of persuasion', πειθώ τις 'sat on his lips'.

1.2.46 *at your very cleverness:* translating δεινότατος ἑαυτοῦ, the reading of A, rightly preferred in the Oxford text to the original reading of B, as a *lectio difficilior.* For the superlative coupled with a comparative genitive of a reflexive pronoun, *cf.* Herodotus 2.8, 4.85, and for the third person of a reflexive pronoun in Xenophon instead of the second person, *cf.* 2.1.20 (where ἑαυτῆς should be read with AB), *Cyr.* 6.2.41, and a *varia lectio* in Plato *Phd.* 101c. The construction is now confirmed by the reading of Π⁶, and its inclusion of ταῦτα (though omitted by A), a limiting accusative, also seems attractive; see *apparatus criticus.*

1.2.47 *being cross-questioned:* the verb ἐλέγχω, though meaning to 'cross-question', 'subject to scrutiny', 'grill', also implies that the chief purpose of the exercise is to 'prove wrong', 'discredit'. See note on 1.2.41. Xenophon used the Alcibiades anecdote to illustrate the misuse of Socratic elenchus by young men which contributed to Socrates' unpopularity and also to portray Alcibiades in a bad light as a youth. Xenophon puts less emphasis than Plato on Socrates' elenchus.

1.2.48 *Crito:* probably Socrates' closest friend, as being of the same age and the same deme, Plato *Ap.* 33e. He attended Socrates' trial along with his son, Critobulus. Both of them volunteered to share with Plato and Apollodorus payment of the fine proposed as his punishment by Socrates, Plato *Ap.* 38b. In *Crito*, Plato represents him as visiting Socrates in prison awaiting execution, but failing to persuade him to escape, although he, Simmias, Cebes and many others would finance it. He and Critobulus were present at Socrates' death as described in *Phaedo.* According to the doubtful evidence of Diogenes Laertius, 2.121, Crito wrote 17 dialogues still (600 years later) extant.

Chaerephon: an eager, impetuous disciple of Socrates, figuring in Plato's *Gorgias* and *Charmides.* He was ridiculed in comedy as a lean, unscrupulous pauper and portrayed in the extant version of *Clouds* as Socrates' chief associate. According to Plato, *Ap.* 21a he consulted the Delphic oracle on the wisdom of Socrates and was told that nobody was wiser; see *Ap.* 14 for Xenophon's expansion of the Delphic response. He was banished by the 'thirty tyrants', but helped to expel them, only to die before the trial of Socrates.

Chaerecrates: Chaerephon's younger brother, and presumably the brother present at Socrates' trial, Plato *Ap.* 21a. In *Mem.* 2.3 Socrates, finding the two brothers quarrelling, urges Chaerecrates to act generously towards his brother, despite his unkindness.

Hermogenes: son of Hipponicus, and Xenophon's source of information for the trial and death of Socrates; see note on *Ap.* 2.

Simmias, Cebes: both Pythagoreans from Thebes who had attended the lectures of Philolaus, still young men in 399, and noteworthy for their significant contributions to the discussions of the *Phaedo.* Simmias in his devotion to Socrates had earlier brought money with him to the prison to finance Socrates' escape, *Crito* 45b, and Cebes was also prepared to help with funds. They were credited by Diogenes Laertius, 2.124–5, with 23 and 9 dialogues respectively.

Phaedondas: also a Theban and present at Socrates' death, *Phaedo*, 59c. The best Platonic mss. give his name as Phaedondes or Phaedonides, and for Xenophon one has to choose between Phaedondas of B and Phaedondes of other mss. Phaedondas seems preferable on the analogy of Epaminondas, a Theban whose military exploits were known only too well to Xenophon, and also on dialectical grounds; moreover Xenophon with a Theban friend in Proxenos should have been better informed on things Theban than Plato.

utter disrespect for their fathers: behaviour portrayed by Aristophanes, particularly in *Clouds*, 1321 ff., and so by implication ultimately to be blamed on Socrates.

to convict one's father: as Euthyphro was doing in Plato's dialogue, though on a different charge, that of murder, and with the implied disapproval of Socrates, *Euthphr.* 4a.

1.2.52 on the subject of friends: the subject of Plato's *Lysis*, a 'Socratic' dialogue, probably known to Xenophon, see note on 1.6.14; *cf.* in particular, the argument of Plato *Ly.* 207–210, well summarised by the Loeb editor, Lamb, as 'a simple introductory talk on the motives of personal affection, which are surmised to depend on a sense of utility and therefore on knowledge.'

53 those who knew...others: those with the precise combination of qualities which Pericles, according to the speech given him by Thucydides 2.60, claimed for himself.

carried out the body... and put it out of sight: for Socrates' stress on the unimportance of the dead body to dear ones see Plato, *Phaedo* 115c–e, (a passage which Xenophon might have had in mind), where Socrates tells Crito he need not be upset at seeing his body cremated or buried, as he himself, the real Socrates, will be gone to the joys of the blessed.

54 everyone loves his own body more than anything else: though this is true enough of mankind in general, the wording seems rather surprising, as coming from Socrates with his emphasis on the tending of the *psychê*, *cf. Ap.* 29c *etc.*, unless the body is to be thought of as only temporarily deserving the greatest love, while it houses the *psychê*.

55 beneficial: translating ὠφέλιμος. See note on *Ap.* 34 There, and again in a final eulogy of Socrates in *Mem.* 4.8.11, Xenophon stresses Socrates' helpfulness to aspirants towards virtue. This quality particularly appealed to the practical Xenophon who throughout his works aimed at being instructive, whether on matters on which he was expert, horsemanship, warfare, hunting *etc.*, or on education, religion and morality. It is small wonder, therefore, that he was so admired by the Romans.

56 his accuser: Polycrates.

evil-doers and tyrannical: perhaps particularly implying Critias.

Hesiod's line: *Op.* 311. I have here translated it as I think Hesiod meant it, with ἔργον and ἀεργίη being contrasted, with οὐδὲν going with ὄνειδος not ἔργον, and with ἀεργίη implying 'wilful avoidance of work', 'sloth', *cf. Od.* 24.251. Note also for Hesiod ἔργον basically meant agricultural work.

the poet...gain: this line could be interpreted by sophistic arguers as condoning all types of activity, but only out of context, because Hesiod goes on to condemn various evil activities, *Op.* 320 ff., and ibid. 352 evilly acquired gains. The line is indeed quoted and discussed in Plato, by Critias, not Socrates, in *Chrm.* 352b, presumably a 'Socratic' and early dialogue, probably preceding *Mem.*; Critias does interpret it as meaning 'no ἔργον is shameful', but then says that Hesiod would not have approved of activities such as cobbling, fishmongering or working in a brothel, and that therefore ἔργα should mean 'works honourably and usefully made'. Socrates, however, passes no comment on Critias' views on the line but reverts to the main subject under discussion, the definition of *sôphrosynê*.

1.2.57 beneficial...harmful: *cf.* ὠφελίμως and βλαβερὰ in Plato *Chrm.* 163c.

played dice...: for Critias' examples of discreditable activities see note on 1.2.56; they were not immoral, but he would have thought them *banausos*, beneath him, degrading, suitable only for the lower classes. Xenophon's example is certainly more creditable to Socrates. Polycrates' aspersions on Socrates in 1.2.56–7 seem completely unfair, but may have originated from memories of the activities of Critias. The dramatic date of *Chrm.* is early, 431 B.C., and I take it to be a 'Socratic' dialogue and a substantially faithful record of an actual discussion. Perhaps later Critias with his sophistic tendencies did reinterpret Hesiod's line less morally for his own purposes, and that was what Polycrates vaguely remembered. In any case on the evidence of *Chrm.*, whether or not it preceded Polycrates' pamphlet, Socrates' only fault was failure to discuss the line with Critias.

In conclusion I think that here Xenophon has used and adapted the passage from *Charmides*.

1.2.58 'When king...war': quoting *Il.* 2.188–191, 199–203. I follow Bandini in printing in the fifth line of the quotation the reading of the Berlin Papyrus and including a second ὄντινα, misquoting Homer, but metrically acceptable by the omission of ἄνδρα and the change to τε before a digamma, and by assuming this change had already intruded into the text used by Xenophon.

In *Iliad* 2, in the tenth year of the war, Agamemnon has been encouraged by a dream to think that he will at last take Troy, but foolishly decides first to test the temper of his army by suggesting they should abandon the siege and sail back home. A rush to the ships follows, but disaster is averted by Athene warning Odysseus of the crisis, so that he makes his way along the ships persuading one and all to stay, but finding most trouble with the ugly, low-born, mutinous demagogue, Thersites, whom he beats up, making him cringe and weep to the amusement of all.

commoners and poor men: Xenophon seems to suggest that Polycrates is merely accusing Socrates of a contemptuous attitude to poor men and commoners; this was not the case, as Socrates, himself the son of a stonemason and midwife, regularly praised the skills and knowledge of artisans in their own spheres. More probably the criticism was of Socrates' attitude to democracy and the fact that amateurs could be involved in government and air their views in the assembly. Xenophon does well to cut the quotation short before *Iliad* 2.204 and omit the phrase οὐκ ἀγαθὸν πολυκοιρανίη, rule by many is not a good thing, which could be used in criticism of a glaring weakness in the Athenian democratic system. For Socrates' views on this see Guthrie 1971(2) 89–96.

For a rejection of the view that Socrates was μισόδημος, a hater of the common people, see Libanius, *Apologia Socratis* 54 ff. This work of the 4th century A.D., though a defence of Socrates addressed to his Athenian jurors, *passim* apostrophises Anytus to counter his opinions. Libanius, like Xenophon, deserves credit for recognising that the prominent and popular democrat Anytus was the chief danger to Socrates and that his trial was mainly politically motivated. See note on Xenophon's *Ap.* 29–31.

1.2.60 never charged any fee: unlike the sophists, *cf.* Plato *Ap.* 31b.

1.2.61 Lichas...Gymnopaidiai: Lichas was an influential Spartan, who had won a chariot victory at Olympia in 420 and served Sparta on foreign embassies, and as adviser to a general in 412–1. He was Argive *proxenos* (see note 7 on p. 12) at Sparta and Plutarch also records his generous hospitality at the *Gymnopaidiai*, a Spartan festival at which boys danced naked and performed gymnastic exercises. See Krentz's note on *HG* 3.2.21.

would try to make: I translate thus to stress the conative and continuous force of the present participle ποιῶν. Even when expecting to be left by them, Socrates' efforts to improve them continued.

62–64 recapitulating that Socrates should have been acquitted of the charges and greatly honoured by Athens, not condemned to death.

1.2.62 honoured by his city: at Athens Olympic victors were rewarded with free meals at the Prytaneum, the magistrates' hall on the Acropolis. *Cf.* Plato *Ap.* 36d, where Plato's Socrates claimed he deserved this honour far more than Olympic victors in horse races, because, though a poor man, he neglected his own affairs in trying to urge his fellows towards personal virtue and wisdom.

thief...temple-robber: *cf. Ap.* 25, where Xenophon's Socrates uses the same argument, but only gives four capital offences, temple-robbery, housebreaking, kidnapping and betrayal of one's city. Now Xenophon, reworking that passage and speaking for himself, starts by adding three less heinous offences, but omits until 1.2.63, the most terrible offence in a city state, that of treason.

63 sedition: translating στάσις, civic discord; on its evils see Thucydides 3.82.

64 of all men: literally 'of the other men', but translating τῶν ἄλλων, to be retained with OCT, though Loeb and Budé prefer πάντων, an easier reading into which it could well have been changed; see Reynolds and Wilson, 150. The genitive is partitive after μάλιστα, most, and the inclusion of ἄλλων, of others, though illogical, is idiomatic, going back to Homer, *Od.* 5.105; *cf.* μόνη τῶν ἄλλων ἐπιστηῶν Pl. *Chrm.* 166e.

his prosecutor: Meletus.

households: here Xenophon, the writer of *Oec.*, lays more stress on the benefits of virtue to households than Socrates himself might have done: *cf.* Plato *Ap.* 36b.

CHAPTER 3 Now Xenophon reverts from dismissing the accusations of Polycrates to general vindication of Socrates.

1.3.1 the ways by which: translating οἷς, instrumental dative neuter plural, Hartman's correction of ὡς; *cf.* 1.4.1 for the same emendation by Jacobs.

custom: translating νόμος, a wide-ranging and elastic term, including both the unwritten laws of customary behaviour and written codified laws, *e.g.* of Solon at Athens. Etymologically '*nomos* is something that νομίζεται, is believed in, practised or held to be right; something that νέμεται, is apportioned, distributed or dispensed', see Guthrie 1971(1) 55. By the time of Socrates sophists had started to exploit the elasticity of the term to argue for and exaggerate a distinction between *physis*, nature and natural law, and *nomos*, man-made customs and laws.

Socrates' observance of the laws of Athens, his one and only home, is best illustrated by his behaviour and attitude as recorded in the *Crito*, when he chooses to remain in prison and accept the death penalty of the Athenian court.

1.3.2 to give what was good: *cf. Cyr.* 1.6.5 where Xenophon makes the father of Cyrus the Great give the same advice to his son about prayers to the gods. Once again Xenophon makes an exemplar talk like Socrates; see note on 1.2.32.

praying for: it is tempting to translate 'praying about', or 'praying for success in', though that is impossible with the text as it stands. It does make some sort of sense to pray to be granted by the gods merely to have a game of dice or a pitched battle.

1.3.3 the following line: Hesiod, *Op.* 336. *Read Κὰδ δύναμιν in the text of Hesiod with Solmsen. κατὰ is here syncopated to κὰδ before a word starting with δ and a short syllable, as in Homeric epic; a sequence of three short syllables would be impossible in the dactylic hexameter metre; *cf.* κὰδ δὲ *Il.* 2.160 etc.

*Text. (1) τὴν, if retained is difficult and goes with παραίνεσιν. (2) Read Κὰδ δύναμιν. The invention of a noun, καδδύναμις, should not be ascribed to Xenophon, who *Mem.* 4.3.16 recommends sacrificing to the gods κατὰ δύναμιν.

1.3.5 manner of life: translating δίαιτα; the simplicity, austerity, asceticism and self-sufficiency of Socrates came to be adopted as basic principles of the Cynic and Stoic philosophies. They were particularly admired and imitated by Socrates' devoted disciple, Antisthenes, who figures prominently in Xenophon's *Smp.*, where 4.34–44 he describes his own austere lifestyle, claiming paradoxically that it makes him a rich man. Antisthenes is called by Diogenes Laertius 6.2 'the first beginner of Cynicism', but his young pupil, Diogenes of Sinope, has a far better claim to have been the founder of Cynicism, because he behaved like a dog, adding to the austerity of Socrates and Antisthenes other distinctive features, many of them anti-social, such as shameless behaviour in public and carrying his love of *parrhêsia* (outspokenness) to the point of rudeness. He was said by Diogenes Laertius, 6.54, and Aelian, *VH* 14.33, to have been described by Plato as 'Socrates gone mad'.

sauce: translating ὄψον, which normally means 'a cooked dish', but can, as here, mean 'sauce', 'relish', 'appetiser'; *cf. Cyr.* 1.5.12, where Cyrus the Great praises the hardy Persians for their use of hunger as a sauce. See note on 1.2.32.

1.3.6 *invitation to dinner: cf.* Xenophon *Smp.* 1.7, where at first Socrates and his companions refused Callias' invitation, but, seeing he was upset, went on to accept it. In Plato's *Smp.* Socrates not only accepted Agathon's invitation, but even persuaded his disciple, the reluctant Aristodemus, to turn up uninvited; Socrates at least was not simply going for the food and drink, as he was in no hurry to get there.

most...overindulging: ὥστε, if text is retained, is difficult Greek, and seems to link ἐργωδέστατον with φυλάξασθαι; τὸ for ὥστε would be more natural.

1.3.7 *characters:* translating ψυχάς personalities, spirit.

Circe...Hermes' advice: Circe, the goddess and sorceress, figures, *Od.* 10.133–574, in Odysseus' account of his adventures in returning from Troy. He tells his audience that, on reaching her island, he sent a party to reconnoitre her palace, but they all, except their cautious leader, had accepted her drugged food, been turned into pigs and confined in sties. Odysseus set out to confront her himself, but was met by the god Hermes who gave him *moly*, a magic antidote to her drugs, and advised him to counteract her drugs with it, draw his sword on her, and refuse to sleep with her, till she had freed his comrades and sworn a mighty oath to plot no more harm against him. He did as instructed, refusing more food till she restored his men to human form and released them. Then for a whole year they all enjoyed her sumptuous hospitality before continuing on the way home.

his...self-control: being ἐγκρατής, having mastery over himself and the temptations of the flesh; see notes on 1.5.1, 1.5.4. Socrates, however, rather exaggerates his praise for Odysseus' self-control, as Hermes with his *moly* and advice was the main factor in Odysseus' success in coping with Circe.

1.3.8 *jest...seriously meant: cf. Smp.* 1.1 and 4.28 for the combination of these two opposites. *Cf.* also Aristophanes' claim, *Frogs* 389–90, to say many things that are *geloia* (in jest) and many things that are *spoudaia* (serious) and Strabo's epithet, 16.2.29, *spoudogeloios* for Menippus.

1.3.8–13 Socrates' warning of the dangers of kissing and sexual contacts with beautiful people as exemplified by the behaviour of Critobulus and the need for self-control. This is closely paralleled by Xenophon's *Smp.* 4.10–26 with much repetition but some variations of detail.

1.3.8 Text. The papyrus Π[1] originally had about 40 lines before ἀλλά most of which have been deleted. As it offers several attractive readings in chs. 10 and 12, I follow Bandini in postulating a lacuna here.

Critobulus, son of Crito: devoted friends of Socrates, both were rich men, see note on 1.2.48; Crito could afford a share in the fine proposed for himself by Socrates at his trial, having earlier failed to persuade him to escape with the connivance of a bribed gaoler. Father and son were with Socrates for his last hours, as recorded in *Phaedo*, and it was Crito who closed the mouth and eyes of the dead Socrates. Critobulus figures prominently in Plato *Smp.* and Xenophon *Smp.* and *Oec.*; Crito had wanted Socrates to help his young son by educating him, Plato *Euthd.* 306d, Xenophon *Smp.* 4.24, and Xenophon's Socrates fulfils that role, *Mem.* 2.6 with advice on choosing friends, *Oec.* passim on estate management, ibid. 3.11–15, on training a wife, and *Smp.* 4.10 ff. on the same subject as this passage.

Alcibiades' son: the object of Critobulus' affection is named by Xenophon, *Smp.* 4.12 as Clinias, a slightly older schoolmate of Critobulus. He was probably not the son of the strikingly handsome Alcibiades, but his cousin, see Plato *Euthd.* 275b; the Clinias of Plato *Euthd.* is about the same age as Critobulus, 271b, and is accompanied by some lovers, but not by Critobulus who has been brought by his father, Crito.

Xenophon: this is the only passage in *Mem.* where Xenophon names himself as taking part in a conversation with Socrates, though he does also claim to have been present in 1.4.2, 2.4.1 and 4.3.2; 1.6.14 and 2.5.1 need only be hearsay reports.

In *Smp.* 1.1 Xenophon seems to be claiming either that he was present or was closely associated at the time with those present (see Bowen's note) at the symposion, the dramatic date of which is 422. It would have needed ten or more years to elapse for Xenophon to be of an age when Socrates' rebuke might have been appropriate. In *Smp.* 4.24 Socrates says he thinks Critobulus has already kissed Clinias, while in this passage Socrates says he has heard from Crito that Critobulus has actually kissed Clinias; so, unless Crito has taken several years to tell Socrates, the situation seems to be of about the same date, and there must be doubts about the chronology, if of nothing else.

1.3.10 ***somersault into a ring of knives:*** the same phrase is used in *Smp.* 2.11.14 more naturally of the dancing girl performing skilfully and boldly at the symposion, but also occurs in Plato *Euthd.* 294e of a feat of *sophia* and knowledge.

jump into fire: cf. *Smp.* 4.16, where Critobulus claims he'd go through fire, if with Clinias.

I am therefore led to believe that in writing *Mem.* 1.3.8–13 Xenophon has reworked material already used in *Smp.*; it follows, therefore, that *Mem.* 1.3.8–1.7.5 must postdate *Smp.* or, more probably, that some or all of *Mem.* 1.3.8–15 was a later insertion by Xenophon into the text of *Mem.* 1. How much fiction is involved it is difficult to say. For a different view see Thesleff.

1.3.11 ***a slave instead of a free man:*** for Socrates' pride in his freedom of spirit and his aversion to servile behaviour see *Ap.* 9, 14 (with Xenophon's version of the Delphic response to Chaerephon) with notes.

1.3.12 *what fearful power a kiss has:* for Socrates on the dangers of kissing *cf.* Xenophon *Smp.* 4.25 ff.; *the word order of Π[1] improves the emphasis; *cf.* Plato *R.* 596c *ὀδύναις τε* and *ὅσον μόνον ἀψάμενα, cf.* Plato, *R.* 607a *etc.*, of Π[1] also seem preferable readings.

1.3.13 *Perhaps...far off:* rightly deleted from the text by Dindorf as unSocratic and an interpolation.

recover from the bite: literally 'become healthy in respect of the bite'; *τὸ δῆγμα* is a limiting accusative to be retained in the text.

1.3.14 *he avoided...easily: cf.* Plato *Smp.* 219c ff. for Alcibiades' account of Socrates' resistance to his charms.

CHAPTER 4 1.4.1 reads like an introduction to a discussion on Socrates' ability to make his associates better men, something Xenophon claims in his final eulogy in *Mem.* 4.8.11, but 1.4.2–19 only gives Socrates' efforts with one man, Aristodemus, giving Socrates' views on divine providence and the need for men to adopt a pious and prudent attitude to the gods. This passage is paralleled by the dialogue with Euthydemus in 4.3.2–18, but with different corroborative examples to prove Socrates' points.

on what: translating *οἷς*, Jacobs' convincing correction for *ὡς*, 'just as', = *τούτοις ἃ*, restoring the dative normal with *tekmairomai*, referring to the evidence on which the judgement is made. *Cf.* note on 1.3.1.

encouraging...to virtue...incapable of guiding to it: the precise criticism of Socrates made by Clitophon, the eponym of a short dialogue found in the Platonic corpus; see in particular its final words, *Clit.* 410e. Clitophon there and perhaps also in *Republic*, Book 1 (where he intervenes in the discussion on justice) seems to be a devotee of Thrasymachus. Platonic authorship is rejected by most scholars, mainly because of the shortcomings of the contents, though the writer is a skilful imitator of Plato's style. See Taylor 538.

searching questions...show up: the verb *elenchô*, like the noun *elenchos* can simply mean 'prove wrong', as in Plato *Ap.* 21c, but more often means 'cross-question' 'test by questioning', usually for the purpose of showing up, proving wrong, exposing ignorance. Socrates was notorious for his persistent use of *elenchos*, which he describes *Ap.* 21c–22e, calling it a 'service to the god', though realising it made him unpopular. See note on 1.2.47.

those who thought themselves omniscient: the sophists, as exemplified by Euthydemus and Dionysodorus throughout Plato's *Euthydemus*, in which Socrates pokes fun at them rather than castigates them; early in the dialogue, 271c, tongue in cheek he describes them as *passophoi atechnôs*, absolutely clever at everything.

2 *'Yes indeed' he said:* literally 'and he 'Yes indeed' said'. *ὅς* (like its feminine *ἥ*) is normally a relative pronoun, but can be used as a demonstrative pronoun to mean 'he' ('she') at the beginning of a clause, when preceded by *καὶ* ('and'), and is often followed by *εἶπε* or a similar verb to mean 'he said', introducing direct speech. An

alternative way of doing this favoured by Plato is ἢ δ' ὅς, using the verb ἠμί.
2 Aristodemus: described by Plato *Smp.* 173b as a small man who was always
barefooted and one of Socrates' most passionate devotees. Socrates in 416, when
invited by Agathon to the *symposion*, not only accepted the invitation but also
persuaded a reluctant Aristodemus, who felt out of place in such distinguished
company, to turn up uninvited. But he was welcomed by Agathon, which was
fortunate for posterity, as it was Aristodemus' account of the *symposion*, which,
via an intermediary, reached the ears of the narrator Apollodorus, who checked
Aristodemus' account with Socrates himself, before confirming its accuracy.

Though here in Xenophon Aristodemus starts off as something of an individualist
with a mind of his own, in Plato's dialogue he remains in the background, making
no significant contribution to the discussion.

the deity: translating τὸ δαιμόνιον, here used in a general sense.
*Text. See notes on p. 106. Marchant's *O. C. T.* should have noted a lacuna after
θεοῖς. AB's reading was corrected by Portus to οὐτ' εὐχόμενον, to which Marchant in
his Loeb added δῆλον ὄντα, 'or could clearly be seen to be praying', *cf. Mem.* 1.1.2,
to take account of the fragmentary Π². Another claim to credit for Π² would be if, as
Bandini thought possible, it read σοφίας, *cf.* Thucydides 6.36, instead of ἐπὶ σοφίᾳ,
cf. Plato *Tht.* 161c; see next note.

cleverness: translating *sophia*, which, like its adjective *sophos*, has a wide range of
meanings from wisdom to cleverness in any craft, menial or otherwise, or *technê*,
musical, poetical, artistic *etc.*; the range of meanings of *sophia* and of the areas
in which it could be shown is well illustrated by Socrates' long discourse in 4.2,
convincing Euthydemus that his pride in his *sophia* was misplaced.
1.4.3 dithyramb: a lyric poem in honour of Dionysus performed by a chorus.
Dithyrambic competitions by choruses of fifty were held at Athens.
Melanippides: like his grandfather of the same name, a dithyrambic poet from the
island of Melos. He was a protegé of Perdiccas, King of Macedon *c.* 450–413, and
noted for musical innovations and for abolishing the complicated triadic dithyramb.
For the scanty fragments of his poetry see D. L. Page *PMG* and D. A. Campbell,
Greek Lyric 5, Loeb Classical Library.
Polyclitus: of Argos, celebrated for his sculptures and for his contributions to the
theory of sculpture. His reputation was already well enough established by the
dramatic date of Plato's *Protagoras, c.* 430, for him to be mentioned at Athens in
the same breath as Pheidias, Plato *Prt.* 311c.
Zeuxis: from Heraclea in Lucania, a leading painter, also mentioned by Xenophon
in *Oec.* 10.1 and *Smp.* 4.3. In Plato *Prt.* 318b, see preceding note, he is already
regarded as an expert painter, though a very young man newly arrived in Athens.

Note the confidence of Aristodemus' reply, see note on 1.4.2, in his eagerness
to suggest that his interests are cultural, with his choice of favourites a blend of the
traditional (Homer and Sophocles) and the up-to-date.
1.4.4 design: translating γνώμην; see Plato *Phd.* 96a ff. for Socrates' initial excitement
on hearing Anaxagoras' theory that *Nous* (Mind) was the arranger and cause of all

things and his disappointment on finding that his 'system was just another set of physical theories' Guthrie 1971(2) 102.

1.4.5 the original creator of men: throughout this passage Xenophon's Socrates talks of the providence of one creator, whereas in his discourse with Euthydemus in 4.3.3 he argues for the providence of the gods in the plural, but see not on *Ap.* 5. Plato in *Timaeus* makes his Socrates talk of a World-Craftsman, a δημιουργός, who organised an ordered world out of chaos and created gods who were instructed, *Ti.* 41d ff., to follow Nature in the fashioning of men.

means of perception: *cf.* 4.3.11.

eyes...ears: *cf.* Plato *Ti.* 45b ff., 47c; both provided by the gods on behalf of the δημιουργός.

1.4.6 eyelids: translating βλέφαρα; *cf.* Plato *Ti.* 45d, where they are provided by the gods, as here, for the protection of the sight.

eyelashes...eyebrows: translating βλεφαρίδας...ὀφρύσι; *cf.* Aristotle *PA* 658a, b on the protection and benefits they exist to afford for men and animals.

the back teeth: the molars, translating γομφίους.

act as molars: translating λεαίνειν, literally 'grind down small'; the English word 'molar' commonly used by dentists comes from the Latin 'molaris' originally meaning 'grindstone' but later used by Juvenal of 'teeth'. *Cf.* Aristotle *PA* 661b on Nature's provision of teeth in humans.

1.4.7 clever craftsman: translating σοφοῦ δημιουργοῦ; see note on 'cleverness' earlier in this chapter. The translation 'wise' seems less appropriate from a grudging Aristodemus, in view of its conjunction with δημιουργοῦ (skilled artisan).

1.4.8 Do you think...: Xenophon's Socrates by his rhetorical questions in this chapter is suggesting that, just as our bodies have something of the elements in the universe, so our *psychai*, see note on 1.4.9, have something of the *Nous* which controls that universe. A remarkably similar line of argument is ascribed by Plato to Socrates in *Philebus* 29a–30d, though at the end of it Plato's Socrates admits he is only confirming the views of earlier thinkers (Diogenes of Apollonia and others?).

and that in your opinion: translating ὡς οἴει which is superfluous as the construction is already accusative and infinitive, after δοκεῖς. Read τινὰ οὕτως οἴει and translate 'owe such good order'. The inclusion of οὕτως adds emphasis; see note on *Ap.* 24.

9 Good Lord, yes I do: translating μὰ Δί'. The particle μὰ followed by the accusative of the deity or thing sworn by, whether or not preceded by οὐ, as just above, is predominantly negative. When used affirmatively, it is usually preceded by ναὶ, as in Xenophon's *Apology* 4; its affirmative use on its own is rare and late. Presumably it has to be explained as virtually negative, with Aristodemus meaning 'No; I won't give the answer expected by your leading rhetorical question.'

Neither do you see your own soul: 'soul' translating *psyché*; see note on *Ap.* 7. Similarly in *Cyr.* 8.7.17 Xenophon makes Cyrus the Great (another of his heroes partly modelled on Socrates and partly on Xenophon himself) say that his *psyché* is invisible, before going on, like Socrates, to discourse on its immortality and how it must be carefully tended.

which controls your body: cf. Plato *Phd.* 80a, *Alc.* 1.129d ff. As later in this chapter, § 17, Socrates tells Aristodemus that his *Nous*, when in his body, directs it as it wishes, to Socrates *Nous* and *psychê* are synonymous; see also note on 1.4.4.

1.4.10 *service:* translating ϑεραπείας. In Plato's *Euthyphro* the eponym offers as his third attempted definition of piety, service to the gods, something which Plato's Socrates, like Aristodemus here, suggests they don't need.

1.4.11 *have a better view of things above:* in a not entirely serious dialogue discussing etymologies, Plato's Socrates, *Cratylus* 399a ff., offers ἀναϑρῶν ἃ ὄπωπε, look up at what he has seen, as the explanation of the word ἄνϑρωπος on the analogy of the name Diphilus (Dear to Zeus), which has lost its second vowel. Xenophon clearly is not waxing etymological here, or he would have replaced ὕπερϑεν with ἄνω.

[and ... mouth]: Delete this clumsy addition. Eyes and ears have already come in 1.4.5.

1.4.12 *it's only:* note again Xenophon's use of the early position of μόνην for emphasis.

articulate the voice: make it utter distinctive sounds. Xenophon's verb is ἀρϑροῦν. Later grammarians suggested compounds cognate with this verb as an etymology for ἄνϑρωπος but this seems even less likely than ἀναϑρῶ, see note on 1.4.11; Xenophon at least is guiltless.

Again...old age: several editors suggested deleting this sentence from the text as inconsistent with Socrates' views on sex as instanced *e.g.* in 1.3.8–15, but even there he did not impose a complete ban on sexual activity.

till old age: presumably till, but not including, old age, at least on the evidence of the views of Polemarchus and Sophocles in Plato *R.* 329a–d, though there Socrates does not make any direct comment on that subject.

1.4.13 *his inner spirit:* translating *psychên*; see note on *Ap.* 7. That its intellectual and rational side is meant is clear from the parallel passage in 4.3.11 where *logismos*, the faculty of reasoning, is implanted in men.

and made it supreme: translating κρατίστην, preeminent in quality and power. Thucydides' Pericles in the Funeral Oration 2.40.3 uses the same superlative applied to *psychê*. Note the emphasis achieved by Xenophon's word order.

remembering in detail all that it hears, sees or learns: cf. 4.3.11 for the gift to men of memory and use of what his various senses have told him.

1.4.15 *advisers, as you say they do:* Aristodemus, though using the plural, seems to be referring to Socrates' *daimonion*, though Socrates in his reply merely talks of omens in general sent to all mankind.

to you: translating Cobet's σοὶ which seems a necessary correction.

what to do: an apparent reference to positive advice from the *daimonion*, see note on *Ap.* 12, but note that here as in *Mem.* 4.3.12 it is Socrates' interlocutor speaking.

1.4.17 *directs your body as it wishes:* see note on 1.4.9.

the intelligence: translating ϕρόνησις, the divine *psychê*; Socrates reverts to the argument of 1.4.8–9 of a parallelism between the divine and human *psychê*.

several miles: literally many στάδια; the stade was the length of a Greek racetrack, roughly a furlong or an eighth of a mile.

the eye of God: Socrates reminds Aristodemus of what Hesiod, *Op.* 267, had told the Greeks, that the eye of Zeus sees and apprehends everything. Similarly Xenophon makes his Cyrus, *Cyr.* 8.7.22, call the gods all-seeing and omnipotent.

here...Egypt...Sicily: Socrates simply means that Aristodemus in Athens is able to take an interest in affairs in very distant places; Socrates chooses as his examples places familiar to Athenians, Egypt to the south-east, and Sicily in the west.

Delebecque suggests the mentions of Egypt and Sicily may be spiteful digs by Xenophon at Plato, but Xenophon would hardly put them into the mouth of his idol, Socrates. A reference to Egypt would hardly make a reader think of Plato, who shows little interest in Egypt except in his late work, *The Laws.* Diogenes Laertius 3.6 does record a visit to priests in Egypt, in Plato's travels after leaving Euclides and Megara, *cf.* also Cicero *Rep.* 1.10.16, *Fin.* 5.29.87, but this, if accepted as fact, would be long before Xenophon was writing *Mem.* 1 at Scillous and Plato was back in Athens, starting his Academy. Plato's connection with Sicily would of course be familiar to every reader, but mainly because of events of 367 and later, after the accession of Dionysius the Second. Plato, however, had visited Syracuse and Sicily for the first time at the age of forty in 388 or 387 and made the acquaintance of Dionysius, as he tells us in his *Seventh Epistle,* and it is possible to imagine him at Athens any time thereafter thinking about Sicily. Plato's publication of *Meno* (388 Delebecque) (386–5 Bluck) must have annoyed Xenophon with its unduly favourable treatment of both Meno, slated in *Anabasis* 2.6.21 ff. for greed and treachery, and of Anytus, the most important of Socrates' accusers. Delebecque thinks that Xenophon's attitude to Plato was uniformly one of hostility, but it seems equally possible that there is no dig at Plato in this passage, that he generally respected him, and the only evidence of jealousy or rivalry was his avoidance of mentioning his name, except in *Mem.* 3.6, when recounting the defects of his brother, Glaucon. See further discussion of this point on p. 17.

1.4.18 *serving them:* translating θεραπεύων, offering θεραπεία; see note on 1.4.10. Euthyphro's definition of piety presumably regarded it as based on self-interest and the hope or assumption of reciprocal treatment from the gods.

repay favours: a basic feature of Socrates' views on friendship; *cf.* 2.3.11 ff. and 2.6.13 ff.; Socrates of course regarded God as his friend.

the divine: translating τὸ θεῖον, but synonymous with the τὸ δαιμόνιον of 1.4.2.

sees and hears all things: see note on 1.4.17.

1.4.19 *escape the notice of:* translating διαλαθεῖν, echoed by Lucian, *Phal.* 1.1.

CHAPTER 5

1.5.1 *self-control:* ἐγκράτεια, see note on 1.2.1.

consider...brought...closer: note the similarity of the two verbs with those of 1.4.1, a longer introductory sentence but with a similar structure and purpose; as the subject now reverts from *aretê* in general to self-control in particular, 1.4 seems something of a digression.

Note that a better way for Xenophon to prove the point he tries to make in both introductions would have been to concentrate not on Socrates' words and example, but on results, viz. instances of improved behaviour by Aristodemus and other associates; but see note in 1.7.1.

we could see: I translate thus rather than 'we saw'; I prefer to retain the ἄν transmitted by the manuscripts, rather than follow many editors in restoring normal syntax by omitting it; *cf.* note on 1.2.6.

unable to resist: literally 'inferior to', 'weaker than'.

gluttony...sleep: there are similar lists of temptations and demands on endurance in 1.2.1 and 2.1.1; this one differs from both in omitting cold and heat, but agrees with 2.1.1 in including sleep. *Cf. HG* 6.1.16, where Xenophon makes a speaker include in his praises of the formidable military prowess of Jason of Pherai his great *enkrateia* over himself and the pleasures of the flesh.

fine and good: translating καλόν τε κἀγαθὸν an appropriate attribute for the perfect man.

*1.5.2 *would we consider:* mistranslating ἡγησόμεθα (should= 'shall we consider') as Marchant has to do in his Loeb. Read ἡγησαίμεθ' ἄν, as one should, in the apodosis of a remote future condition, when the protasis has εἰ with the optative.

a slave lacking self-control: similarly Xenophon makes Ischomachus demand self-control about food, wine, sleep and sex in a female housekeeper, *Oec.* 9.11 and about food, drink and sex in overseers on his estate, ibid. 12.10 ff.

*supervision: the meaning of both ἐπίστασιν and ἐπιστασίαν, Stobaeus' rare noun. Stobaeus seems more reliable in this passage.

*a man like that: read τὸν τοιοῦτον, already in Athenaeus' text of Xenophon, over two hundred years before Stobaeus.

1.5.3 *destroy...one's...soul:* for Socrates' insistence on the need to look after one's *psychê* see *e.g.* Plato *Ap.* 29d, 30a.

1.5.4 *self-control the basis of virtue:* κρηπίς, literally the groundwork, foundation or basement of a building or altar, is here used figuratively for the essential basic feature, as in Plato *Lg.* 736a, *Plt.* 301e: *cf.* Tigranes' similar tribute to *sôphrosynê* in *Cyr.* 3.1.16.

Enkrateia and its corresponding adjective and adverb do occur just occasionally in Plato, but for Xenophon *enkrateia* is of immense importance, *cf.* in particular the long conversations with Aristippus and Euthydemus in 2.1 and 4.5. Xenophon, the moralist and man of action, see note on 1.4.2, most admired Socrates for his moral strength and the way he behaved, but Socrates was also an intellectual and that was the side of him that most appealed to Plato. Xenophon clearly accepted the Socratic paradox that virtue is knowledge, making his Socrates say that justice and all other aspects of *aretê* are *sophia*, wisdom, 3.9.4, and equating that with *epistêmê*, knowledge, 4.6.7.

Another Socratic paradox, that nobody willingly does wrong, causes greater problems, because it is untrue of real life and opposed to common sense; the words of Ovid's Medea in *Met.* 7.21–2, *video meliora proboque, deteriora sequor*, put it in a nutshell. If the paradox is carried to its logical conclusion, the only opposite of *aretê* is ignorance, and so vices such as *akrasia*, lack of self-control, do not exist or are irrelevant. Xenophon could not accept this paradox, and so in 4.5.4–6 makes his Socrates say that men often choose to do wrong when their perception of good and bad is stunned by *akrasia*. Its opposite is *enkrateia*, which for Xenophon is virtually synonymous with *sôphrosynê, cf.* 4.5.7. Xenophon's commonsense answer to the paradox was to ignore it, and stress the vital importance of *enkrateia* as an essential prerequisite of *aretê*.

Whether the arguments of Xenophon's Socrates are genuinely Socratic is another matter. The concept of *enkrateia* is entirely absent from Plato's Socratic dialogues, *Charmides* in particular, but occurs twice in *The Republic*, once, *R.* 430e, in association with *sôphrosynê*. In Plato's last work, *The Laws*, 709e ff. the Athenian, whether to be taken as Plato himself or someone like-minded, refers to *sôphrosynê* as the necessary accompaniment of all the parts of virtue and specifies two distinct concepts of *sôphrosynê*, one that of those who dignify it and identify it with wisdom, *phronêsis*, and the other that of common men who regard it as something inborn in children and animals, which makes its possessors act with self-control, ἐγκρατῶς, in dealing with pleasure. This second type of *sôphrosynê* the Athenian dismisses as of no account. Perhaps, therefore, Plato, despite giving *enkrateia* a favourable meaning in *The Republic*, has reverted to some sort of contempt for the concept, and may perhaps be aiming a dig at Xenophon.

For a full discussion of these problems see Guthrie (2) 130–142.

character: translating *psychê*: see note on *Ap.* 7.

1.5.5 by our Lady: literally 'by Hera', a favourite oath of Socrates, to which W. M. Calder, see Bibliography, has devoted a useful study. It was generally used by Plato's Socrates for ironical and feigned admiration, as Calder recognised, but not exclusively, *cf. Phdr.* 230b. Here Xenophon's Socrates uses it seriously, but most, if not all, of seven later usages by Socrates himself in *Mem. Smp.* and *Oec.* seem ironical. Perhaps, when writing *Mem.* 1, Xenophon remembered it as a Socratic oath, or was reminded of it by reading Plato, *e.g. Ap.* 24e, but later, on reading more Plato, came to appreciate its usual ironic significance.

The 1996 supplement to LSJ deleted its statement that this was an Athenian woman's oath. Calder had already accepted that it was a woman's oath and that seems reasonable enough, even if almost all the examples are of men using it in Xenophon and Plato. Hera was not honoured as much in Athens as in Argos, but as Zeus' long-suffering consort she might be particularly honoured by any woman in a male dominated society. Socrates might have adopted the oath ironically to convey the humble impression that like women he was inferior. Perhaps, however, Socrates' best known use of the oath was in Plato *Phdr.* 230b in praising the beauty of the shady resting place under the plane tree, and there at least the oath seems sincere, as addressed to a goddess beautiful herself and a good judge of beauty.

Xenophon, however, never allowed his Socrates to swear by the dog, as Plato did, or by the goose, as Plato's Socrates never did despite LSJ.

anyone enslaved: translating δουλεύοντι which should be read with B and Stobaeus as dative of the agent with ἱκετευτέον

CHAPTER 6

Three conversations with Antiphon the Sophist, who sought to attract Socrates' disciples to himself by criticising him for his miserable standard of life, his refusal to charge fees and his personal abstention from politics.

1.6.1 *Antiphon the Sophist:* scholarly controversy has long raged on whether Antiphon the Sophist is the same man as Antiphon of Rhamnus, praised by Thucydides 8.68; he was prominent in the oligarchical revolution of 411, but after its fall was recalled to Athens, tried and executed despite his brave and eloquent speech in his defence. Though Athenian himself, in most other respects he could be regarded as a sophist, as his extant works include defence speeches for others, and three *Tetralogies* (quadripartite sets of model speeches for the two prosecutors and the two defendants in imaginary cases), and Plato *Menexenus* 236a indicates he was a teacher of rhetoric; moreover Thucydides noted his reputation for cleverness. Pseudo-Plutarch, *Lives of the Ten Orators*, 833c, records him as Socrates' interlocutor in this passage.

However Antiphon was a common Attic name, and we know of an Antiphon as a tragic poet, as a soothsayer, and as a writer about dreams, whether one, two or three people. Hermogenes (third century A.D.) records *DKA* 2, that Didymus (first century A.D.) had already noted another sophist as author of *Truth, Concord* and *Politicus*. These works are lost but fragments indicate the writer to be an extreme democrat and protagonist of the claims of *physis* as opposed to *nomos*; the Rhamnusian, however, was an ardent oligarch and upholder of conventional ideas and the laws. Despite this J. S. Morrison *PCPS* 1961 argued strongly that the Rhamnusian was the author of *Truth* and *Concord* and figured in this passage, but, despite evidence in his favour in the career of the Rhamnusian and the complaint at the end of this passage about Socrates' personal avoidance of politics, he has not completely succeeded in proving his case. For a fuller discussion see Guthrie (1) 285–294.

1.6.2 *your food and drink:* for Socrates' abstemious eating habits see 1.3.5–9, a passage with many similarities to sections 5–11 of this chapter, except that here it is Socrates talking himself. *The neuter forms σιτία and σῖτα, a heteroclyte plural of σῖτος, have parallels in Xenophon, and Plato, but on the evidence of the mss. σιτία seems marginally preferable.

your cloak is poor: cloak, translating ἱμάτιον, the outer garment worn above the χιτών (tunic), the inner garment worn next to the skin.

unchanged summer and winter: as confirmed by Alcibiades' account of Socrates' hardiness at Potidaea during terrible frost, Plato *Smp.* 220b.

you never wear shoes or a tunic: Socrates was regularly mocked by the comic poets for his bare feet, and he even trod the snow at Potidaea, Plato *Smp.* ibid., unshod, and according to Phaedrus, Plato *Phdr.* 229a, he was always barefooted; but for 'never', 'hardly ever' would be more accurate, as he made an exception for a special occasion, Plato *Smp.* 174a.

1.6.3 *make their disciples copy themselves:* *cf.* 1.2.3, 8, 17.

a teacher of misery: this complaint is appropriate, if from the Antiphon credited by Pseudo-Plutarch, *loc. cit.* with a *technê alupias* (*Art of avoiding Pain*, whether a system or a published work) and by Philostratus, *Lives of the Sophists* 499, with *nêpentheis* (pain-banishing) lectures, though both writers include these details in biographies of the Rhamnusian. Guthrie 1971(1) 290–1 cautiously suggests that these details may refer to the author of *Truth*, whose philosophy of life was 'a refined and intellectual hedonism'.

1.6.5 *lifestyle...victuals:* translating δίαιτα in its normal general sense, as in 1.3.5, to include all the points made by Socrates up to § 10, but inclusive of the meaning 'diet' (as in modern English), 'eating habits' (a specialised use of the word in medical writers), and taking the cognate word διαιτήματα in the more limited sense of 'victuals' 'food'.

relish: translating ὄψον: see note on 1.3.5, where Xenophon makes the same point about Socrates, as here he makes for himself.

1.6.6 *cold...sore feet:* see note on 1.6.2.

1.6.7 *physical training:* Socrates, when not in the *agora*, was often to be found at *palaistrai*, wrestling grounds, *cf.* Plato *Chrm.* 153a, though using them mainly for discussions, Plato *Ly.* 204a. He even approved of dancing as a means of keeping fit, Xenophon *Smp.* 2.17. See also 1.3.5 ff.

1.6.8 *gluttony...lust:* *cf.* 1.3.7, 1.3.8–15.

1.6.9 *military service:* for Socrates'own fitness for military service see Alcibiades' tribute to his hardiness and endurance in severe wintry conditions at Potidaea early in the war, Plato *Smp.* 219e, and to his courage and composure and his saving of Alcibiades' life at Delium in 424, and also Laches' praise of his behaviour there, Plato *La.* 181b; Plato's Socrates also mentions soldiering at Amphipolis in 422 (at the age of 47), *Ap.* 28e.

1.6.10 *needing nothing:* being self-sufficient; see note on 1.3.5.

1.6.11–12 Antiphon's interest in money is typical of a sophist. Socrates was at pains in Plato *Ap.* 19e ff. to reject his portrayal in *Clouds* as charging fees; see also Xenophon *Ap.* 16.

1.6.13 *amongst us:* in the circle of my friends and disciples. E. R. Dodds, *CR* 1954, 94–5 revived a theory that the meaning is 'amongst us Athenians', and that therefore the addressee is a non-Athenian, and so not the Rhamnusian, but has failed to convince most scholars, including J. S. Morrison.

brand as: translating ἀποκαλῶ (call by an uncomplimentary name).

a perfect man: translating *kalon te kagathon*, as later in this chapter; see note on 1.1.16.

a man of character: translating σώφρονα, having *sôphrosynê*, see note on 1.1.16.

sophists: for Xenophon's low opinion of contemporary sophists see his treatise on hunting *Cyn.* 13, where he stigmatises them as immoral hunters of young men, as opposed to philosophers who are friends to all and share with all. Plato, in a late work, *The Sophist*, 231d, e gives six different definitions of 'sophist'.

[as resembling prostitutes]: I follow Ruhnken in omitting this as an interpolation.

1.6.14 *horse...hound...bird:* Xenophon's account of Socrates' delight in good friends seems to be indebted to an early work of Plato, *Lysis*, where, 211e, Socrates describes his passionate desire for the possession of friends, and his valuing a good friend more highly than the best quail or cock in the world or even more highly than any horse or dog. In *Mem.* 2.4 Socrates returns to the subject, saying that no other possession can compare with a good friend, who is to be valued above any horse, yoke of oxen or faithful slave. (Note how Xenophon there omits Plato's quail, having criticised, 2.1.4–5 its excessive amorous propensities.) Xenophon's picture of Socrates as a loyal, useful and helpful friend compares favourably with the Socrates of at least *Lysis*, who gives rein to his notorious irony to pretend, *Ly.* 212a, that he has no friends and doesn't know how to acquire one.

unroll: open up the papyrus scrolls and read.

1.6.15 The criticism of Socrates' avoidance of personal involvement in politics is well suited to the Rhamnusian; if so, the dramatic date is no later than 411. However all sophists concentrated on rich young men with political ambitions, and so any dramatic date for this criticism prior to the affair of the Arginusai generals in 406 is possible. For Socrates' opposition as a *bouleutês* to the block execution see note on 1.1.18.

CHAPTER 7

1.7.1 encouraged: Xenophon here uses the active form of προτρέπω, as opposed to the middle in the similar context of 1.4.1, but there seems no difference in meaning, *cf.* 2.1.1. Throughout 1.3–7 Xenophon concentrates on Socrates' efforts and example for the benefit of his disciples; thus even the preceding discourses with Antiphon are relevant, because held in the presence of his companions and for their instruction. One topic, however, which Xenophon avoids is the success of Socrates' efforts, *cf.* 1.4.1 and note on 1.5.1. Xenophon does at least avow Socrates' verbal competence in expositions and definitions in 4.8.11; see pp. 158–9.

imposture: translating ἀλαζονεία, the noun cognate with ἀλάζων, defined by Aristotle, *EN*, 1127a 20 ff. as 'one who claims to have creditable qualities he lacks or to have them to a greater extent than he does.' The translation 'impostor' is appropriate for Xenophon, see D. M. MacDowell, *The Meaning of alazôn, Owls to Athena*, Oxford, 1990, 287–292, and indeed for Aristotle, though 'pretentious' or even 'boastful' might serve in Theophrastus, *Characters*, 23.

For Aristotle the opposite of the ἀλάζων is the εἴρων who misses the virtuous mean of truthfulness and sincerity by self-depreciation, though for him, when the motive for εἰρωνεία is not gain but the avoidance of ostentation, it is less culpable and he seems to include Socrates in this category; indeed even the μεγαλόψυχος, man with greatness of spirit, may use it for honourable motives. Theophrastus' *eirôn*, however, in *Characters* 1, if judged by the examples of his behaviour, is a nasty contemptible dissembler.

In this chapter Xenophon's Socrates gives advice (to be repeated to Critobulus in 2.6.38 ff. and to Euthydemus in 4.2.8 and put into the mouth of Cyrus' father in *Cyr.* 1.6.22) that there is no short cut to a good reputation in any sphere of action; one must actually become good in it; otherwise he will be exposed and disgraced and the consequences will be disastrous, whether he be a pipe-player, a helmsman or a general.

1.7.2 pipe-player: player of the αὐλός, the double pipe.

fine equipment: translating σκεύη τε καλὰ of the manuscripts: Cobet's correction to σκευήν τε καλὴν is printed in Marchant's Loeb, but σκευή commonly means 'dress', 'costume', and surely good instruments are also necessary. Moreover κατασκευάς, used in the parallel passage in *Cyr.* 1.6.22, has a more general meaning; similarly σκευάρια in Aristophanes *Acharnians* 451 and *Wasps* 1313 means 'props', 'equipment'.

1.7.3 to be a good general: *stratêgos* means 'army-leader' and here for the moment Socrates merely refers to military duties. At Athens, however, ten *stratêgoi* were chosen by vote annually. A *stratêgos* might be given charge of an army or a fleet, but he also was heavily involved in state duties and would be expected to address and advise the assembly.

1.7.5 persuading others...the state: by getting himself elected to the *stratêgia* or another important office. Socrates reverts to the topics of this chapter, military command and political leadership, in 3.1–7 and 4.2, repeatedly making the point that political skills only come to those with the right basic qualities and then only after long and serious study and preparation and, 4.3.1, after first acquiring prudence (*sôphrosynê*). Socrates also regularly objects to ignorant and unqualified men speaking in the assembly to offer advice on matters of state.

XENOPHON'S SOCRATES

Any educated person of the twenty-first century need not be a philosophical specialist or classical scholar to have some conception of who Socrates was and of his characteristic behaviour. This is entirely due to Plato, not Xenophon. Plato started writing about Socrates before Xenophon, and was better qualified to do so, almost certainly having been closer to Socrates and having had a longer association with him, whereas Xenophon was absent from Athens for the last two years of Socrates' life and for many years thereafter. Moreover Plato was of a philosophical bent, interested in arguments and thought processes and able to describe them clearly and in detail. But above all he could be described as a prose dramatist, whose graphic literary skills made his hero come alive for his readers. Plato's portrayal of Socrates should, therefore, be more accurate, reliable and detailed than that of Xenophon.

Plato assigned a leading role to Socrates in all his works, except his last one, *The Laws*, but, as time went on, he began to use Socrates as a spokesman for his own philosophical theories, though these were often logical developments of Socrates' original views. Most scholars, therefore, believe that only in Plato's earliest works does he represent the real Socrates arguing and thinking for himself. These so-called 'Socratic' works probably precede the *Phaedo* but include the *Apology* and dialogues such as *Charmides*, *Crito*, *Euthyphro*, *Hippias Minor*, *Laches* and *Lysis*.

One argument in favour of Plato's honesty and truthfulness in these Socratic works is that Socrates is far from idealised, but depicted as sometimes using illogical, fallacious or even immorally based arguments against opponents; for details see D. W. Graham, 152–3, who is justified in concluding 'Plato portrays Socrates, then, as dialectically devious and at least willing to maintain a questionable moral stance.'

Aristotle, however, did describe Socratic discussions as μιμήσεις, imitations, representations; even Plato's works, therefore, might contain a certain amount of fiction. Vlastos, 1980, 3–4, argues convincingly that the *Apology* is 'a reliable recreation of the thought and character of the man that Plato knew so well', but stresses that it is 'recreation, not reportage'. One fiction in *Apology* might well be 'Plato's invention' of the Chaerephon story, see Stokes 115–6 and Waterfield 88. That fiction, however, if fiction it is, is considerably less than Xenophon's embroidery of the Delphic response in *Ap.* 14. But it is not for me to speculate on fictitious elements in early works of Plato, only to suggest that Xenophon did have a precedent for fiction in his Socratic works.

Xenophon's knowledge of Socrates came from three main sources. Firstly there were personal memories of Socrates up to 401BC. Secondly there was what Hermogenes, and perhaps other friends, told him in the years after Socrates' death, but only after Xenophon settled at Scillous would there be much likelihood of encounters with friends or visits from them, except every fourth year during the Olympic festival. Thirdly there would be the works of Plato, when published. Some of the information from friends would be based on them. Eventually Xenophon might have been able to read them for himself, whether from copies lent to him or, just possibly, acquired by himself.

It would seem therefore that the Socratic works of Xenophon are a less reliable and less valuable source of information about Socrates than those of Plato. Xenophon, however, is a useful supplement to Plato in illustrating the various factors which contributed to Socrates' condemnation. One of the main reasons for that was, as both Plato's *Apology* and Xenophon's adaptation of it make clear, Socrates in his two speeches at his trial made not the slightest effort to court the goodwill of the jurors or coax them into acquitting him or deciding against the death penalty. Note, however, how Xenophon, by adding probably fictitious remarks by Socrates about Anytus to his *Apology*, drew readers' attention to Anytus as the most formidable of the three accusers and a major threat to Socrates, see notes on *Ap.* 29–31.

Memories of the harm done to Athens by Critias and Alcibiades must have contributed to Socrates' unpopularity, as they had once been his associates. Neither politician was mentioned by Socrates in Plato's *Apology* or in Xenophon's adaptation of it, perhaps because, as suggested by Malcolm Willcock, it was avoided as a weak spot in the defence. It may be, however, that Socrates felt no guilt about them and his silence about them was truthfully recorded by Plato. In any case Xenophon found this topic in Polycrates' exercise and deserves credit for realising its importance and rebutting this feature of Polycrates' accusation so fully in *Mem.* 1.2.12–47.

I continue the discussion of Xenophon's portrayal of Socrates by giving a translation of his final eulogy of Socrates in *Mem.* 4.8.11 recapitulating his virtues and services to devotees of virtue for readers to admire and emulate.

Of those who know what sort of man Socrates was, all who seek after virtue still, even to this day, miss him more than they do anyone else, thinking him the greatest of benefactors towards the pursuit of virtue.

Indeed, in my opinion, because he was the sort of man I have described, so pious that he did nothing without the approval of the gods, so just that he did not do even the least of harm to anyone, but conferred the greatest benefits on his companions, so self-controlled that he never chose the pleasanter option in preference to the better one, so prudent that he made no mistakes in judging the better things and the worse things, and did not need anyone's help, but relied on himself for knowing about these things, capable in his verbal exposition and definition of such matters, and capable too in putting others to the test and proving them wrong when they were in error, and in encouraging them to seek virtue and become perfect men, he therefore seemed to be an example of a superlatively good and fortunate man.

But if anyone disagrees with this, let him compare the character of others with these qualities of Socrates and then judge.

The second paragraph, which amplifies the simpler final eulogy of *Ap.* 34, consists of 102 Greek words and is perhaps the most impressive and effective sentence Xenophon ever wrote. Carefully constructed, elaborate and detailed, it clearly and comprehensively summarises the impression of the character, life-style and behaviour of Socrates, the perfect man and exemplary educator, which Xenophon has striven to convey throughout *Mem.*

Some comments:

pious: typically Xenophon makes piety the first virtue, or component of the virtue, of Socrates, just as in *Mem.* 1.3.1 he starts the main part of *Mem.* with Socrates' attitude to religion.

without the approval of the gods: the *daimonion* would have come to veto any contemplated action.

did not do even the least of harm to anyone: 'anyone' should include enemies. So here Xenophon is closer to Plato's Socrates than in *Mem.* 2.6.35, where he seems to approve of the view that it is virtuous to excel in harming enemies.

self-controlled: translating ἐγκρατής; Xenophon prefers to stress ἐγκράτεια rather than σωφροσύνη, when enumerating virtues or parts of virtue; *cf.* *Mem.*, 1.3, 1.5, 2.1, *etc.*

prudent: translating φρόνιμος not σώφρων.

knowing about: translating γνῶσις. Note that this is Xenophon, not Socrates, speaking. Plato's Socrates might have preferred to use irony and pretend he knew hardly anything, *cf., Ap.* 22c, *etc.*

relied on himself: translating αὐταρκής, self-sufficient, the attribute of Socrates which particularly appealed to Antisthenes and the Cynics.

capable in ... definition: Xenophon gives his own abbreviated version of Socrates arriving at definitions in *Mem.* 4.6, see p. 60. Plato, Xenophon and Aristotle all emphasise the importance Socrates gave to definitions. Socrates' capability in this area could be questioned. The early dialogues of Plato which should reveal the true Socrates in search of a definition involve a succession of long and complicated arguments and tend to end in an impasse, so that they have been labelled as *aporetic* because they reduce the participants to *aporia*, a state of helplessness, or what A. R. Lacey, in Vlastos, 1980, p. 38, calls 'apparent bewilderment'.

when they were in error: stressing that the elenchus was justified. In *Mem.*, Xenophon gives several examples of a helpful elenchus with positive results, *e.g.* involving Aristodemus 1.4 and Euthydemus 4.3, 4.5 and 4.6 and Hippias 4.4. The least useful elenchus in *Mem.* is conducted not by Socrates, but by the objectionable Alcibiades in 1.2.40–46.

encouraging them to seek virtue: by emphasising Socrates' capability in this respect Xenophon gives a positive answer to the enquiries he conducted in 1.4, 1.5 and 1.7.

Differences between the two representations of Socrates

The differences between the two representations of Socrates can partly be explained by the interests and motives of the two writers. Plato, the intellectual, took a special interest in the thoughts and arguments of his mentor. Xenophon, however, though showing in *Mem.* 1 some skill in philosophical or theological exposition in his account of Socrates' dialogue with Aristodemus, was less interested in Socrates the philosopher than in Socrates the teacher, who taught how to lead a virtuous, self-sufficient and happy life, not just by his words but by the example he set. Throughout his writings, Xenophon was instinctively a moraliser, and occasionally for his readers, a would-be teacher himself, interested in education and training as a practical means towards a virtuous and happy life. Socrates, therefore, was a subject very much to Xenophon's liking.

When Xenophon started writing *Mem.*, he was already established as a prosperous landowner at Scillous, and as he had no doubts about his own piety with his particular devotion to Artemis, or about his military record, he could well regard himself as a *kaloskagathos* and, as I see it, he made it his purpose to make his Socrates a flawless example for fellow *kalokagathoi* to imitate; he already at this early stage planned the main details of the comprehensive portrait of Socrates he was to place at the end of *Mem.* 4, and he worked reasonably consistently throughout *Mem.* with this plan in mind. On the subject of the relationship of Xenophon's Socrates to a *kaloskagathos* see also Waterfield's useful article. The term was normally limited to aristocrats or upper-class men, see note on 1.6.14, but Xenophon broke new ground in using the term more freely of men of whom he thoroughly approved, *e.g.*, of a devoted teacher of virtue to a friend, *Mem.* 1.6.14, of soldiers who died bravely in battle, *An.* 4.1.19 and even made his Ischomachus, *Oec.* 14.9, treat a virtuous slave like a *kaloskagathos.* He could therefore have no hesitation in applying the term to Socrates despite the poverty of this lifestyle, as he had earlier been prosperous enough to be a hoplite, had many aristocratic friends, and was thoroughly at ease as the guest of wealthy men such as Callias and Agathon.

Xenophon's tendency to idealise and disregard historical facts, which he was to show in his *Agesilaos* and *Institutio Cyri*, can be seen, though to a lesser extent, in his representation in *Mem.* of a Socrates without any faults.

Vlastos 1980, p. 1 came out with the statement that 'Xenophon's Socrates is a Socrates without irony and without paradox. Take that away from Plato's Socrates and there is nothing left.' Of course the second sentence is a grave underestimation of Xenophon's Socratic works, but Xenophon knew very well what he was doing in depicting a Socrates without much irony or paradox. He and the *kaloikagathoi* for whom he was writing would regard the ironical man, the dissembler, as Theophrastus was to do, as someone nasty and dishonest; but see notes on *Mem.* 1.7. Unfortunately for readers however, the comparative lack of irony made Xenophon's Socrates less humorous.

One particular example of the irony of Plato's Socrates, his pretence of ignorance, was also a paradox unlikely to be acceptable to normal, sensible men of the world. How could Socrates teach others, if ignorant himself?

Therefore only rarely, as in *Mem.* 1.2.34, does Xenophon make his Socrates pretend ignorance, though in *Mem.* 1.2.36 Critias justifiably in the context accuses him of asking questions to which he knows the answers. Xenophon generally depicts Socrates as knowledgeable and wise, but prefers to call him σώφρων or φρόνιμος rather than σοφός, a word often applied pejoratively to quibbling sophists.

Another paradox that Xenophon avoided was the assertion by Plato's Socrates that 'no one willingly does wrong' and that there was no such thing as ἀκρασία, incontinence, lack of self-control. Xenophon gave particular emphasis to the existence and importance of its opposite ἐγκράτεια as the basis of virtue; see note on *Mem.* 1.5.4.

Because Xenophon was a practical man who placed great store on successful results, he made his Socrates into a more positive and effective figure than his Platonic counterpart. Thus Xenophon describes him as competent in verbal exposition and definitions, unlike the Socrates of dialogues like *Euthyphro* and *Charmides* which end most inconclusively, see note on *Mem.* 4.8.11 on p. 157. Similarly, though Xenophon does give examples of his Socrates using elenchus, something which made him many enemies, they usually are helpful and beneficial to the recipients of the elenchus, see note on 4.8.11 on p. 157. Positive as well as negative instruction was also a feature of the *daimonion* of Xenophon's Socrates; see note on *Ap.* 4.

Other differences may be due to Xenophon, perhaps sometimes inadvertently, making Socrates think or talk like himself by showing greater interest in, and knowledge of, Sparta, *Ap.* 15, *Mem.* 1.2.61., and Persia, *Oec.* 4.5, 14.6, than one would expect from the man who had never left Athens, except when on military service. Similarly in *Mem.* 1.5.2 Xenophon's Socrates discussed the sort of slave we should trust to look after our flocks or our money, just as he is later to show an interest in running as estate in *Oec.*, unlike the Socrates of Plato's *Apology* 36b who had disclaimed interest in money-making or running an estate. Xenophon had earlier, in *Ap.* 30, made his Socrates sneer at tanning as a servile occupation, *cf.* also *Oec.* 4.2, but this seems unlikely as Socrates himself was trained as a stone-mason and thoroughly approved of the expertise of cobblers, carpenters, smiths and their like, as long as they did not presume to advise on matters of state in the assembly.

Xenophon in his version of the Delphic response to Chaerephon gives first place to a virtue of Socrates rather less noted by Plato, that he was ἐλευθέριος, which I translated as 'free-spirited', but an alternative translation might sometimes be 'generous' as in *Smp.* 4.15, where Socrates says that 'we handsome men' (note this magnificent touch of humour by the ugly Socrates), 'make them' (sc. 'our lovers') ἐλευθεριωτέρους εἰς χρήματα, 'more generous as regards money'.

There can be two main objections to Socrates fully deserving the description *kaloskagathos*, firstly that in appearance he was not *kalos*, handsome, but brutally ugly; Xenophon, however, preferred to think, as we Britons do today, that 'handsome is as handsome does'. Secondly Socrates was far from rich and prosperous, normal prerequisites for a *kaloskagathos*, but Xenophon's thoughts, when he was completing *Mem.*, were along the same lines as in *Smp.* where, 1.34–44, Antisthenes boasts about his wealth, which he says he had acquired from Socrates, by following his frugal, hardy lifestyle, implying that they were both as rich as their host Callias. Xenophon, therefore, by his characterisation of Socrates, has provided one more Socratic paradox, by suggesting to his readers that the ugly Socrates who claimed in Plato's *Apology* to be living in abject poverty, was really a *kaloskagathos*.

Finally, Plato's most distinctive contribution to philosophical thinking, his 'Theory of Forms' or 'Ideas', expounded by his Socrates in the *Phaedo* and later dialogues, was too far-fetched for Xenophon to accept or to let his down-to-earth Socrates use.

SUPPLEMENTARY NOTES ON THE TEXT

Changes from Marchant's Oxford Classical Text incorporated in this text (see pp. 20, 62).

Ap. 7	κατακριθῇ μοι
Ap. 8	τότε μὲν for τότε μου
Ap. 23	διεψηφίσθη
Ap. 33	τἄλλ' ἀγαθὰ for τἆλλα τἀγαθὰ
Mem. 1.1.18	ἐννέα στρατηγοὺς without brackets
Mem. 1.2.6	ἂν without brackets
Mem. 1.2.23	σωφρονήσαντας ... δυνηθέντας
Mem. 1.2.35	brackets removed
Mem. 1.2.46	ταῦτα added
Mem. 1.2.58	ὅντινα for ὃν; ἄνδρα omitted
Mem. 1.3.1	Οἷς for Ὡς
Mem. 1.3.3	p. 100 l.8 Κὰδ δύναμιν
Mem. 1.3.10	ἐγώ μοι δοκῶ for ἐγὼ δοκῶ μοι
Mem. 1.3.10	ὑποστῆναι for ὑπομεῖναι
Mem. 1.4.11	deletion of καὶ ὄψιν ... ἐνεποίησαν
Mem. 1.4.15	σοὶ for σὺ
Mem. 1.5.1	ἂν without brackets
Mem. 1.5.5	δουλεύοντι
Mem. 1.6.2	σιτία for σῖτά
Mem. 1.6.10	δὲ νομίζω

Further recommended changes from Marchant's Oxford Text. These are indicated by asterisks.

Ap. 11	ἄλλοι οἱ for οἱ ἄλλοι οἱ
Ap. 16	διέλιπον
Ap. 24	ὀνομάζων
Ap. 28	μᾶλλον ἂν
*Mem.*1.2.12	add καὶ φονικώτατος
*Mem.*1.2.12	add καὶ βιαιότατος
*Mem.*1.2.30	προσκνήσασθαι and ὑΐδια
*Mem.*1.3.3	p. 100 l.6 read Κὰδ δύναμιν
*Mem.*1.3.8	add lacuna
*Mem.*1.3.12	trs. δύναμιν to before εἶναι; trs. ὄντα ante τὸ; read ὅσον μόνον ἀψάμενα; read ὀδύναις τε
*Mem.*1.4.1	Οἷς for Ὡς
*Mem.*1.4.2	after θεοῖς add οὔτ' εὐχόμενον δῆλον ὄντα
*Mem.*1.4.8	οὕτως for ὡς
*Mem.*1.5.2	ἡγησαίμεθ' ἂν for ἡγησόμεθα
*Mem.*1.5.2	ἐπιστασίαν for ἐπίστασιν
*Mem.*1.5.2	read τὸν τοιοῦτον

INDEX

Plain numbers refer to pages of the whole volume.
A = Apology, text and commentary.
M = Memorabilia, text and commentary.

accusative absolute *M* 1.2.20
Aeschines, Socratic writer 8,16,134, *A* 1
Agesilaus 5, 10
agnostics *M* 1.1.4
akrasia 160, *M* 1.5.4
alazôn, alazôneia A 1, *M* 1.1.5, 1.7
Alcibiades 8, 12, 16, 132–4, 156, *M*
 1.2.9, 1.2.12–26, 1.2.39–47, 1.3.8
Anabasis see Xenophon
anaphora *A* 1, 17, *M* 1.2.32
Anaxagoras *A* 10, *M* 1.1.11, 1.4.4
anthrôpos etymology of, *M* 1.6
Antiphon, a sophist *M* 1.6
Antisthenes 8, 16, 134, 162, *A* 16, 18,
 M 1.3.5
Anytus 8, 17, *A* 10, 29–31, 157, *M*
 1.2.9, 1.4.17
Apollo 9, 10, *A* 14; see also Delphi,
 Pythia
Apollodorus *A* 28, *M* 1.4.2
apologia 17, *A* 1
aretê 155ff., *A* 29, *M* 1.1.5, 1.2.18,
 1.5.4
Arginusae 8, 133, *M* 1.1.16
Aristippus 16, 59, *M* 1.5.4
Aristodemus *M* 1.4
Aristophanes 60, 133, *A* 20, *M* 1.1.5,
 1.1.11, 1.1.14, 1.2.5, 1.2.31, 1.2.48,
 1.3.8, 1.6.11, 1.7.2
Aristotle 155–6, 158, *A* 1, *M* 1.1.16,
 1.4.6, 1.7.1
Arrian 1
Artemis 10

artisans, skilled *A* 20, *M* 1.2.37, 1.4.7
assembly, see *ecclêsia*
atheism, atheists *M* 1.1.5, 1.1.14
atomists *M* 1.1.14
Athenaeus *A* 14, *M* 1.5.2
aulêtês, aulos M 1.2.27, 1.7.2
Aulus Gellius 15
autarkeia, self-sufficiency 155ff., *M*
 1.3.5, 1.7.2
banausos, degrading *A* 30, *M* 1.2.57
Boeotia 87, 12, see Cebes, Simmias,
 Thebes
boulê, bouleutês, council, councillor *M*
 1.1.18, 1.2.35
carpenters 160, *M* 1.2.37
cavalry 6, 7
Cebes *A* 23, *M* 1.2.37
Chaerecrates *M* 1.2.48
Chaerephon 19, 155, *A* 14, *M* 1.2.48
Charicles *M* 1.2.31
Charmides 8, 15, 59, *M* 1.2.48
Charmides, see Plato
Cicero 1, *M* 1.1.16, 1.4.17
Circe *M* 1.3.7
Clinias *M* 1.3.8
Clitophon *M* 1.4.1
Clitophon, see Plato
cobblers 160, *M* 1.2.37, 1.2.56
Corinth 11
Coronea, battle of 10
cosmology *M* 1.1.11
council, councillor, see *boulê*
Cratylus, see Plato

Creator, the, see *dêmiourgos*
Critias 8, 12, 131–2, 156, *M* 1.1.14, 1.2.12–38, 56–57
Crito 16, *A* 1, 23, *M* 1.2.48, 1.3.8
Crito, see Plato
Critobulus *M* 1.3.8
cross-questioning, see *elenchos*
Cynegeticus, see Xenophon
Cynics 8, 16. *A* 16, *M* 1.3.5
Cyreniacs 16, 197
Cyrus the Great 1, 5, 6, 14–15, *A* 1, 5, *M* 1.2.23, 1.2.32, 1.3.2, 1.3.5, 1.4.17
Cyri Institutio, see Xenophon
daimonion 8, 18, 19, 157, 160, *A* 4, 10, 13, *M* 1.1.1–2, 1.4.2, 1.4.15, 1.4.18
definitions 60, 158–9, *M* 1.1.16, 1.2.41
Dêlia A 1
Delium, battle of, 12
Delphi 9, 19, *M* 1.2.48, 1.3.1; see also Apollo, Pythia
dêmiourgos M 1.4.5, 1.4.7
Diagoras of Melos *M* 1.1.14
diaita M 1.3.5, 1.6.5
Diodorus, son of Xenophon 10, 11
Diogenes, the Cynic *M* 1.3.5
Diogenes Laertius 7, 8, 10–12, 15, 16, 59, *A* 1, 10, 23, 28, 29, *M* 1.1.16, 1.2.9, 1.2.43, 1.3.5, 1.4.17
Dionysodorus, the sophist *M* 1.4.1
doctors *A* 20
ecclêsia, the assembly *A* 20, *M* 1.1.18, 1.2.9, 1.2.37, 1.2.58
education, of sons *A* 31
Egypt *M* 1.4.17
eirôneia see irony
ekkleptô A 22
Eleatics *M* 1.1.14
elenchos, elenchus, *elenchô* 157–160, *A* 10, *M* 1.2.14, 1.2.41, 1.2.47, 1.4.1
Empedocles *M* 1.1.14

enkrateia, enkratês, self-control, self-controlled 60, 157, *M* 1.2.1, 1.2.23, 1.3.7, 1.5
epiteleisthai A 5, 33
Erasinides *M* 1.1.18
Erchia 7
estate management 5, *M* 1.1.7; see *oikoi*, Xenophon, *Oec.*
Euclides of Megara 16
Euripides 132, *A* 26, *M* 1.1.14
Euthydemus, a disciple of Socrates 60, *M* 1.2.29–30, 1.5.4
Euthydemus, the sophist *M* 1.4.1
Euthydemus, see Plato
Euthyphro, *Euthyphro*, see Plato
exile, Xenophon's 10, 11
farming, see Xenophon, *Oec.*
fees, not charged by Socrates *M* 1.2.5–7, 1.2.60, 1.6
freedom of spirit 155ff., *A* 9, 14, 16, *M* 1.2.6, 1.2.29, 1.3.11, 1.5.5
friendship *M* 1.2.7, 1.2.52, 1.4.18; see Lysis
generals see *stratêgoi, stratêgia*
Glaucon 15, 59, *M* 1.2.37
God, gods *A* 5, 8, 13, *M* 1.4.2ff.; see also *daimonion*, oaths, omniscience, providence
Gorgias *A* 26, *M* 1.1.14
Gorgias, see Plato
Gryllus, father of Xenophon 7
Gryllus, son of Xenophon 10, 11, 15
Gymnopaidiai 11, *M* 1.2.61
haplography *A* 14, 32
Hellenica, HG, see Xenophon
Hera, oath by *M* 1.5.5
Heraclitus *M* 1.1.14
Hermes *M* 1.3.7
Hermogenes 17–19, 60, 156, *A* 2–27, *M* 1.2.48
Hesiod *M* 1.2.56, 1.3.3, 1.4.17

Hiero, of Xenophon 6
Hippias, the sophist 60
Hipponicus *A* 2
Homer *A* 30, *M* 1.2.58, 1.3.7
horses, Xenophon and 6, 7
hyperbaton, see word order
Ideal Theory of Plato *M* 1.1.6
imposture, see *alazôneia*
irony, of Socrates 155ff., *A* 1, 9, 14, *M* 1.1.18, 1.2.34, 36, 1.7.1
Ischomachus 10, 14
Isocrates 12, *M* 1.2.9
juries, citizen *A* 3, 14, 23
justice 155ff., *A* 5 , 14, 16, *M* 1.1.16
kainos, new *A* 10, *M* 1.14.1
kaloskagathos, the perfect man 8, 12, 157–8, 161, *M* 1.1.16, 1.2.2, 1.2.7, 1.2.18, 1.2.23, 1.2.29, 1.2.48, 1.3.11, 1.5.1, 1.6.13ff.
knowledge 158, *M* 1.1.16
kybernêtês, steersman *M* 1.7.3
Lacedaimon, see Sparta
Laches, see Plato
Lamprocles 59
Leucippus *M* 1.1.14
Leuctra, battle of 11–14
Libanius *M* 1.2.58
Lichas *M* 1.2.61
lot, election by *M* 1.2.9
Lucian *M* 1.4.19
Lycon *A* 10
Lycurgus *A* 15
Lysander 14
Lysias 16
Lysis, see Plato
Mantinea, battle of 15
megalêgoria, boastfulness *A* 1, 9, 16–21, 32
Melanippides *M* 1.4.3
Meletus 17, 18, *A* 10, 11, 19, 20
Melissus *M* 1.1.14

Meno *M* 1.4.17
Meno, see Plato
monotheism, see God, gods
nomizô A 10, 24, *M* 1.1.1, 1.1.3
nomos M 1.2.41–45, 1.3.1
oaths, of Socrates *A* 10, *M* 1.5.5
Odysseus 60, *A* 26, *M* 1.3.7
Oeconomicus, see Xenophon
oikoi 160, *M* 1.1.7, 1.2.64, 1.5.2
Olympia 10, 11
omens 14, 19, *A* 12, 13, *M* 1.1.3
omniscience, of gods *M* 1.1.19, 1.4.18
ôphelimos, helpful, useful, beneficial 1 58–60, 159ff., 1.2.55
opson M 1.3.5, 1.6.5
oracles, see Delphi
Ovid, *M* 1.5.4
Palamedes 18, *A* 26
Parmenides *M* 1.1.14
Pausanias, the traveller and writer 11
perfect man, the, see *kaloskagathos*
Pericles *M* 1.2.40–46, 1.2.53, 1.4.13
Pericles, the younger 59
Phaedo, see Plato
Phaedondas *M* 1.2.48
Philasia 10
Philebus, see Plato
Philostratus *M* 1.6.3
phronêsis, *phronimos* 157, 159, *A* 20, *M* 1.4.17
physis, nature *M* 1.3.1
physiologoi M 1.1.14
piety 157, 159, *A* 5, *M* 1.1.16, 1.3.1–4; see also *Euthyphro*
Plato 1, 13–19, 155ff., *A*, *M* passim
Alcibiades 1, *M* 1.4.9
Apology 13–19, 160, *A*, *M* passim
Charmides 14, 160, *M* 1.2.12, 1.2.56–57, 1.5.4, 1.6.7
Clitophon M 1.4.1
Cratylus A 2, *M* 1.4.11

Crito A 1, 23, 27, *M* 1.2.48, 1.3.8
Epistle, Seventh M 1.4.17
Euthydemus 14, *M* 1.2.9, 1.2.29,
    1.3.8, 1.4.1
Euthyphro 60, 160, *A* 1, *M* 1.2.49,
    1.4.10, 1.4.18
Gorgias M 1.2.48
Laches M 1.6.9
Laws 15, 155, *M* 1.4.17, 1.5.4
Lysis 15, 59, *M* 1.2.25, 1.2.52,
    1.6.7, 1.6.14
Menexenus M 1.6.1
Meno 13, 14, 16 *A* 1, 29, *M* 1.2.20,
    1.4.17
Phaedo A 1, *M* 1.2.53, 1.4.4, 1.4.9
Philebus A 32, *M* 1.4.8
Protagoras 12, *M* 1.2.12, 1.2.20,
    1.2.37, 1.4.3
Republic 60, *M* 1.1.16, 1.3.12,
    1.4.1, 1.4.12, 1.5.4
Symposium 15, *M* 1.2.1, 1.2.12,
    1.3.6, 1.3.12, 1.3.14, 1.4.2, 1.6.2,
    1.6.9
Timaeus M 1.4.5–6
Plutarch M 1.2.12. 1.2.22, 1.2.38
Polycrates, accuser of Socrates 13, 16,
    157, *M* 1.2.9, 1.2.56
Polyclitus *M* 1.4.3
polytheism, see gods
preSocratic philosophers *M* 1.1.14
president of the council, *prytanis M*
    1.1.16
Prodicus 8, 59, *M* 1.1.14
Protagoras *M* 1.2.31
Protagoras, see Plato
providence, divine, *M* 1.4.2–198
proxenos 10, *A* 7, *M* 1.2.61
Proxenos of Thebes 8, 12, *M* 1.2.48
prytanis, see president of the council
psychê, soul, spirit *etc.*, *A* 7, 8, 30, 33, *M*
    1.2.4, 1.2.198, 1.2.53, 1.3.5, 1.3.7,

1.4.8, 1.4.9, 1.4.13, 1.5.3, 1.5.5
Pythia, Pytho *M* 1.3.1; see also Apollo,
    Delphi
sacrificing *M* 1.1.2
Scillous 10, 14
sêmainô, sêmeion, Socrates' divine
    sign, signalling orders *A* 4, 12, 13,
    M 1.1.18, 1.1.19, 1.2.19
servility, see slavishness
Sextus Empiricus *M* 1.2.12
Sicily *M* 1.4.17
Simmias *A* 23, *M* 1.2.37
slavery to pleasure *M* 1.4.17, 1.5.5
slavishness, Socrates' abhorrence of
    servile behaviour, attitudes and
    occupations 161, *A* 9, 14, 16, 30, *M*
    1.1.16, 1.2.9, 1.2.29, 1.3.11, 1.5.5
smiths 161, *M* 1.2.37
Socrates, accusers of, see Anytus,
    Lycon, Meletus, Polycrates
    as example of the perfect man, see
    kaloskagathos
    charges against *A* 10, *M* 1.1.1
    Delphic response about *A* 14
    not charging fees *M* 1.2.5–7,
        1.2.60, 1.6.132
    freedom of spirit of 156ff., *A* 9,
        14, 16, 30, *M* 1.1.6, 1.2.9, 1.2.29,
        1.3.11
    hardiness of *M* 1.6.2
    helpfulness of, see *ôphelimos*
    justice of *A* 5, 14, 16,156ff.
    life-style of *A* 18, *M* 1.6, see also
        diaita, enkrateia
    military service of *M* 1.6.9
    on appointment of officials by lot
        M 1.2.9
    on sex *M* 1.3.8–15, 1.4.12
    piety of 156ff., *A* 10, 22, 24, *M*
        1.1.1, 1.1.3,
    pride shown at trial by A 1, 2, 32

prudence of, see *sôphrôn,*
    sôphrosynê, phronimos
sacrificing, on *M* 1.1.2
self-control of, see *enkrateia*
wisdom of *A* 14, 16
Socratic writers 13–16, *A* 1
sophia, sophos 159, *A* 16, *M* 1.4.2ff.
sophists *M* 1.1.11, 1.2.60, 1.3.1, 1.4.1,
    1.6
Sophocles *A* 26
sôphrôn, sôphrosynê, A14, *M* 1.1.16,
    1.2.23, 1.3.8, 1.5.4, 1.6.13
soul, spirit, see *psychê*
Sparta 10, 11, 14, 160, *A* 15, *M* 1.2.61
Stobaeus 19–20, *A* 25, *M* 1.5.2, 1.5.3
Strabo 11–12
stratêgos, stratêgia A 20, *M* 1.2.20,
    1.7.3, 1.7.5
symboloi, chance meetings *A* 13
Symposium, see Plato, Xenophon
Thebes 14, 15, *A* 23, *M* 1.2.37, 1.2.48
Themistogenes of Syracuse 12
Theognis *M* 1.2.20
Theophrastus 160, *M* 1.7.1; see irony
Thersites *A* 29
Thrasybulus 8
Thrasyllus 8, *M* 1.1.18
Thucydides *M* 1.2.53, 1.2.63, 1.4.13
thunder, omens via *A* 12
Timaeus, see Plato
tynchanô A 1
tyrant, tyrants *M* 1.2.32, 1.2.432
Vectigalia, Ways and Means, see
    Xenophon

word order *A* 1, 5, 24, *M* 1.3.2, 1.4.12,
    1.4.13
Xanthippe 59, *A* 28
Xenophon, encounters with Socrates 8,
    9, *M* 1.3.8
Agesilaos, Ages. 1, 5, 10
Anabasis, An. The March up
    Country 5, 8, 10, *M* 1.4.17
Cynegeticus, Cyn., On Hunting with
    Dogs 6, 10
De Equitandi Ratione, On
    Horsemanship 6, 7, 10
De Equitum Magistro, On
    Commanding Cavalry 6, 7, 10
Hellenica, Historia Graeca, HG,
    5, 7, 8, 10, 11, *M* 1.1.18, 1.2.20,
    1.2.24
Hiero, Hier. 6
Institutio Cyri, Cyropaedeia, Cyr.,
    The Education of Cyrus 1, 6, *A* 1,
    5, *M* 1.2.23, 1.2.32, 1.3.2, 1.3.5,
    1.4.9, 1.4.17, 1.7.1, 1.7.2
Oeconomicus, Oec., On Estate
    Management 1, 5, 7, 10, 14–16,
    160, *M* 1.1.7, 1.2.64, 1.3.8, 1.4.3,
    1.5.2
Respublica Lacedaemoniorum,
    Lac., On the Spartan State 6
Symposium, Smp., The Banquet 5,
    15, 16, 18, *M* 1.2.9, 1.2.20, 1.3.5–
    14
Vectigalia, Vect., Ways and Means
    6, 11
Zeuxis *M* 1.4.3